Multi-Domain Master Data Management

Multi-Domain Master Data Management

Advanced MDM and Data Governance in Practice

Mark Allen
Dalton Cervo

AMSTERDAM • BOSTON • HEIDELBERG • LONDON
NEW YORK • OXFORD • PARIS • SAN DIEGO
SAN FRANCISCO • SINGAPORE • SYDNEY • TOKYO

Morgan Kaufmann is an imprint of Elsevier

Acquiring Editor: Steve Elliot
Editorial Project Manager: Amy Invernizzi
Project Manager: Priya Kumaraguruparan
Cover Designer: Mark Rogers

Morgan Kaufmann is an imprint of Elsevier
225 Wyman Street, Waltham, MA 02451, USA

ISBN: 978-0-12-800835-5

British Library Cataloguing in Publication Data
A catalogue record for this book is available from the British Library

Library of Congress Cataloging-in-Publication Data
A catalog record for this book is available from the Library of Congress

For information on all MK publications
visit our website at www.mkp.com

Working together
to grow libraries in
developing countries

www.elsevier.com • www.bookaid.org

To Bobbie, Matt, and Kim, and in memory
of my mother and father,
who always encouraged me to write.

—Mark Allen

To my wonderful family: my wife Milene, my sons, Ettore and
Gian Lucca, for all their love and support.

—Dalton Cervo

Endorsements

"Multi-domain Master Data Management represents a significant challenge to practitioners due to the myriad of disciplines required. Sadly, many organizations fall short of their MDM vision by taking shortcuts with these key disciplines. With their latest publication, Mark Allen and Dalton Cervo provide a complete blueprint for understanding each discipline and how it should be executed in the multi-domain MDM journey. This is a landmark publication and should form essential reading for any organization or practitioner about to embark on a multi-domain MDM initiative."

—**Dylan Jones,** Founder and Editor of Data Quality Pro

"One of the best ways to approach a complicated problem is to break the problem down into its component parts and attack each part individually. Multi-domain MDM is a complicated implementation with lots of moving parts. Multi-domain Master Data Management describes and addresses each aspect of multi-domain MDM in a very thorough and straightforward way. It is easy to understand the specifics of each part, but, more importantly, it is clear how the parts fit together to address the whole of this difficult challenge. The thing I like most about Mark Allen and Dalton Cervo's books is how they approach issues from a hands-on, implementation-oriented point of view. Multi-domain Master Data Management is packed with practical implementation guides to help you establish the organization, processes and technologies to be successful with multi-domain MDM. It is a required guidebook to anyone that is embarking on this type of initiative."

—**Tony Fisher,** VP of Data Collaboration and Integration at Progress Software, and author of The Data Asset: How Smart Companies Govern Their Data for Business Success

"Pundits, software vendors, and consulting firms today aren't exactly shy about espousing the benefits of Big Data. Amazon, Facebook, Google, and Netflix are making sense of petabytes of unstructured data. These companies remain, however, the exception that proves the rule. Organizations cannot begin to harness the power of Big Data until they effectively manage its smaller counterpart. MDM may not be as sexy as Hadoop and other newfangled technologies, but make no mistake: Organizations that cannot master practical, step-by-step blocking and tackling are very unlikely to realize any value from one of its most valuable assets: its data. In Multi-domain Master Data Management, Allen and Cervo provide a veritable MDM playbook."

—**Phil Simon,** author of The Visual Organization and Message Not Received

Contents

Acknowledgments

I want to start by thanking my good friend and coauthor Dalton Cervo for his tremendous contribution and dedication to this book. As part of my acknowledgments with our previous book, I had said that I can only hope for more opportunity to work with Dalton in the future. Well, good fortune prevailed, and once again I had the great pleasure to collaborate with him on this book. As always, Dalton's experiences and knowledge provided the balance and compliment needed to successfully work through many months of sharing thoughts, editing, and delivering this work.

My knowledge of data management and data governance comes primarily from the practical experiences that I have had in my career with implementing, supporting, and managing programs and projects with very talented and dedicated colleagues. A special thanks also goes to the many past and present coworkers at Sun Microsystems, Oracle, WellPoint, and Anthem who I have enjoyed many journeys with.

Special thanks go to Dylan Jones, Phil Simon, and Tony Fisher, whose endorsements we are very proud to have; and to Evan Levy, for reviewing the manuscript and providing some great feedback.

I am deeply grateful to my lovely wife, Bobbie, and our wonderful children, Kim and Matt, for all their patience and support during the many weekends and evenings I spent working on this book.

I also would like thank David Loshin, who first suggested we contact Morgan Kaufmann Publishers regarding their interest in a book of this nature, and of course my thanks go to Andrea Dierna, Kaitlin Herbert, Steve Elliot, Charlie Kent, and Priya Kumaraguruparan at Morgan Kaufmann and Elsevier for all their assistance throughout the development and production of this book.

—Mark Allen

Acknowledgments

First, I want to thank my coauthor, Mark Allen, for his outstanding contribution, dedication, and friendship. This is our second book together, and once more we have had a very enjoyable and complementary collaborative experience. It is always an honor to work with Mark and share our knowledge.

I want to thank my wonderful wife, Milene, and our extraordinary children, Ettore and Gian Lucca, for their love and support. Thanks to my caring mother, Aracy, and my late father, Dan, for their remarkable dedication, teachings, and nurturing.

I also humbly thank the recognized experts who kindly have agreed to endorse this book: Tony Fisher, Phil (Rush) Simon, and Dylan Jones. Big thanks also go to Evan Levy for his review and feedback.

Last, but not least, thanks to Steve Elliot, Charlie Kent, Kaitlin Herbert, Priya Kumaraguruparan, and Andrea Dierna at Morgan Kaufmann and Elsevier for all their assistance throughout the development and production of this book.

—Dalton Cervo

About the Authors

Mark Allen has over 25 years of data management and project management experience, including extensive planning, deployment, and management experience with master data and data governance. Mark manages the Enterprise Data Governance program at Anthem/WellPoint Inc. Prior to this, Mark was a senior program manager in customer operations groups at both Sun Microsystems and Oracle Corporation. At Sun Microsystems, Mark served as the manager and lead data steward throughout the planning and implementation of Sun's enterprise customer data hub. Throughout his career, Mark has championed and implemented many data management programs establishing data governance, data quality management, data stewardship, and change management practices. Mark is the coauthor of *Master Data Management in Practice: Achieving True Customer MDM* (John Wiley & Sons, 2011), has been a speaker at data governance and information quality conferences, and has served on various customer advisory boards focused on sharing and enhancing MDM and data governance practices. Mark can be contacted at mark.allen@ mdm-in-practice.com, or you can visit http://www.mdm-in-practice.com for additional guidance.

Dalton Cervo has over 24 years of experience in data management, project management, and software development, including architecture design and implementation of multiple MDM solutions, and management of data quality, data integration, metadata, data governance, and data stewardship programs. Dalton is the founder of Data Gap Consulting, which provides data management services to a wide variety of industries, such as automotive, telecom, energy, retail, and financial services. Prior to this, Dalton was a consultant for SAS/DataFlux, which provides expertise in MDM, data governance, data quality, data integration, and data stewardship. Dalton was also a senior program manager at Sun Microsystems and Oracle Corporation, serving as the data-quality lead throughout the planning and implementation of Sun's enterprise customer data hub. Dalton has extensive hands-on experience in many data management, change management, and continuous improvement programs. Dalton is coauthor of *Master Data Management in Practice: Achieving True Customer MDM* (John Wiley & Sons, 2011), and contributor to a chapter on MDM to *The Next Wave of Technologies: Opportunity in Chaos* (John Wiley & Sons, 2010).

Dalton has been a speaker at multiple data quality and data management conferences, and has served on customer advisory boards focused on sharing and enhancing MDM and data-quality practices. Dalton has BSCS and MBA degrees, and is PM certified. Dalton can be contacted at dalton.cervo@datagapconsulting.com, or you can visit www.datagapconsulting.com for additional information.

Preface

Master data is data critical to a company's operations and analytics because of how the data is shared and how it interacts with and provide context to transactional data. Master data are inherently nontransactional and are usually identified and organized within data domains that reflect key business entities, such as customers, partners, products, materials, finance, and employees.

Master Data Management (MDM) is the application of discipline and control over master data to achieve a consistent, trusted, and shared representation of the data. This is often referred to as achieving a "single version of the truth." In MDM, business and information technology (IT) disciplines such as data governance, data stewardship, data integration, Data Quality Management (DQM), and metadata management are applied to ensure that there is accuracy, consistency, stewardship, and control of the master data in these domains.

MDM is often thought of as a technical discipline, and it is certainly more familiar to those in IT roles than those in business roles. But a closer look at a well-functioning MDM program reveals that while technology is an integral component that provides MDM with capabilities to operate more efficiently, it is actually the underlying organization and cohesiveness of people and processes associated with the business and IT practices that form the foundation by which MDM becomes a core competency and enterprisewide discipline.

In our first book, *Master Data Management in Practice: Achieving True Customer MDM* (John Wiley & Sons, 2011), we presented a practical, ground-level-view orientation and guidance for the planning and implementation of MDM with a focus on the *Customer* domain. We indicated that as the MDM market was emerging, so was the opportunity to deliver more guidance and instruction based on common approaches and techniques inherent to the MDM philosophy and discipline. The *Customer* domain is typically the first MDM data domain that most companies will address before expanding to other key MDM domains. But regardless of how or where a company gets started with its MDM approach, moving toward a multi-domain scope is a common practice. According to the TDWI 2012 Best Practices Report "Next-Generation Master Data Management":

> *61% of organizations surveyed have already deployed MDM solutions, and more than one-third practice multidata-domain.*

Few organizations practice MDM with an enterprise scope. Most start with a few silos and then connect the silos later, suffering much rework in the process.

Consequently, many interest groups, vendor products, and professional forums have emerged in support of the multi-domain scope. Therefore, it is clear that there continues to be opportunity to deliver more practical guidance and instruction as MDM matures into multi-domain strategies.

Consider a scenario where someone recently had a serious medical condition where treatment involved hospitalization, various procedures, and medications. This person has just received her Explanation of Benefits (EOB) statement indicating what will be covered under her medical plan and what she will be responsible to pay. She carefully reviews the EOB and finds that it is complete and accurate according to her medical plan coverage, as well as being in line with what her care management advisors had suggested during initial consultations prior to treatment. In other words, there are no surprises. This is an example of well-coordinated data management across various business domains such as *Providers, Claims, Care Management, Finance,* and *Contracts.*

In another scenario, a person applies for a financial loan to buy a new car through a dealership. However, the applicant makes an honest mistake and incorrectly enters his address. The automotive finance company receives the information from the dealer, correctly identifies the vehicle make/model/year being financed, automatically corrects the mistakenly entered address, properly evaluates the person's credit, calculates pricing that can be offered according to his credit history, applies any potential dealer incentive to final pricing, and issues an approval. Within weeks after the application is approved and executed, the new customer receives his welcome package with all the correct details of the new loan. This is another example of well-coordinated data management across various business domains: in this case, *Prospects, Applications, Dealers, Vehicles, Customers, Finance,* and *Contracts.*

These scenarios are examples of multi-domain MDM. Often, MDM-type activities may be referred to as *enterprise data management* or *enterprise information management,* or are associated with a large Business Process Management (BPM) project that may be more recognized by its project name than as an MDM activity. The question of whether these activities are formally recognized as MDM is less important than the ability to understand and implement MDM-type practices to achieve more enterprisewide organization and control of master data. We will discuss these type practices in the context of an MDM program, but keep in mind that not seeing the term *MDM* formally in a company's vocabulary or strategic plans does not mean that MDM practices are not occurring. Looking closely at a company's continuous improvement initiatives, data management strategies, and IT practices will typically reveal various plans or existing activities that in fact reflect MDM practices. These are practices that need to be identified and examined when building a multi-domain MDM program and strategy.

There are many cross-functional challenges inherent to the planning and execution of a multi-domain MDM program. It is critical for a company to determine what practices and capabilities can be repeatable and scalable across various data domains and associated business functions. This book will deliver practical guidance and specific instruction to help guide planners and practitioners through the challenges of a multi-domain implementation. It is important to emphasize that the multi-domain topic is a more advanced level of MDM intended for those already generally familiar with the fundamental concepts and practices associated with it, or who are already using MDM in a single-domain initiative.

Unfortunately, repeating MDM success from one domain to another can be very difficult due to differences in system architecture, data architecture, executive sponsorship, business processes, and data context. In other words, one size and approach does not fit all. For example, most rules and solutions for handling customer master data do not apply to product master data, or there may be a champion for MDM in one domain, but not in another domain. Many of the basic concepts and approaches related to the practices of data governance, metadata management, and DQM can be applied and translated across domains, but in each domain, the data context, reference data, quality-improvement needs, and tactical approaches to MDM can vary significantly.

This book is aimed at providing strategies, examples, and insights connected with building a more cohesive multi-domain MDM plan to avoid the silos and reworking referred to in the TDWI report. Throughout this book, we will present examples of how to assess these variances and how to construct plans to address this while still maintaining a cohesive, cross-domain MDM strategy. The key objectives of this book are the following:

- Provide a logical approach to planning, implementation, and ongoing management of multi-domain MDM from a program manager and data steward perspective.
- Provide a comprehensive set of topics and practical guidance centered on the key MDM disciplines of Data Governance, Data Stewardship, DQM, Metadata Management, and Data Integration, which, if coordinated properly in a multi-domain initiative, will lead to a successful outcome.
- Deliver context and content in a business-friendly style with sufficient program-planning guidance, business-engagement techniques, and change-control and quality-control examples that will afford MDM practitioners insights that they can apply to their strategies, plans, and processes.
- Provide a comprehensive level of program management insight and technique that they can apply to their internal MDM initiatives to ensure more successful implementations.
- Provide useful models and measuring techniques to evaluate the progress and maturity of the MDM program.
- Cover advanced MDM strategy and instructions that can improve DQM, lower data-maintenance costs, and reduce corporate risks by helping to foster increased efficiency in data management practices.
- Provide guidance for developing more advanced data governance and data stewardship practices to enable an organization to more successfully control, manage, and maintain their master data, metadata, and reference data.

We want to emphasize up front that there is no single approach or best practice that a multi-domain MDM strategy can follow end to end without alteration or modification. A multi-domain strategy requires patience, persistence, adaptation, maturity, and the ability to act on opportunities as they emerge across the enterprise. Multi-domain MDM can be very much like a jigsaw puzzle, with a big picture that you want to piece together. These parts can come from various places in the puzzle, but putting the puzzle together should not be a random process. A MDM strategy has to consider how to address certain parts of the MDM plan first and others later. We hope that this book will assist readers with identifying their MDM "big picture" and implementing sound strategies for building a successful multi-domain framework.

Overview of the Book
Part I: Planning Your Multi-domain Initiative

This section (which includes Chapters 1–5) addresses the underlying strategy, scope, and planning considerations associated with defining an enterprisewide multi-domain MDM program. In this part, we provide perspective on the following points:

- Where common approaches should be applied across the data domains while recognizing and supporting flexibility where unique requirements, priorities, and deliverables can exist within each domain, and discuss the importance of establishing collaboration and alignment across data governance, project management, and IT.
- Approaches for evaluating and defining the guiding principles of data governance, data stewardship, data integration, DQM, and metadata management to create scalable approaches that will drive a successful multi-domain initiative.
- Identifying master data and prioritizing the data domains in the multi-domain scope, including cross-domain dependencies and how to determine domain implementation order.
- Exploring process and implementation issues that can occur if the implementation order is not executed correctly.
- Addressing different architectures and where current technologies can help support and enable a multi-domain model.
- Determining capability needs and use cases for the technology solutions, as well as limitations such that one platform or even multiple tools cannot address all requirement and capability needs.
- Planning and structure for creating a Program Management Office (PMO) to oversee the MDM program, including roles and responsibilities of the PMO in relation to resources, budgets, tools, and change management processes.
- The need to establish a MDM maturity model, how to define the right MDM maturity model, and how to apply it consistently across a multi-domain model.
- How to measure maturity in a more granular manner.

Part II: Implementing the Multi-domain Model

This part (which includes Chapters 6–10) delves deeper into what we consider the five key disciplines associated with implementing a multi-domain initiative:

- *Data governance:* Discusses multi-domain governance dynamics and processes, including how and where various MDM and data governance gate points can be established within IT and project life-cycle models. Also addresses the need to establish consistency and transparency with governance agendas and decisions.
- *Data stewardship:* Discusses the various roles, responsibilities, and investments needed to develop multi-domain data steward model practices. Also addresses the need for stewardship to be effective at the tactical and operational levels.
- *Data integration:* Discusses the need to establish consistent techniques for data profiling, quality assessment, data validation, and standards when integrating data into a MDM environment. Also addresses the need to appropriately engage data governance teams and data stakeholder/consuming groups to help fully evaluate requirements and impacts associated with data integration projects.
- *DQM:* Discusses how to define and apply a data-quality-measurement model consistently across a multi-domain environment and how to establish standard guidelines and definitions for data-quality dimensions, profiling, and reporting. Also covers how to establish a cross-domain process to manage DQM strategies, decisions, and execution.
- *Metadata management:* Discusses a standard approach to define, identify, and manage enterprise-level metadata assets, such as enterprise business terms, reference data, data models, data dictionaries, and other artifacts that express the data flow and life cycle. Also covers how well-organized and -maintained metadata is critical to the efficiency and success of data governance and data analysis.

Part III: Sustainability and Improvement

This part (which includes Chapters 11–12) addresses the aspects of MDM program performance and sustainability that are necessary to keep the multi-domain program on track to reaching its maturity goals. We cover the following points:

- *Performance measurement:* Discusses how to establish a robust performance-measurement model, including examples of various types of metrics needed to measure MDM activity and performance factors consistently across domains and in relation to the disciplines of data governance, data quality, metadata management, reference data management, and process improvement. Addresses performance measurement from a strategic, tactical, and operational perspective.

- *Continuous improvement:* Covers the need and opportunities for continuous improvement in a multi-domain MDM program. Discusses the reasons that MDM and governance maturity can be slowed down or even stopped, what are maturity inhibitors, and how to achieve or regain momentum. Explains that improvement targets should relate to the program's roadmap and be part of annual budget-planning reviews, and how multi-domain MDM practices can be applied more generically across data management practices.

Planning Your Multi-Domain Initiative

CHAPTER 1

Strategy, Scope, and Approach

This chapter covers the strategy, scope, and approach associated with planning an enterprisewide, multi-domain Master Data Management (MDM) program. Although companies are increasingly recognizing the value and need for MDM, they still often struggle with being able to fully or consistently implement MDM strategies and objectives for multiple domains or subject areas. They find this so difficult because they fail to recognize the many components, functions, and services that are either required to make MDM work correctly or are created as a consequence of an integrated set of disciplines and shared data. Many companies see MDM only as a data integration discipline, which is a mistake.

This chapter sets the foundation for MDM services, components, and disciplines by defining the guiding principles of data governance, data stewardship, data integration, data quality management, and metadata management to create scalable approaches that will drive a successful multi-domain initiative. It discusses where common approaches should be applied across the data domains, while recognizing and supporting flexibility where unique requirements, priorities, and deliverables can exist within each domain. It also covers the importance of establishing collaboration and alignment across program management, data governance, business units, and information technology (IT), all supported by a strong, high-level executive sponsorship.

Defining Multi-domain MDM

A *data domain* reflects the organization of key business entity areas such as customers, products, vendors, partners, service providers, financial accounts, patients, employees, and sites. *Master data* is data most critical to a company's operations and analytics because of how it is shared and how it interacts with and provides context to transactional data. Master data is nontransactional in nature. Multi-domain MDM is concerned with managing master data across multiple domains. While some MDM functions and disciplines can and should be leveraged across multiple domains, some of those functions and disciplines within each domain are still specific enough or have distinct business requirements, so they need very specific management and implementation. Even technology use and maturity can vary widely across domains, as will be described in more detail in Chapter 3. This fact alone directly influences how companies have to adapt their MDM practices for different domains.

Imagine a small software company, with 10–20 employees, selling a single, very specialized application to a handful of customers using prepackaged software components from certain vendors. This company is unlikely to need MDM software or MDM automation to manage its master data. Why? It certainly knows its customers very well, and its managers have a clear understanding about what vendors they use and where to get what they need from them. They have their contacts clearly established. The multiple versions of their application can be managed by a good software configuration system. More important, chances are that they utilize a minimum set of internal software applications to maintain their operations, or even use a single cloud computing service such as Salesforce.com to support most of their IT functions. The bottom line is that the company's volume, redundancy, and fragmentation of information are very low. Furthermore, business intelligence is simplistic. MDM automation would not add much value to this type of company.

Now imagine a large automotive finance company. This company does business with millions of prospects and customers, finances and leases millions of cars from multiple manufacturers, manages millions of financial accounts and a multitude of financial products, handles negotiations with thousands of dealerships and related contacts, maintains relationships with thousands of vendors and other firms (e.g., auction houses, appraisal companies, bankruptcy courts and trustees, and collection agencies), uses services of thousands of insurance companies, deals with thousands of attorneys representing either them or their customers when disputes occur, and hires thousands of employees. Just from these specifications, it is possible to identify a multitude of domains that such a company would have: prospects, customers, vehicles, manufacturers, financial accounts, financial products, dealers, contacts, vendors, attorneys, and employees. It is clear that the volume of information is large, and it is easy to figure out that the number of attributes and data systems maintaining all the information would probably be quite large. This company very likely can benefit from MDM because chances are that there is data redundancy and inconsistency across many data sources. But do *all* those domains need MDM?

There are many factors to consider when determining where to prioritize an MDM focus. Chapter 2 will detail how to identify and prioritize data domains, but let's take a quick look at the key drivers that influence MDM decisions and priorities.

Figure 1.1 indicates the key factors that should drive the priorities and business case decisions for where MDM should be focused in a multi-domain model. However, regardless of the business case or the domain, there are key data management practices and disciplines that need to be scoped, planned for, and implemented in any MDM program. Each of the five major practices—data governance, data stewardship, data integration, data quality management, and metadata management—is important enough to be addressed by its own chapters in Part 2 of this book (Chapters 6 through 10, respectively). In addition, entity resolution, create-read-update-delete (CRUD)

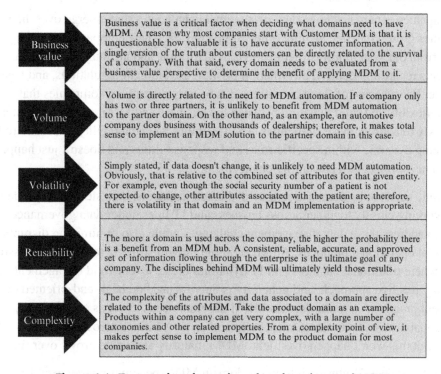

Business value — Business value is a critical factor when deciding what domains need to have MDM. A reason why most companies start with Customer MDM is that it is unquestionable how valuable it is to have accurate customer information. A single version of the truth about customers can be directly related to the survival of a company. With that said, every domain needs to be evaluated from a business value perspective to determine the benefit of applying MDM to it.

Volume — Volume is directly related to the need for MDM automation. If a company only has two or three partners, it is unlikely to benefit from MDM automation to the partner domain. On the other hand, as an example, an automotive company does business with thousands of dealerships; therefore, it makes total sense to implement an MDM solution to the partner domain in this case.

Volatility — Simply stated, if data doesn't change, it is unlikely to need MDM automation. Obviously, that is relative to the combined set of attributes for that given entity. For example, even though the social security number of a patient is not expected to change, other attributes associated with the patient are; therefore, there is volatility in that domain and an MDM implementation is appropriate.

Reusability — The more a domain is used across the company, the higher the probability there is a benefit from an MDM hub. A consistent, reliable, accurate, and approved set of information flowing through the enterprise is the ultimate goal of any company. The disciplines behind MDM will ultimately yield those results.

Complexity — The complexity of the attributes and data associated to a domain are directly related to the benefits of MDM. Take the product domain as an example. Products within a company can get very complex, with a large number of taxonomies and other related properties. From a complexity point of view, it makes perfect sense to implement MDM to the product domain for most companies.

Figure 1.1: Factors that determine what domains need MDM

management, reference data management, data security, and data architecture are major topics and vital functions that also need to be covered within the overall MDM program strategy and scope. Let's understand all these key areas before going any further.

Multi-domain MDM Strategy and Approach

Data is considered a strategic asset to a company, and it needs to be managed accordingly. Data supplies companies with the information and knowledge it needs to compete and thrive amid increasing pressure to succeed. Consequently, there is no dispute how valuable data is to a business. But the challenge is that the IT department has predominantly owned data management, and business organizations have not taken sufficient responsibility for data quality. Data is maintained within technology-enabled applications but created and changed by business processes, so any data issue requires as much of a business emphasis as it does a technical emphasis. Multi-domain MDM programs need an effective engagement and collaboration between business and IT. Collaboration is cultural, but it can be stimulated with proper organizational structure, robust communication channels, and an effective change management process.

Large companies experience huge data management challenges that emerge over the years as companies grow, constrict, acquire other companies, face new competitive challenges, transition from old system infrastructures to new platforms, and are subject to increasing requirements regarding security, information privacy, government regulations, and legal compliance. Because any of these conditions can be very disruptive, companies that can maintain a flexible and fluid dynamic between the business and IT roles will be most able to adapt quickly to address these challenges. The flexibility and adaptability needed here has to be an existing dynamic within specific roles and responsibilities and doesn't just happen with initiating a new project or a consulting engagement.

This dynamic needs to be demonstrated by dedicated managers, data stewards, and data analysts working closely together across business and IT lines under data governance authority to address these data management challenges while also minimizing disruption to the normal operational practices. An MDM program will struggle to gain a successful foothold, where traditional business and IT dynamics create a very rigid engagement model, has a mostly reactive approach, and generally is only focused on back-end-oriented data management practices. A multi-domain MDM program needs to act as a bridging dynamic to create collaborative data management roles and responsibilities across business and IT functions. But this won't happen overnight. MDM maturity and value grows over time.

MDM is not a project. Venturing into multi-domain MDM becomes a large exercise in Business Process Management (BPM) and Change Management. The planning and adoption of cross-functional disciplines and processes necessary for the support of MDM needs to be well orchestrated. This process can be greatly aided by leveraging a consulting partner well versed in MDM, particularly during the discovery and planning phases where capability needs, gap analysis, stakeholder assessment, and project planning deliverables need to be addressed and clearly articulated to a steering committee for review and approval.

With that said, Figure 1.2 is an example of the type of cross-domain model that must be carefully considered when creating your own model. It is also used to exemplify typical scenarios, but they must be adapted to each particular situation.

In Figure 1.2, the four boxes at the top represent the management organization functions required to support a successful multi-domain MDM model. Domains are represented by round boxes labeled "Domain 1," "Domain 2," and "Domain *n*." Those constitute the data domains within the MDM program scope. The square boxes completely inside the rounded boxes are functions that are likely to require high specialization for a particular domain. In data synchronization, for example, one domain might require real-time synchronization among all sources, while another domain might meet business needs with nightly batch synchronization.

The vertical boxes crossing the domains represent functions that are likely to be generic and can be used by various types of master data. For example, a data governance program and charter can include scope and authority broader than just the master data focus.

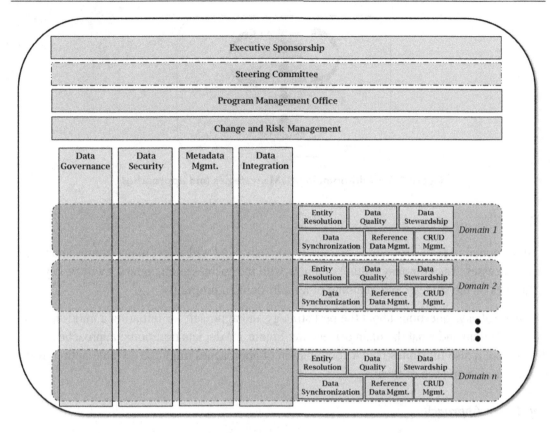

Figure 1.2: Multi-domain MDM—A cross-domain model

Similarly, data security is likely to be a cross-functional component focused on policies and management related to data access and data protection. The platform where the domain data exists is irrelevant, and data security disciplines are very reusable.

Every component will benefit from economies of scale. As MDM is applied across more domains, these functions and their associated tools and processes become more reusable or adaptable. Certain functions, such as data quality, are extremely broad. Most of the disciplines inside data quality are indeed reusable across multiple domains, but they still have domain-specific requirements for activities such as data profiling, data matching, and data cleansing.

How and Where to Start?

First, it is important to clarify there is no one-size-fits-all approach to multi-domain MDM. As indicated in Figure 1.2, there are too many factors that will differ from one company to another or within a company from one domain to another for that to be possible.

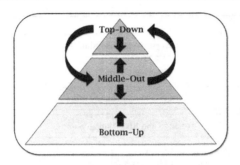

Figure 1.3: Multi-domain MDM strategies and approaches

A multi-domain MDM program is extremely pervasive and will affect many groups and their processes. The company culture and how well the business units interact will be key influences on the strategy and planning of a multi-domain program.

There are always questions about the best strategy and approach for initiating a multi-domain MDM program and what the main drivers are. Figure 1.3 depicts traditional approaches and drivers, but it also illustrates how a combination of approaches might be a viable option. Next is a discussion on each of them.

Top-Down Approach

A top-down approach is the ideal scenario. It assumes that there is an active executive steering committee overseeing the MDM program and providing consistent and visible, top-down sponsorship across the various MDM domains in scope. There are many benefits to building the executive-level engagement process as soon as possible:

- Demonstrates visibility and commitment to MDM and data governance in general.
- Some areas, such as legal, finance, human resources (HR), and compliance, may not need a full domain team structure initially (or even at all), but can still provide representation for strategic plans and tactical direction.
- Leaders associated with future domain areas are still likely to be interested in or affected by MDM decisions. Their participation in strategic decisions is important, and they can observe a working MDM and data governance model occurring with the active domains. This will help shape interest and planning for future domains.

If there is no active steering committee level, the following disadvantages can result:

- Executive leadership/sponsorship is not visible.
- Data governance may appear fragmented and/or only as an inconsistent process in some areas rather than being viewed as an enterprisewide model with an expanding plan.

- Being able to address cross-domain issues will be a more difficult and often ad hoc process if there is insufficient participation and commitment to give input when needed.
- Other business areas may not be aware of where good MDM and data governance practices exist.

Over time, one or two domains will typically command higher priority, budgets, and attention than other domains. What domain area and MDM initiatives gets the most corporate funding and highest level of attention at any given time should not be a largely dominant or limiting factor for defining and planning a multi-domain program strategy and model.

In a multi-domain plan, there will typically be leading and lagging domain scenarios. Therefore it's important to leverage the leading cases to lay down the MDM foundation and value propositions while also planning how MDM principles and practices will be able to be applied and scale across other domains over time. If MDM is successfully executed in the leading cases, then MDM practices will become more valued and incorporated into ongoing data management strategies, therefore requiring less top-down engagement. In other words, as MDM practices mature, execution of MDM practices across multiple domains should require less top-down attention and take on more normalized processes through IT and program planning.

Middle-Out Approach

Although a top-down approach can provide the most thrust for initiating an MDM program, it may be difficult to establish or sustain a top-down approach across all domains in scope. MDM initiatives don't necessarily require a top-down model. Often, there are sufficient existing business case needs, budgets, planning processes, resources, and decision authority within an operational or analytical area to plan and drive an MDM initiative without need for top-level executive engagement. A middle-out structure is a viable option in these cases.

A middle-out approach is often triggered in cases where new business systems or analytic platforms are being funded or in progress and, through those projects, the need for MDM practices are identified and covered by the project plan. However, finding these project-driven scenarios across multiple domains can be a hit-or-miss affair and might have fixed time and budget constraints. Having a MDM program office with visibility into the company's project planning and solution design processes can greatly enhance the ability to identify and support MDM growth opportunities from a middle-out perspective.

Bottom-Up Approach

Bottom-up is neither recommended nor likely to be a sustainable approach. Any MDM capabilities or practices stemming from localized projects and efforts are most likely to reflect one-dimensional solutions that may service the local needs well, but will not have sufficient scope or budget—for expanding the solution across other operational and organizational areas.

Movement to an enterprise model needs to be driven by executable enterprise strategies and projects acting as forcing functions to migrate localized functions. Without these enterprise drivers, there is little incentive and opportunity for localized departmental functions to move into an enterprise model. During a transition period, there may be support for both local and enterprise models until the local model is decommissioned. But generally, localized data quality and governance functions are not going to make the leap to an enterprise level unless broader factors and business strategies can enable this.

Top-Down and Middle-Out Approach

A strategy supporting a combination of top-down and middle-out can also be a realistic approach. A MDM multi-domain plan and program office should certainly look to establish the top-down approach for each domain to gain the initial momentum and sponsorship, but where top-down sponsorship is lacking for a given domain, the plan should be flexible enough to also work middle-out to recognize and promote MDM opportunities in domain areas where there are existing project opportunities that can provide fertile soil for MDM growth.

Although top-down is considered the best-practice MDM and data governance approach, history tells us that there can be significant industry swings in a company's health, priorities, executive leadership, and employment stability. These swings will drive changes in longer-term IT and business strategies. Therefore, it's actually prudent to build an MDM program strategy without being overly dependent on a consistent level of executive sponsorship or a fully executed enterprise architecture. A top-down and middle-out strategy will enable a more flexible approach with emphasis on aligning the MDM initiatives and priorities with the existing domain specific data management, platforms, and project roadmaps where IT investment and business process initiatives will likely be more tangible and in progress.

Multi-domain MDM Scope

Typically, an MDM program is initiated to address certain fundamental issues. Data is duplicated, fragmented, and inconsistent across multiple sources. IT systems are usually built to support a certain business function, and data is primarily maintained for that business function alone. There is very little regard to cross-business needs or systems depending on this data—aka *downstream systems*. Furthermore, data lacks quality because not all disparate systems and processes across the company are built with data quality in mind. Mergers and acquisitions, which bring more disparate, fragmented, and inconsistent systems from other companies into the mix, only add to the problem. Finally, volume keeps increasing at a faster pace.

The bottom line is that there are multiple sources of information with similar (but not exactly the same) data, representing a single entity. Some of that information is outdated and therefore incorrect. MDM helps by formally establishing and governing rules to define what common set of data elements should be used to match entities across multiple sources, as well as techniques to cleanse and consolidate the disparate information, and create a single version of the truth.

However, data offers a large number of challenges, and as such, there are numerous disciplines geared toward addressing their many aspects. Figure 1.4 depicts the primary multi-domain MDM functions, which are described next.

Data Governance

Data governance is the exercise of authority and control over the management of data assets. It's important to note when planning a MDM program strategy that a data governance discipline can and should exist in a company whether it has a MDM program in place or not. As much as data governance does not require MDM, the opposite is not true, especially in an inherently complex multi-domain MDM. All the MDM functions shown in Figure 1.4 require strong data governance engagement and support in many occasions. As MDM expands into more domains and covers a larger amount of entities and master data, data governance

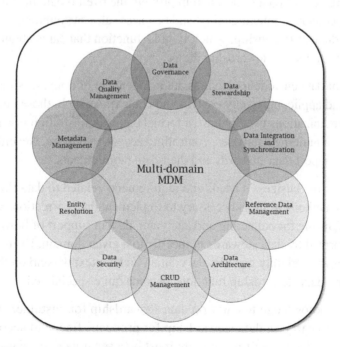

Figure 1.4: Multi-domain MDM functions

becomes even more critical because the volume of activities, need for decisions, and prioritization of work naturally increases.

The good news is a well-established data governance program can cover many data domains and be leveraged to provide the data governance support required in the multi-domain MDM program. Even though one domain will typically have ownership of the master data associated with that domain, master data is intended to be a controlled and shared asset, often having various data creation and consuming processes across the business model. Because of this, it is important that the data governance component in a multi-domain model is prepared to support the MDM program not only for a given domain's governance needs, but also on a cross-domain level where master data awareness, quality management, issue resolution, policies, and standards need to be addressed across applications and process areas. Data governance is the glue that holds MDM together. Without it, cross-domain MDM will not be a cohesive, sustainable program.

How to leverage data governance across multiple domains is discussed in detail in Chapter 6.

Data Stewardship

Data stewardship encompasses the tactical management and oversight of the company's data assets. It is generally a business function facilitating the collaboration between business and IT, driving the correction of data issues, and improving the overall data management process. Their interest is in content, context, quality, and business rules surrounding the data. That's different from the data custodianship, which is an IT function that cares about storage, safety, transportation, and support of stewardship duties.

The vast majority of data custodian activities are independent of domains since they are mostly technical and applicable to any content and context. As such, those tasks are reusable across domains. Organizations usually have a formal data administration organization that is responsible for maintaining databases, controlling access, and more. Nevertheless, these groups do need to support data stewards and their data requirements.

Data stewards gather the business's needs and requirements related to data fitness for use and translate them into methodical steps necessary to implement data corrections and adjustments. They are also responsible for collecting and analyzing data in support of business activities. All this work performed by data stewards is specific to a given domain. Even though data analysis techniques are certainly generic, the content and context depend on the domain in question. Therefore, data stewardship functions become quite specialized.

That means that the knowledge to carry on data stewardship for customers differs from the knowledge needed to carry on data stewardship for products, financial accounts, vendors, partners, and others. That doesn't mean there must be a separate data steward team for each domain. As stated previously, a lot of the data management techniques are quite similar and should be shared. Just keep in mind that subject matter expertise is a must and should be accounted for when planning and building a data stewardship organization.

More information about data stewardship will be given in Chapter 7.

Data Quality Management

Data Quality Management (DQM) is about employing processes, methods, and technologies to ensure the quality of the data meets specific business requirements. DQM is a very extensive function, with far-reaching results if employed consistently, continually, and reliably. Trusted data delivered in a timely manner is the ultimate goal. DQM can be reactive or preventive (aka *proactive*). More mature companies are capable of anticipating data issues and preparing for them. To prevent such issues, a company must create a culture of data quality. It is not only about having a data quality team. It is about encouraging quality at many levels—from a physical data model design, which is a technical function, to data entry, which is a business function.

Bad data model design will open the door for data quality issues in the future. The key is to start with a solid data architecture team and solid data design. Companies usually hire system architects to integrate their applications but fail to recognize the need for data architects. They hire data modelers, but those roles typically remain contained within their specific applications. Data architects are better prepared to understand the implications of poorly designed data models and data interfaces.

Other preventive aspects of DQM are embedded within multiple processes throughout the company. Technical and business processes must be designed and executed with data fitness in mind. Remember that it is not about data quality for its own sake. It is about fitness for use. It is about achieving the best data quality possible as required by the business. If the cost to prevent a data quality issue is higher than the cost of using bad data, you must reconsider your methods. This is by no means a green light to accept bad data. It is simply an indication to review what is being done, identify the root causes of issues, and find more efficient ways to achieve desired goals. Plus, you may not be measuring the value of your data correctly. Companies underestimate the value of good data, as well as the cost of bad data.

Nonetheless, no matter how mature a company is, there will always be a need to perform reactive data quality maintenance tasks. Again, it is about data adequacy to a business need, not perfect data. Data correction projects must have clearly established requirements, objectives, and metrics to measure success. Furthermore, every data issue has a root cause. When correcting existing data issues, make sure to identify why and how the issue occurred and implement corrective actions to prevent similar anomalies in the future.

DQM techniques are vital to many activities related to entity resolution, data governance, data stewardship, data integration and synchronization, data architecture, data security, reference data management, and CRUD management. It is a foundation to just about every MDM data component. Even though this book treats DQM as a multi-domain MDM function in itself, it is important to realize its pervasiveness across the other functions.

Besides being broad, DQM is also diverse. Techniques for designing high-quality data models are different from techniques for profiling data, which in turn are different from methods to augment information, and so on. Remember that even software designers and developers must employ proper techniques to ensure that their final product preserves high-quality information.

From a multi-domain MDM perspective, DQM will have many subjects that can be leveraged and planned for across domains and entities. But due to its diversity, some DQM subjects will still be quite specific depending on the domain being implemented. The main reason for this is that quality of information depends on business requirements, context, and subject matter expertise and its associated tools and references. For example, record linkage within entity resolution can vary widely depending on the domain being implemented. Record linkage for individuals is quite different from record linkage for products. Since data matching is the foundation for record linkage and data matching is a DQM topic, it is easy to see how specific certain DQM subjects can be for a given domain.

DQM will be covered in great detail in Chapter 8, as well as in other chapters within other disciplines as applicable.

Data Integration and Synchronization

It's been stated already that the fundamental issue MDM addresses is the duplication, fragmentation, and inconsistency of data across multiple sources behind systems that are continuously operating in silos. Since data integration involves combining data from several sources, it becomes a required core competency in MDM programs.

There are many flavors of data integration, but they can be largely placed into either the physical or the virtual category. *Physical data integration* implies making a copy of the data, while *virtual integration* doesn't. An enterprise data warehouse is a typical physical data integration implementation, while data federation is a technique to virtually integrate multiple data sources. In a pure sense, data migration doesn't necessarily mean data integration because you could be moving data around without truly integrating any data. However, if data migration is in the context of an MDM program, it will certainly carry physical data integration aspects with it.

Data synchronization is the process to establish consistency among systems and ensuing continuous updates to maintain consistency. According to this definition, data synchronization presupposes an ongoing integration effort. Therefore, data synchronization is the continuing realization of a data integration activity. Because of its maintenance characteristics and associated costs and risks, data synchronization has a huge influence on the selection of an MDM architecture. This consideration will be expanded in Chapter 3, where multi-domain technologies are explored, as well as in Chapter 8, as part of a discussion of data integration.

When looking to leverage data integration and synchronization across multiple domains, it is necessary to remember the difference between their definitions: data synchronization implies ongoing data integration, while data integration in itself doesn't have the reoccurring aspect to it. This matters because domains will have different requirements about how data is brought together, as well as how often they need to be kept in sync when data is replicated.

As with all other functions, the more mature a company becomes in one particular area, the more capable and nimble it will be to reapply related knowledge, experiences, methods, processes, and procedures in successive domains. With that said, certain aspects of data integration and data synchronization can indeed be generic for multiple domains, while others are not so much. It also depends very heavily on the type of the MDM implementation. For example, if one domain is implemented using a federated system, there is a need for initial data integration to achieve proper data linkage, but there is no need for data synchronization. There are many nuances that will be covered in a lot more detail later in this book. Generically, however, there is always a need for integration since the starting point is discrepant sources, but there may not always be a need for synchronization since a single copy might exist after data is integrated into a multi-domain MDM hub.

Metadata Management

Metadata management is likely the most overlooked data component of multi-domain MDM, data governance, and data management in general. This is largely to do with low level of maturity about how to effectively implement a metadata management program that yields short- and long-term results. The following are the main reasons why companies fail with their metadata programs:

- Unclear goals, policies, standards, or roadmaps
- Unclear who are the owners and users of the metadata
- Not setting the right priorities on what needs to be documented first
- Wasting too much time with data elements that are of little interest to consumers of metadata information
- Unsuitable technology
- Wrong personnel skills
- Underestimating the effort to maintain an up-to-date metadata repository
- Treating all metadata the same way

Most of the issues described here stem from a lack of true understanding about what metadata management is and how it is used. *Metadata* is briefly defined as data about data, which can be considered a bit ambiguous or vague. There are different categorizations of metadata. Some experts will separate metadata into either structural or descriptive metadata. Structural metadata is about documenting the design and specification of data structures, while descriptive metadata is about documenting the data content. Others will classify metadata into technical, business, and operational areas. Technical metadata is related to physical data structures and interfaces. Business metadata is related to a glossary of business definitions and business rules. Operational metadata is related to statistics on data movement.

The description about metadata thus far has been regarding its documentation aspect, which is obviously of huge importance. Imagine how much easier it would be to start a multi-domain MDM program if all the master data attributes were properly documented from both a technical perspective and a business perspective. That's the ideal scenario, but it almost never happens. As said earlier, companies struggle with metadata management. They often don't have a metadata repository solution, or if they do, it is not up to date and therefore not trustworthy. This is considering a metadata repository as an important input to an MDM program. However, there is also the importance of a metadata repository as an output of a multi-domain MDM program.

It has been stated before how MDM is about bringing data from multiple lines of business (LOBs) together, and as such, data governance is a must not only to support entity resolution, but also to manage the ongoing usage of shared master data. Business metadata becomes a critical part of supporting data governance with the appropriate channel to publish enterprise business definitions and rules for widespread understanding of shared data elements. Knowledge about information and its usage is the cornerstone to solid governance.

In addition to the documentation aspect of metadata, both as an input and as an output to a multi-domain MDM program, metadata is an important piece of some MDM architectures. Data federation requires a metadata component to virtually connect data elements from multiple sources. Therefore, depending on the technology chosen, metadata management can play an even bigger role.

Metadata management is described in more detail in Chapter 10.

Entity Resolution

Entity resolution is one of the reasons why MDM is so complex and why there aren't many out-of-the-box technical solutions available. It is a relatively simple concept, but it is very difficult to achieve. Conceptually, the objective of entity resolution is to recognize a specific entity and properly represent it uniquely, completely, and accurately from a data point of view. Entity resolution is important because it addresses the issue of multiple versions of the truth. It encompasses processes and techniques to identify and resolve the many occurrences of an entity across many sources.

What's an entity? This book defines *entity* as an object, individual, unit, place, or any other item that should be unique within a certain domain. For example, in the *Customer* domain, either a business or an individual with a contract could be considered an entity. In the *Product* domain, a single unit or a collection of parts could be considered an entity. In the *Health Care Provider* domain, a hospital, a doctor, or a pharmacy could be considered an entity. Not all domains will have multiple entities within them. Take the *Account* domain as an example. It is very possible that some companies will have only the account entity in their account domain. Even with the *Customer* domain, a certain company might only do business with other companies, not individuals. In those cases, the terms *entity* and *domain* are practically equivalent and could be used interchangeably.

Domains and their related entities are typically quite obvious to determine because they are key to a company's core business. They are intrinsically nontransactional but are almost always associated with a particular transaction. For example, a person finances a vehicle with specific contract terms on a particular date, or a patient is seen by a doctor at a certain hospital on a precise day and time. Person, vehicle, contract, patient, doctor, and hospital are the entities in these two examples.

Once an entity is determined, the process to find and resolve the many occurrences and many forms of that entity across the company needs to be handled. The following is a brief description of the steps behind the entity resolution process:

1. **Recognize the sources of master data:** Identify what sources have master data to gather.
2. **Determine what attributes to gather for a given entity:** Decide what master data attributes will be in the MDM hub.
3. **Define entity key attributes (identity resolution):** Determine what attributes will be used to uniquely identify an entity.
4. **Conduct entity matching (record linkage):** Link records and attributes associated to same entity.
5. **Identify the system-of-record (SOR) for each attribute:** Define the best source for a given attribute or set of attributes. A SOR is the authoritative data source for a given data element or piece of information.
6. **Compile business and data quality rules:** Assemble a set of rules that will be used to cleanse, standardize, and survive the best information.
7. **Apply business and data quality rules:** Execute the rules collected previously.
8. **Assemble a golden record:** Create a single version of the truth for an entity (the "golden record").

Notice that these steps are very much data oriented. Since data varies extensively from one industry to another, from one company to another, or even from one source to another within a single company, it is easy to see how difficult it is to have a one-size-fits-all solution for entity resolution. Moreover, data differs from one domain to another, which makes the process of entity resolution unique for each domain. Obviously, the entity resolution process itself is reusable, but much within those steps is domain specific, such as data classification and organization, reference data availability, entity identity, business rules, data quality rules, data fitness for use, and data ownership.

Much about entity resolution is quite specific for each entity. Other functions, on the other hand, might have more overlapping activities. Data governance, for example, has many overlapping practices and procedures across multiple domains. Therefore, the effort to govern multiple domains does not increase at the same rate as the effort to solve for entity resolution for them.

Figure 1.5 illustrates that concept. Entity resolution is unique for each domain. Therefore, the effort to execute entity resolution is expected to grow almost linearly as more domains are added. Obviously, as companies mature, they get better at entity resolution, meaning that this task does get a bit easier with time, and effort starts to flatten out. Data governance evidently matures as well, and some of the flattening is due to that. However, most of the flattening comes from leveraging existing processes, procedures, and practices established with multiple LOBs from previously implemented domains.

Keep Figure 1.5 in mind in relation to the other MDM functions that have been identified. Logically, the more a discipline is reused, the lesser the effort associated with it. As each component is explained, a sense regarding its reusability across multiple domains is also covered.

Entity resolution is described in more detail in Chapter 8.

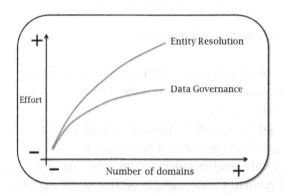

Figure 1.5: Data governance vs. entity resolution: Effort as domains grow

Reference Data Management

Some experts use the terms *reference data* and *master data* interchangeably. In a way, all master data is reference data because it should meet the data quality standards expected from a reference. On the other hand, not all reference data is master data because, even though they are also likely to meet data quality standards, they are not necessarily directly tied to transactional processes. This book has a broader and simpler definition of *reference data:* It is any data that can be used to validate, classify, or categorize other data. In that regard, any data can be used as a reference, depending on its trustworthiness and context. Reference data can be simple lists, such as International Organization for Standardization (ISO) country codes or two-character U.S. standard postal code abbreviations for states. Reference data can be more complex as well, such as a vehicle catalog with make, model, year, trim, and options.

Database normalization is used fairly often to maintain reference data. It enables the creation, update, and deletion of a given data set in a single location. Therefore, it facilitates the governance and stewardship of that data. However, it is not uncommon for companies to replicate reference data as they do with master data. That means that you have challenges integrating and synchronizing reference data as well.

A vast majority of reference data is used as a lookup method to either validate an entered value or to serve as a list of possible options from where to select only the correct values. Database-driven applications normally have these lookup lists created in local tables to expedite response time. For example, you don't want to have a web service call every time you need to create a drop-down list of valid country codes. Therefore, you should store that list as a database table that is directly accessible to that application. Since the same list might be needed in multiple applications, you end up creating tables with the same content in multiple databases. Obviously, a list of ISO country codes is relatively static. Consequently, updating multiple database tables infrequently is not such a daunting task. On the other hand, other references are less static.

Let's take a look at a vehicle catalog as another example. There is a total of close to 50 car makes, most of them with over 10 models for a given year. Per model and year, there is a multitude of trims, colors, engine type, number of doors, transmission, manufacturer's suggested retail price (MSRP), fuel economy, and more. Considering the catalog for new cars is updated yearly with a considerable number of changes, and manufacturers release their new cars at different schedules, one can see how dynamic this list can be. If you create a catalog of both new and used cars, the number of updates is even larger. If a company has many applications using the vehicle catalog, it makes sense to centralize this information in a single place for easier maintenance. Of course, there is always the option to obtain the vehicle catalog information via a vendor service. But in case it is necessary to create local drop-down lists for quick selection, one must use caution on how to duplicate this information internally and keep it synchronized with a possible external source.

The two examples described here are extreme, and recognizing their level of challenge can be obvious. But there are many cases in between: reference data lists that are less static or less dynamic. Recognizing the difference between these types of lists will help with the decision on how to design and maintain them. A vast majority of reference data doesn't have the same visibility and intrinsic value as master data, which makes companies even more careless about them than they normally are with master data in terms of duplication and consistency.

In addition to static versus dynamic characteristics of reference data, there is the internal versus external aspect of it. The quantity of external reference data varies widely not only per domain, but also per industry. From example, in the *Customer/Vendor/Partner* domain, there is quite a bit of reference data related to companies and individuals from D&B, Acxiom, and OneSource; there is U.S. Postal Service reference data through address verification services from Vertex, DataFlux, and Trillium. Other domains can get even more specific depending on the industry. The *Product* domain is a good example. In the automotive industry, which is used frequently in this book, vendors such as Chrome, Kelley Blue Book, and Black Book provide reference data and services for vehicle related information validation. With that said, subject area expertise and industry experience are valuable knowledge to have when either evaluating or selecting a vendor for reference data.

Create-Read-Update-Delete (CRUD) Management

It is necessary to understand the full lifecycle of an entity to plan for its MDM implementation and ongoing maintenance. Since the ways that data records are created and used vary widely depending on the domain, it is easy to see how this aspect can be very specific for each domain being implemented and how it can influence the actual design of each one.

For example, let's say that all vendors for a given company are created only in the enterprise resource planning (ERP) system, since that's where they are sourced for payment information. Let's also suppose that all other sources do not update or delete any vendor data: they simply consume what's in ERP via a service. If that is the case, a SOR for vendor data clearly exists, and there is no fragmented or inconsistent data as all nontransactional information related to vendor comes in real time from ERP. Do you really need MDM for vendors in this example? No—you can actually use ERP as your master hub for vendor data. Even though this example is possible, it's not what happens a good deal of the time. Other sources may create vendors as well, or they may copy some of the vendor data from ERP into a local database, change it, and augment it with what's needed locally.

These scenarios illustrate an important aspect that will be covered in this book. A multi-domain MDM program doesn't imply a single hub for all domains. It also doesn't imply same integration and synchronization techniques. The data life cycle of all master attributes associated to an entity is a big driver behind fundamental decisions regarding the MDM architecture and governance of a given domain. Data governance is also affected since the who, how, and when of the data life-cycle operations are of great interest to management.

In essence, the more sources create, update, and/or delete data, the more difficult it is to keep it synchronized. In other words, the more sources only read data, the easier it is, since there is a lesser need for synchronization. Due to its technical complexity, data synchronization is intrinsically high risk and consequently very expensive to maintain.

It is repeated throughout this book that MDM is both a business and an IT issue, and that it requires constant and effective collaboration. MDM is as much a technical solution as it is a business solution. Therefore, as much as CRUD is inherently technical because you have applications and data sources collecting and propagating data, there is a business aspect to it as well. Business process requirements have a great influence on what systems are used to maintain data. Maintaining business processes streamlined and minimizing the need for CRUD in many applications will certainly simplify MDM implementation and maintenance, and consequently will lower costs and risks.

A good deal of the time, business teams will define their processes according to what systems are primarily accessible to their users. Using the vendor example presented previously, let's say that the services team needs to modify certain attributes related to vendors. Instead of providing access for their users to ERP, which is clearly the SOR for vendors, they add a requirement to allow changes for certain attributes to be possible in CRM. That may simplify their process, but it complicates the synchronization between ERP and CRM. Balancing technical and business feasibility is a constant, and tradeoffs always have to be considered.

CRUD management is explored further when applicable when other MDM functions are discussed in this book.

Data Security

In an ever-growing reality of cyberattacks, lawsuits, stiff competition, and marketing strategies, companies must protect their data. Data security is by no means an MDM issue alone. It is a vital data management competency, and more than ever, companies must face the challenge of safeguarding their information or they could go out of business overnight. Data access control, data encryption, and data masking are just some of the subjects associated with information security.

Data security practices are quite generic and independent of domains. Companies decide what piece of information should be protected based on requirements related to privacy and confidentiality rules, government regulations, proprietary concerns, strategic directions, and other aspects. Those are not a direct consequence of an MDM implementation. What MDM brings to the picture is an increase in data sharing and data exposure across systems. Of course, the higher the data exposure, the higher the security risk.

When IT systems are operating in silos without MDM, most of the data security activities are actually simpler due to the following points:

- **Access control is implemented at that particular system level.** Most robust IT applications provide solid and granular capabilities to control user access, which facilitates data security management. Granted, without MDM, a single piece of information might be duplicated across many sources, which requires protecting the duplicated information in multiple places.
- **The number of user groups is smaller on a system basis.** Obviously, each IT system has a smaller number of users than the overall combined users of all systems.
- **Data usage is more specific because each system is more specialized.** Data fragmentation works in favor of security, as systems only carry data that they need.

The moment data is shared across systems, either physically or virtually, the concern increases because data now must be protected as it is transported as well as where it resides. Furthermore, as data is consolidated, more complete records are shared among more systems, which potentially increase the need to protect data in a location not in scope previously.

As it will be discussed later in this book, it is necessary during entity resolution to define what values will be used to link records from multiple sources. Care must be taken when using values that are subject to high security regulations. If those values need to be encrypted or masked, consider the impact of using them as keys to your entity.

Finally, a lot of data quality measurements and data stewardship activities might require direct database access to query raw data in bulk, which can be seen as a big security risk by many IT organizations. Consider those implications and analyze in advance how this can affect your overall multi-domain MDM and data governance design, implementation, and ongoing maintenance.

Data Architecture

IT applications are regularly replaced as they become obsolete, and data is migrated into new applications with different physical structures. An MDM data model will likely have to survive these regular application upgrades and their accompanying schemes. Very likely, MDM will have the responsibility to define the standard enterprise data model for a set of master data attributes. As such, cross-dependencies will arise, and systems that could possibly be replaced independently before now have to conform to the multi-domain MDM model as well. This increases the need for a well-designed multi-domain MDM data model to support a scalable, robust, and consequently successful program.

Furthermore, this enterprise data model will likely affect internal and even external interfaces. Carefully designing and validating the model so that it both meets current needs and is flexible enough to support future needs are not easy tasks and should not be taken lightly. A well-managed data architecture discipline needs to be in place to ensure that rigorous practices are being followed.

Companies don't carry out important IT projects without a system architect. Similarly, multi-domain MDM programs should not be performed without a data architect. A system architect is also important for MDM, as it does have many integration challenges. Those two roles need to work in tandem to assure all facets are covered.

Conclusion

Planning an enterprisewide, multi-domain MDM program offers many challenges. The right strategy and approach ultimately dictate that the proper foundation is set to fully, repeatedly, and successfully implement MDM strategies and objectives across the enterprise. This foundation is key to delivering trusted data in a timely manner to help the business gain a competitive advantage in an ever-growing, aggressive marketplace.

Data is a corporate asset. Master data, being key to business operations, require proper management. MDM is not exclusively a technology issue, but it is also a business capability. The scope of MDM is quite large as a consequence of an integrated set of components, functions, and services required for creating, maintaining, and governing critical shared data.

In a multi-domain MDM, it is important to balance when to leverage common approaches, components, functions, and services across data domains, while recognizing and supporting flexibility where unique requirements, priorities, and deliverables exist within each domain. Still, suitable business and IT collaboration lies at the core of successful implementation.

CHAPTER 2

Defining and Prioritizing Master Data

This chapter covers how to identify, define, and prioritize master data and data domains in a multi-domain model. It discusses the cross-functional usage of master data, how to address conflicts with the business definition of master data, how to determine domain implementation order, and the process and issues that can occur if the implementation order is not executed correctly.

The term *Master Data Management (MDM) domain* refers to a specific data domain where identification and control of the master data is focused. *Customer, Product, Locations, Finance,* and *Employee* domains have been among the most commonly targeted data domains where MDM initiatives are focused. The focus on these domains has evolved from data management practices associated to customer data integration (CDI), product integration management (PIM), accounts receivable (AR), and human resources (HR) practices. These data management practices have paved the road for the introduction of MDM as a more common discipline using a data domain based approach.

Companies will typically begin their MDM focus in one domain area, and then expand to more domains with implementation of a multi-domain program model. In some cases there may be a multi-domain strategy from the start, but usually a single domain like *Customer* or *Product* will still be the starting point and set the tone for subsequent domains. When taking this multi-domain leap, it is critical to determine each domain's master data elements and what aspects of MDM planning and execution are repeatable and scalable across the domains. With that in mind, this chapter offers guidance and questions that are important to consider when pursing a multi-domain model.

Ideally, the domains where master data analysis and MDM practices can be applied will be clearly defined in a company's enterprise architecture, such as in an Enterprise Information Model (EIM). However, such an architecture and models often reflect a target state that is only partially implemented and without firm plans for how other key pieces of the architecture design will be implemented. To be successful, a MDM program needs to lock into and provide value to current state operations and where enterprise level or operational initiatives are in progress. Master data exist regardless of how advanced a company is with its enterprise architecture strategies. If an enterprise architecture design cannot provide a firm point of reference for defining MDM domains, it can instead be derived from other reference points, such as from a review of subject areas in an enterprise data warehouse or from the operational model and functional architecture.

Identifying Domains

Although certain domains, such as *Customer, Product, Locations,* and *Employee,* are the most commonly referenced, the domain types and mix can vary due to a company's industry orientation and business model. They may also be influenced by system architecture, such as if a company has implemented an integrated business suite of applications that has an underlying data architecture and predefined data models.

Here are some industry-oriented examples of how domains are often defined:

*   **Manufacturing domains:** *Customers, Product, Suppliers, Materials, Items, Locations*
*   **Health care domains:** *Members, Providers, Products, Claims, Clinical, Actuarial*
*   **Financial services domains:** *Customers, Accounts, Products, Locations, Actuarial*
*   **Education domains**: *Students, Faculty, Locations, Materials, Courses*

Identifying Master Data

Regardless of how the domains are determined, the concept of master data and how this data is identified and managed needs to be consistent across a company's systems and processes. Master data should be clearly defined and distinguished from or related to other types of data, such as reference data and transactional data. Here are definitions for these types of data.

*   **Master data:** Data representing key data entities critical to a company operations and analytics because of how it interacts and provides context to transactional data
*   **Transactional data:** Data associated with or resulting from specific business transactions
*   **Reference data:** Data typically represented by code set values used to classify or categorize other types of data, such as master data and transactional data
*   **Metadata:** Descriptive information about data entities and elements such as the definition, type, structure, lineage, usage, changes, and so on

While each of these types of data will be used together for operational and analytical purposes, and all may be in the scope of a data governance charter, the source control and quality management of the master data will have different priorities, requirements, challenges, and practices than will the other data types. MDM is the application of discipline and control over master data to achieve a consistent, trusted, and shared representation of the master data. Therefore, reference data and metadata associated with a master data element should also be included in the MDM scope if any control or consistency problems with the reference data or metadata data will affect the integrity of the master data element. For example, many code sets act as reference data to qualify a master data element or provide a list of values expected to be populated in the master data field. In such cases, the reference data associated with the master data element should be in the MDM scope.

The MDM and data governance programs work together to focus on managing and controlling the elements, definitions, and business processes that influence the creation and change of master data. Clearly recognizing and defining this are perhaps the most challenging and foundational actions within a MDM program. MDM and data governance efforts can be and often are initiated with objectives to pull the business entities and definitions together, but this is a much more complicated process that requires attention from many resources to ensure a coordinated approach. If the MDM Program Management Office (PMO) and data governance are not prepared with sufficient resources and support to help pull this information together and coordinate the analysis process, the progress and maturity of the MDM program will be impeded until this work can be completed. The MDM PMO scope and its relationship with data governance are discussed in more detail in Chapter 4.

To fully evaluate the master data and the master data characteristics within a domain, the following artifacts should be inventoried, gathered, and reviewed for each domain:

- **Data models:** Conceptual, logical, and physical models that organize and document business concepts, data entities, and data elements and the relationships between them
- **Data dictionary:** A listing of the data elements, definitions, and other metadata information associated with a data model
- **Functional architecture:** Depicts how systems and processes interact within each other within a functional scope
- **Source to target mapping:** Describes the data element mapping between a target system and source system
- **Data life cycle:** Depicts the flow of data across application and process areas from data creation to retirement.
- **CRUD analysis:** Indicates where permissions to create, read, update, and delete have been assigned to various groups for certain types of data

All of these are artifacts are extremely valuable for evaluating the scope, consistency, and use of master data. Unfortunately, not all these artifacts are likely to be available or in a complete form for each data domain in scope. The data governance or MDM program management office should consider opportunities to assist with the initiation or completion of any of these artifacts where needed. Figure 2.1 shows an example of inventorying these artifacts with each data domain in the MDM program scope.

These artifacts should also be the basis for defining key metrics that will demonstrate the value and progress for how MDM practices can drive the alignment and consistency of the master data across these areas and artifacts. For example, an initial analysis of these types of artifacts and data assets is likely to reveal many gaps or conflicts with master data definitions,

Data Domain	Data Models	Data Dictionaries	Functional Architecture	Source to Target Mappings	Data Life Cycle	CRUD Analysis
Domain 1	X	X	X	X	X	X
Domain 2	X	X	X	X		
Domain 3	X	X		X		
Domain 4	X	X	X		X	X
Domain 5			X	X		

Figure 2.1: Sample inventory of artifacts

alignment, lineage, usage, and control. From this type of assessment, current state baselines can be determined, leading to quality improvement objectives that can be implemented and tracked as ongoing quality metrics for each domain. Examples of these type measurements are provided in Chapter 11. This type of data asset inventory and analysis by domain should also be leveraged to help scope the data governance, data quality management, and metadata management practices needed for the MDM plan and approach for each domain.

Identifying Sources of Master Data

Within a company there can be many silos of information. For the most part, lines of business (LOBs) operate autonomously. Granted, they have distinct objectives, budgets, targets, processes, and metrics which justify most of their independent operations. But when it comes to data, LOBs are highly dependent on data from multiple domain areas that can have various degrees of quality and present different systems of reference.

Take the *Customer* and *Account* domains as examples. Certain entities within the *Customer* domain, such as individual customers or business customers and the associated contacts are spread throughout the company with a multitude of different transactions attached to them at the many disparate systems, such as customer relationship management (CRM), enterprise resource planning (ERP), supply chain management (SCM), asset management, service management, and data warehouse.

The *Account* domain is no different. In many industries, a customer may have multiple accounts. For example, a couple finances a car, and the father is a cosigner with a son (who is not living with them) on another car financing. In this example, there are three customers (father, mother, and son); and two accounts (one for the couple's car, another for the son's car financed with the father). If the parents are still making the payments for their son's car, they may want to have the billing address for that account to be different from their son's home address, even though the son might be the primary person on the account. Many other combinations are possible. In any event, many nontransactional attributes remain associated at the account level, not at the customer level. Therefore, there is a need to have a master account as an independent entity. Like data related to customer entities, the account entity will have duplicated, fragmented, and inconsistent information spread across multiple-source systems.

Recognizing a certain entity exists within the major information technology (IT) systems is not difficult. Business units will know immediately what category of information they need and use. The problem lies at the granular level. Unless a company has implemented a data hub architecture and has a comprehensive metadata management solution in place, there is unlikely to be a centralized location or team with detailed information about all elements across the enterprise applications that relate to a certain entity and their degree of completeness, uniqueness, validity, consistency, and accuracy. That should not be confused with lack of business understanding of their functions. Business users do understand their processes and what pieces of information are needed to complete a given task. But a clear, enterprise-level understanding of the data and the source of truth is typically missing in the absence of an MDM focus and comprehensive data-quality-analysis capabilities.

For example, a particular task might be to mail correspondence to customers. All that is needed for someone to perform this process is the customer name and billing address. Furthermore, this person cares about it on a unit basis. That means, to send one correspondence, he or she needs one customer name and one address. There is no need to look at other attributes of the customer, nor is it necessary to know whether the same customer exists multiple times in the system, and if so, if all the records have the same address. However, if the same customer exists multiple times and all the addresses are the same, it means sending multiple copies of the same correspondence to the same person, which incurs additional costs (and probably annoys the customer). And if the addresses are different, it is likely that only one is correct—therefore, the extra copies are sent to the wrong location, also wasting money and effort.

When evaluating sources of information, remember to consider the many locations and forms where data is maintained. It is not unusual for companies to have pockets of data in diverse locations and forms of storage. Organizations might even have full-blown business processes that totally depend on manually maintained spreadsheets or local databases. The business need normally starts small (e.g., a newly created or recently improved process requires a new piece of information related to a certain entity). Modifying existing software applications might be too expensive or take too long. That particular LOB decides to take the matter into its own hands and augment some existing information with the new data needed, maintaining it on a local data store or spreadsheet. Later, more data is added. All of a sudden, what started small becomes large and extremely critical to business operations. Those sources of information cannot be ignored. They need to be accounted for and leveraged accordingly.

Conduct a data life cycle and CRUD analysis to identify a comprehensive list of all sources. Don't ignore anything. Until all elements for the entities in scope are evaluated thoroughly, no data source should be underestimated, but in the final analysis, not all elements associated with a domain are necessarily in scope as master data. This topic is discussed next.

Determining the Master Data Elements

Once the sources of master data are identified, the next step is to determine what master data elements will be in scope. What is in scope should be an exercise that coordinates PMO and data governance, with appropriate data stewards and business analysts involved who are familiar with the domain's data and business process areas. Keep in mind that while the business areas will be able to identify what data entities and elements they rely on, they may not have a sufficient understanding about all the elements associated with those entities, nor may they understand the level of quality. That happens for the following reasons:

- Operational business processes use only a subset of all entity attributes at a time—i.e., a narrow view of the data
- Operational business processes use only a few rows of information at a time—i.e., a shallow view of the data

Figure 2.2 shows a narrow and shallow view of domain data due to specific business processes that use just a small percentage of an overall data set at a time.

There is nothing wrong with business processes having a narrow and shallow view of the data. They fulfill a certain business need very well. Obviously, however, there are certain business groups that want or need to analyze data a bit more deeply. Those are usually analytical teams looking for particular trends within an overall data set. However, those analyses can still be narrow and segmented by source.

The next step is to compile a comprehensive list of master elements in a given domain. To do this, it is necessary to conduct a very detailed, wide, and deep analysis of the many elements associated with those entities at the various sources. Data must be profiled at length from a technical and business point of view. Once the comprehensive list is compiled, a simple approach is to classify the elements as master data (nontransactional), transactional data, or reference data. Transactional attributes will generally be out of scope, whereas some reference data may be in scope. Ultimately, it should be a PMO and data governance decision as to what elements are classified as master data.

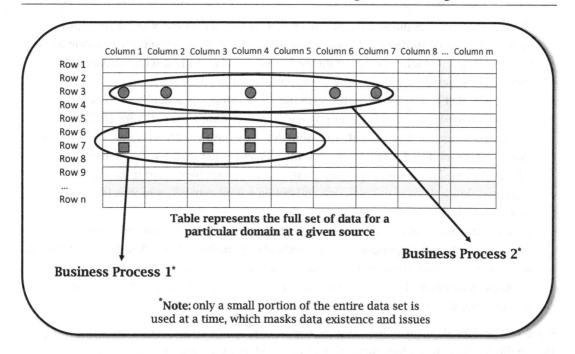

Figure 2.2: Narrow and shallow view of domain data

For example, the following types of assessments should be performed to help with the final analysis and the master data decisions:

- If a data element is not populated at all, that is a strong indication that it is not used and can be disregarded. The data elements in this group can be categorized as out of scope for data mastering. Also, keep in mind that a data element may not be populated but still could be a candidate for master data classification. For example, the data exist in the source system but were not pulled across into a data hub or data warehouse, or a new data entity was modeled to support new data elements expected in the future, but the data have not yet been made available.

- If an element is only scarcely populated, that indicates that the element is most likely not used and could potentially be disregarded. However, the scarce population of an element may be due to its definition and intended usage. This needs to be evaluated before disregarding the element. For example, let's say that a populated end date indicates that a contract has expired, while lack of an end date indicates an active contract. If the end date is scarcely populated, that means there are many active contracts, and so a scarcely populated end date field should not be ignored. However, depending on the type of business and contract term expectations, if contract expirations should frequently occur and those end dates should trigger specific contract renewal attention, the fact that this element is scarcely populated may indicate that there is a data entry or business process issues that must be further examined. Exercise caution before completely ignoring a data element. When in doubt, confirm with the business and provide it with the data profile results. Those results are invaluable to supporting a well-made decision.

- An element that is always populated with the same value is practically in the same category as an element that is never populated. It is common for software applications and database rules and constraints to assign default values to certain fields. It the default value is never modified, chances are that the element is not used by the business and can be ignored. Treat elements in this group as you would treat them if they were never populated. Mark them as out of scope and obtain a final sign-off, which is likely to happen with little dispute.
- Typical data profile techniques should be applied to help with the data analysis. Frequency distribution, pattern analysis, redundancy analysis, type identification, primary and foreign key evaluation, and other statistical measurements are just a few of many methods that support the evaluation of data fields and the making of a final decision on in-scope or out-of-scope exercises.

Some master data elements will exist in one source but not in others, and some will overlap. The quality of the data (or lack thereof) will vary widely by source, which means that every source must be profiled independently and meticulously. IT and the business must work together in this activity. The data-profiling activity can be quite technical, but it is necessary to have a wide and deep view into the data for proper analysis. Proper alignment and collaboration between data governance and IT are critical factors. Figure 2.3 depicts a simple template example of inventorying the master data with each domain, including the most critical data elements (CDEs). An actual inventory list may have many more columns to capture additional source and reference information that is helpful for the analysis.

Defining the Most Critical Data Elements

The master data elements were identified in the previous discussion, but the question now is: What set of information from multiple sources (or even within a single source) belongs to the same entity, and which of the elements are most critical to the business and analytical operations? While conducting the narrow/shallow analysis, this is an opportunity to also have these business process areas identify their CDEs. As part of compiling the master data list, the identified CDEs should be clearly tagged, as this will be a valuable subclassification of the master data that can be leveraged later for focusing on data quality measurement and business term standardization efforts.

The compiling of a master data element list is likely to reflect various data inconsistencies that exist within and across the sources involved. These data issues will need to be examined

Domain 1

Business Concept Area	Data Entity Name	Data Element Name	Business Term Definition	Critical Data Element (Yes/No)	System of Reference

Domain 2

Business Concept Area	Data Entity Name	Data Element Name	Business Term Definition	Critical Data Element (Yes/No)	System of Reference

Figure 2.3: Master list inventory template

in relation to the data quality management, data integration, and entity resolution practices. Those practices will be covered in detail in later chapters of this book, but certainly the outcome of the exercise to identify and list a domain's master data can help raise the initial visibility to many data quality and consistency issues.

Business Definition Conflicts

When analyzing the master data, it would not be unusual to find variations with the definition of the subject areas, data entities, and the business terms for the data elements. This is because siloed applications and their data models will have been defined and implemented without the benefit of many, if any, enterprise standards. Engaging data analysts and information architects to conduct an enterprisewide analysis to evaluate the semantic consistency of a domain's key entities and business terms should be a planned activity supported by the MDM PMO and data governance. The master data inventory previously described and represented in Figure 2.3 will also support the ability to evaluate the business term definition conflicts and overlaps that are likely to exist within or across domains. How to address these conflicts and build enterprise standard definitions will be discussed further in Chapters 6 and 10.

Prioritizing Domains

MDM business case and investment decisions should be driving the overall MDM strategy based on priorities that are typically associated with risk mitigation, revenue growth, cost reduction, or business efficiency. However, there can be many strategic, operational, and technical reasons that influence domain implementation order. The MDM priorities will also be influenced by the IT roadmap, business process needs, analytical needs, and executive sponsorship.

Starting an MDM initiative with focus on the *Customer* or *Product* domain certainly makes sense since the operability and sustainability of most companies rests on customer and product dynamics. Almost all the manufacturing, sales, marketing, financial, service, and analytical functions in a company are tied to these customer and product master elements; therefore, this typically is a natural starting point for MDM. And once these most critical domains are addressed, it will be easier for other domain programs to follow suit as part of a broader MDM strategy and plan.

When planning a multi-domain program, sufficient time is needed to work out the right implementation approach, examine business impacts, determine critical path dependencies, and to define the ongoing program management model. Not fully addressing these items will likely lead to various program impacts and priority adjustments. It is the business functions and transactional areas that are the primary creators and consumers of the master data. And since most transactional areas will interact with master data from multiple domains, the domain implementation plan and order can have a significant impact on business operations. Although the result of a successfully executed MDM initiative will provide many benefits for business operations and analytic functions, these initiatives will drive data and process changes that can be disruptive if the changes are not handled well. Quotes, orders, fulfillment, claims, payment, and service delivery are all major process areas that can be easily disrupted by master data changes due to MDM initiatives. And, of course, if not handled well, such changes can cause customer abrasion that will negatively affect customer satisfaction and loyalty, which in turn can affect a company's bottom line and become a very unwanted, highly visible problem.

For all domains in the scope of an MDM program, it is critical to inventory the business processes, consumer areas, and life cycle of the master data. Be sure to understand how MDM changes will affect these dynamics and ensure that these stakeholders are represented in the domain MDM plans and data governance structure. More discussion of this point will be provided in the subsequent chapters of this book.

Conclusion

This chapter covered how to identify and define master data, how to associate master data with data domains, and how to prioritize the implementation of data domains in a multi-domain model. This included a discussion about when metadata, reference data, scarcely populated data elements, or even some unpopulated data elements may need to be included within the MDM scope. Also explained was how to address cross-functional conflicts with the business definition of master data and how to identify the most critical master data elements to ensure that these elements will have the highest priority for quality control across the MDM practice areas.

Be sure to define, analyze, plan, and prioritize master data wisely. Ensure that the MDM domain definition is well aligned with enterprise architecture strategies and business model concepts. When considering domain priorities, review the business impacts and change management needs associated with the MDM objectives. Stay focused on the overall multi-domain strategy and plan, but also aim at the near-term objectives that can establish quick successes and be executed within a reasonable time frame. Longer-term objectives can change, and they are often influenced by the execution and success of the nearer-term objectives.

CHAPTER 3

Architecture and Technology Considerations

As stated often in this book, Master Data Management (MDM) is about people, process, technology, and methodology. The right technology is critical to success. This chapter makes no attempt to provide a comprehensive list of vendors or cover all available MDM technologies. That information, as well as product evaluations, is widely available through various websites. The primary purpose of this book is to provide general guidelines on key aspects that should be considered when planning an enterprisewide technological landscape that can sustain a scalable multi-domain MDM solution. Chapter 1 exposed the many functions and disciplines behind a complete multi-domain MDM program. The fact is that there is no single MDM solution or vendor that will provide an entire suite of applications that will provide all those moving parts—it is important to remember that. Furthermore, technology maturity varies widely across domains, as well as across the multiple activities and disciplines behind all MDM functions. This chapter addresses those issues and highlights the important aspects to contemplate when designing an effective infrastructure that truly solve your business problems.

Multi-domain MDM Technological Background

As just mentioned, there is no single product that will address all the capabilities necessary to meet multi-domain MDM needs. Even a single domain requires multiple technologies. MDM can be implemented in many different ways, depending on the problem that it is trying to solve, as well as how an eventual MDM hub will integrate with other enterprise applications. Information technology (IT) organizations typically have existing architecture and rigid processes to manage and integrate current and new enterprise applications. However, adding a multi-domain MDM to the mix is about more than just adding a new application. It is about adding a capability that will most likely affect the most important data elements across all existing systems.

From a technology perspective, no single solution on the market today can address all of them. Therefore, when evaluating multi-domain MDM products, it is necessary to understand what they offer. Most of the time, when a vendor sells an MDM product with the ability to identify and match master data, the core functionality being sold is entity resolution. Naturally, though, entity resolution presupposes some sort of data quality and data transformation activity to more effectively identify when two or more entities are truly the same. But you will not necessarily get all the data quality pieces needed to strongly support other MDM functions. For example, a product solving for entity resolution might include a deterministic fuzzy-logic algorithm to resolve the situation when two people have the same name or nickname. That is clearly a data-quality function. However, the same product may not provide other data-quality-oriented capabilities such as tools for data profiling, quality measurement, or dashboards that are essential for data analysis and data governance.

Product maturity is also another big consideration. Some vendors offer better solutions for certain domains, but not so much for others. That is not only due to product maturity, but also because certain domains are more difficult to generalize than others. Customer MDM is usually the most popular for many reasons. One is because use cases and data elements are more uniform across multiple companies when it comes to creating a product that will solve for customer MDM. Therefore, vendors have a better opportunity to create a solution that requires less customization and can be deployed more quickly and efficiently. On the other hand, product MDM is much more specific. Companies will have very unique requirements, which complicates MDM product offerings. Customer and product MDM are just two examples, but almost every company has customers and products. As other domains become even more specific, product offerings and maturity will suffer.

In addition to product value and applicability at the domain level, vendor product applicability and maturity are also issues across MDM disciplines and functions. Vendors have been slow to respond to certain data management needs. In particular, data governance and metadata management products lack sufficient maturity. Data federation has made great strides recently but still has a long way to go. Certain aspects of data integration and data quality are advanced, but there is still room for improvement. Data quality management has a very broad focus, and certain aspects of it are far more evolved than others. For example, data quality for structured data is relatively more advanced than it is for unstructured data. The integration of data quality and data governance is still at the very early stages, with product solutions still very fragmented.

Nonetheless, some vendors will offer a suite of products with functionality designed to address many data management components required to support MDM. In truth, however, these types of integrated tools all have strengths and weaknesses, with underlying design assumptions and dependencies that can make certain components fail to interoperate well with other vendor solutions. Some solutions are more mature and flexible than others, but this needs to be carefully examined.

A lot of this tendency has to do with the nature of MDM. MDM offerings do not often integrate as well with existing IT infrastructure as other applications do. Vendors must balance a solution that will address a problem and simultaneously fit an existing IT model that does not quite support what is needed to truly solve that problem. IT is typically prepared to support vertically aligned applications within distinct lines of business (LOBs). Vertically aligned applications look at a particular facet of the data to satisfy the need of a certain organization. For example, a financial department might rely solely on an enterprise resource planning (ERP) system for all its data needs. But MDM requires a horizontal view across many disparate systems to truly expose a consistent version of master data. Granted, most IT organizations will have some type of middleware technology to provide integration among systems, but using them for MDM requires customization that will add to the complexity, delivery schedule, and cost.

Therefore, companies looking for MDM solutions should not be surprised to find products that lack maturity, have insufficient functionality, and are difficult to integrate. In some cases, the only solution is to combine multiple products to cover all MDM functions, which has obvious drawbacks. In such cases, it is necessary to work with multiple vendors to create custom code to integrate products that were not naturally designed to function together. In parallel, companies need to adapt their processes and train their people to use the new product or products. With all that happening, a multi-domain MDM implementation becomes extremely difficult to achieve without proper expert guidance.

The bottom line is that evaluating technologies is a very complex task. It is best to rely on highly specialized and very experienced consultants to guide your company in this venture. Preferably, when considering a multi-domain MDM implementation, it is ideal to start with vendor-agnostic consultants with a proven track record in delivering comprehensive MDM use case analysis, planning assistance, and recommendations for how and where vendor solutions can add value. Getting objective, unbiased advice is important because that way, you're more likely to obtain a solution that fits your specific needs.

With that said, let's look at multi-domain MDM from an architectural point of view.

MDM Architectures and Styles

Multi-domain MDM can evolve from many different scenarios, often without a comprehensive enterprise strategy or plan. Some MDM implementations start in nonoperational environments that do not directly affect upstream applications. In these cases, it often begins as an expansion of a data warehouse or an operational data store (ODS) implementation, leveraging existing data integration capabilities but adding more formal data quality capabilities to cleanse, standardize, consolidate, and augment existing information. Those cases can be best described as analytical MDM, with its primary purpose to improve analytics, reports, and business intelligence. If a company's business case for MDM is to increase revenue, an analytical MDM approach can be a viable option. Improved analytics will certainly help with better-informed business decisions and more precise company strategies.

Business analytics in itself is focused on improving market strategies based on increased knowledge about a company's own data. Analytical MDM goes a step further. It establishes the opportunity to evaluate the same data, but increase internal efficiency. Data quality metrics become the foundation for data governance and data stewardship programs. It allows companies to recognize how their data lack the proper quality management rigor to meet desired outcomes. Trusted, consistent metrics provide data governance with solid information to evaluate data quality and pursue appropriate corrective actions and improvement activities with application and business process owners. Figure 3.1* depicts a typical analytical multi-domain MDM implementation.

However, the analytical MDM model has only limited benefits and cannot be considered an enterprise solution. Operational systems rarely access data contained within an analytical system. From the analytical systems perspective, operational systems are upstream, read-only environments. Therefore, operational systems do not automatically

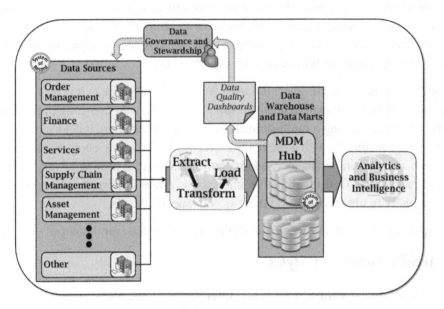

Figure 3.1: Analytical multi-domain MDM

---

* A disclaimer about the figures presented in this chapter depicting MDM styles: There are many variations of multi-domain MDM, and these illustrations are meant to convey conceptual ideas. Data governance, for example, is a function that should be acting across all data sources and related business units at all times. The figures here will show data governance acting in particular areas, but that is just to indicate the location where data governance efforts would make the greatest impact related to master data for that particular style. For example, in Figure 3.1, data governance also should obviously be an active function with the data warehouse processes. However, the picture shows data governance working with upstream data sources to correct master data at the source by using data-quality dashboards generated from the MDM hub.

benefit from data improvements or from the entity resolution in the analytical environment. Therefore, data quality improvements have to be duplicated in multiple sources, so they become scattered and inconsistent.

The concept of an operational MDM is a natural evolution. An operational MDM encompasses an MDM hub that can be directly referenced by operational sources. But an MDM hub within an operational environment can be implemented in different styles. There are many variations and different nomenclatures, but fundamentally they are

- Registry style or virtual integration (VI)
- Transaction/persistent style or single central repository architecture (SCRA)
- Hybrid style or central hub-and-spoke architecture (CHSA)

Certain MDM styles will be less intrusive than others, primarily due to architectures that vary from loose to tight coupling. A loose-coupling architecture requires less reengineering of existing systems to integrate them with a multi-domain MDM hub. Conversely, a tight-coupling architecture requires much more reengineering of the existing applications for such an integration. Therefore, a loose-coupling architecture will be much less intrusive than a tight-coupling architecture. Let's cover each of them in more detail next, and discuss which styles are more intrusive than others. To be sure, a complete enterprise MDM solution is achieved when the results of an operational MDM is also captured at the analytical level for maximized benefits.

Registry-Style MDM

In a registry style, the MDM hub maintains only the minimum set of information necessary to identify data related to an entity and locate it at the many original data sources. In this style, the hub maintains identity information and source system keys. All other data relative to a given entity is kept at their respective sources and it's not duplicate in the MDM hub. In essence, the hub serves to find instances of a given entity at their many sources. Notice that the hub is not truly a system of record (SOR) for an entity and its attributes. It is simply a system of reference. Figure 3.2 depicts a Registry Style Multi-domain MDM implementation.

The hub does not directly update the data sources. It is a federated system that builds a master record during operation to be consumed by downstream systems. This style is not very intrusive, as it does not affect the original sources of data. However, it can suffer from performance issues due to latency as a result of dynamically collecting many attributes from multiple sources and assembling a golden record. Furthermore, if the same piece of information related to the same entity exists in multiple locations, a set of business rules must exist to clearly define a SOR or to resolve conflicts during operations.

This style has a relatively low cost and can usually be delivered quickly. It creates a solution based on loosely coupled systems, where minimal knowledge is shared across components. It is low risk since sources are left intact and act as read-only sources. The latter facilitates ongoing maintenance since it doesn't require two-way synchronization. This style might be a good option in companies with many data sources and LOBs that are highly sensitive about ownership and changes to their data. However, if data sources are of poor quality, they won't directly benefit from improvements and consolidation happening in the hub. This doesn't necessarily diminish the impact of MDM; it simply points to the fact that not all source systems can accept nonapplication-centric changes.

Entity resolution is obviously a key factor in all MDM styles. But it is even more critical in the registry style because entity identification happens dynamically. Any automated matching algorithm will suffer from false positives and false negatives, and they can be higher or lower, depending on the quality of the existing data and the particular domain being mastered. Therefore, this particular style will be more effective in certain companies than others. It will also be more effective for certain domains than others, as the identity of an entity can be more straightforward for certain entities than for others.

In this style, the ability to create a robust metadata model for a particular domain is directly related to its successful outcome. Since this is a federated model and data is not copied to the hub, a metadata model must be established to dynamically represent an entity that is physically distributed in multiple places. As the attributes of that entity are physically changed or augmented at these multiple sources, their metadata representation needs to be upgraded accordingly. This factor is also more critical in some domains than others. However, not all domains must be implemented using the same MDM style, as will be discussed later in this chapter.

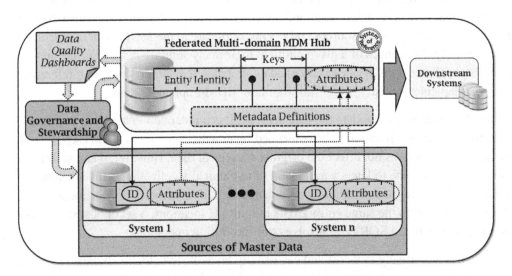

Figure 3.2: Registry-style multi-domain MDM

Transaction- or Persistent-Style MDM

In a transaction-style hub (aka a *persistent hub*), the MDM hub physically stores all attributes of an entity. The hub becomes a centralized single source of truth, and it is used to publish master attributes to other application systems. This style presupposes an initial loading of the hub with entity data from multiple sources. After initial loading, data are created and maintained directly in the hub and consumed by other applications, which have to be modified to use master data from the hub. This style consists of a highly coupled architecture, which is a major drawback since it is likely to require massive changes to existing applications in order to access data from the hub instead of data that is maintained locally.

Another challenge is to create a data model that satisfies all consumers of the master data in the hub. One option is to create a data model that encompasses all attributes needed by all applications. However, it is easy to see how difficult it can be to agree on a single model that can support very specific applications, created by many vendors, with clearly distinct functional requirements.

Nonetheless, this style has obvious advantages. Data is created and maintained in a single location, which increases the ability to prevent potential data issues. Remember that the most effective way to ensure data quality is through prevention. Data-quality efforts to cleanse and consolidate data after the fact can be very time consuming and have ripple effects, particularly related to risk and compliance. Data stewardship is also simpler, as there is a single location to manage information related to a domain and its entities. Finally, data synchronization is a nonfactor since multiple copies are not maintained. This is a huge advantage because data synchronization is highly risky due to its complexity and susceptibility to defects.

In summary, this style is highly intrusive and typically the most expensive and time consuming to implement. It might even be impossible to implement, depending on existing applications and their flexibility to be customized to consume data from the hub. One must consider how data will be distributed to other sources, typically through an enterprise service bus (ESB) and service-oriented architecture (SOA) due to time constraints. However, if this style is indeed achieved, ongoing maintenance is simplified when compared to other models. Data governance and stewardship will directly benefit from an authoritative source that is clearly defined, which will avoid future disputes.

Figure 3.3 depicts a possible architecture implementing the transaction-style multi-domain MDM. Notice both real-time and batch-mode interfaces are represented, but they do not necessarily have to coexist. Nonetheless, it is not uncommon for certain sources to consume data from certain domains in batch form, while consuming data from other domains in real time. It is also possible for some sources to consume data from certain domains in real time

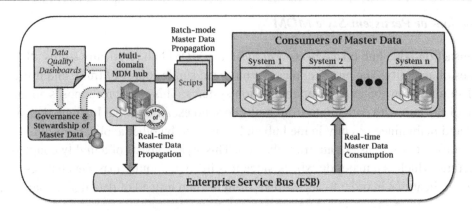

Figure 3.3: Transaction- or persistent-style multi-domain MDM

while other sources consume the same data from the same domains in batch mode. Overall, several combinations are possible.

Hybrid-Style MDM

The hybrid model of MDM is a compromise between the registry and transaction styles. It recognizes the shortcomings of a registry model and its latency issues and the shortcomings of a transaction model and the need to modify applications to query a MDM hub for all master data. In a hybrid style, more than just identity attributes are kept in the hub. A copy of many attributes related to an entity is maintained in the hub, which speeds up queries to the hub. Also, since the information is a copy, existing systems can continue to use their own version of the data.

In this model, the hub is not the SOR since data creation and maintenance continue to happen at the original sources, and attributes replicated in the hub are kept refreshed. The MDM hub is a system of reference, integrating many sources, applying entity resolution and other data quality functions to master data, and making available a single version of the truth to consuming systems.

The hybrid MDM is loosely coupled and came into existence because tight coupling is not always practical in today's multivendor, multiproduct IT environments that frequently use internal and external application systems. IT organizations can't be expected to completely reengineer their existing applications, as required by the transaction-style MDM.

Although the hybrid model overcomes certain issues with the registry and transaction styles, it does have its own problems. The most glaring one is related to maintaining a copy of some attributes. Any time data is replicated, there is the risk of inconsistency. The hybrid model is popular and deployed very successfully in many setups, but if it is not implemented carefully, it can almost contradict what MDM is set to achieve. MDM is about solving issues related to having multiple copies of master data across multiple sources. Yet, the hybrid MDM does so by creating another source. Granted, in theory, it is a source setup with the capabilities to resolve conflicting information. Still, if proper precautions are not taken, it could become another source of contention.

The hybrid style shares the challenge of the transaction style with regard to creating a data model that meets the requirements of many data sources, but to a lesser extent. Since not all attributes have to reside in the hub, the hub needs to model only a minimum set of information, seen as enterprise master data attributes. Other more specific master attributes are still kept only at their original sources, supporting specific application functionalities. Those specialized attributes, although also nontransactional in nature, are considered extensions to the enterprise model. Relative to application usage, the distinction of what attributes are global and which are local can be overwhelming.

This style also presupposes an initial loading of the hub. There is a need for ongoing synchronization and its many facets, such as batch or real-time synchronization, what interfaces are bidirectional, conflicting updates from multiple sources, what attributes are affected for each source, and so on. Because original sources are kept relatively untouched, the hybrid style can be quick to deploy, but in general, it does take longer than the registry style. Figure 3.4 depicts a possible implementation of a hybrid multi-domain MDM. Notice both real-time and batch-mode interfaces are represented, but they don't have to coexist.

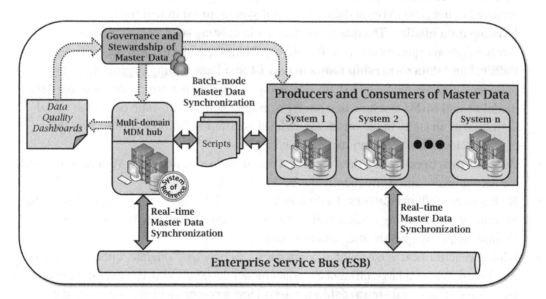

Figure 3.4: Hybrid multi-domain MDM

Nonetheless, different synchronization mechanisms or combinations thereof might exist between sources and domains.

Multi-domain MDM Technical Implementation Considerations

Before a particular style is identified for your multi-domain MDM solution, it is important to consider some fundamental aspects that are critical to making the right decision.

In very simple terms, MDM is technically about integrating master data into a data structure, creating a single version of the truth, and propagating or synchronizing this cleaner information. From a technical perspective, it is possible to say that MDM is about the following:

- Data models
- Data integration
- Entity resolution
- Data synchronization or propagation

Granted, some of these items will be implemented differently depending on the MDM style chosen. But realizing that those are the actual technical components can help you evaluate vendor solutions, as well as decide which one best fits your enterprise architecture. A company will have certain cultural and operational characteristics, some of which can affect the foundational technical components. Here are some examples:

- **IT infrastructure:** Companies with higher capabilities in SOA and ESB are more prepared to integrate existing data and keep it synchronized in real time.
- **Existing data quality:** The quality of the data in existing sources will influence synchronization requirements, as well as the capabilities required to carry out entity resolution.
- **Political and data ownership issues across LOBs:** How willing organizations are to build an enterprise model and share ownership of the data is a strong driver to the data model behind MDM and how that model is fully integrated. In some cases, the actual definition of an entity at the organization level is different from its definition at the enterprise level due to operational idiosyncrasies.
- **Business practices:** Where data is created has an influence on which system is the SOR for each domain, and consequently on the MDM style itself.
- **Risk and compliance factors:** Certain industries and domains will be more susceptible to scrutiny by governing bodies, which can directly affect how much leeway there is to cleanse, and consequently alter, existing data.
- **Global reach:** Local versus global companies, and how they operate, either centralized or distributed, wields a large influence on data model designs and overall system integration.
- **Data governance and stewardship models:** How a company plans to execute data governance and how stewards will manage data are highly dependent on MDM styles.

These points are just some factors to consider. An enterprise and LOB balance must be found, as technical decisions will affect the business; at the same time, business practices, requirements, and company culture must be evaluated to dictate the technical implementation that best fits their needs. To be sure, it is always about solving a business problem, and in the end, any technical solution must satisfy that need. But sometimes there are multiple ways to solve the same problem, and some approaches are more suitable than others. Considering what is technically already available or what best fits an existing IT model might justify concessions on business requirements.

Let's take a further look at the four foundational technical components mentioned previously.

Data Model

One of the reasons why it is difficult to find an existing MDM solution that fits your needs is because it is impossible to create a universal data model that will reflect every company's business requirements. Data inside a company is very specific, both structurally and from a content point of view. Obviously, content is what makes data an asset to an organization, but structure is directly tied to business requirements. For example, some companies might use a customer-centric model while others use an account-centric model; and some companies might use the concept of a party to represent every person and company with any type of relationship with them, while other companies might model employees, individual customers, business customers, vendors, and partners completely independently.

Therefore, data normalization, cardinality, and integrity constraints are all relevant factors for both existing systems and for a newly created MDM system. Remember that MDM is integrating data from multiple sources, and in most cases, keeping it synchronized as well. Understanding how data is modeled across multiple sources and its create-read-update-delete (CRUD) management is critical to understanding how data should be modeled in MDM. Data is most likely already modeled differently within existing systems. Creating a master data model that integrates well with all those systems can be overwhelming.

The reason data models are important is that they translate business concepts into concrete technical terms. That is where the risk is. If a business concept is not clearly defined, its technical representation is flawed and further maintenance is prone to error. The challenge increases when modeling multiple domains and their relationships. Existing multi-domain MDM solutions will include a predefined physical model, but they usually allow customizations to extend their models since their existing design will not fit every company's needs.

Vendors may or may not provide conceptual or logical models. These models can be fundamental tools for business teams, as they provide the right level of abstraction to facilitate understanding and validation, but they can also be very specific to each company and its business. Often, conceptual and logical models are never fully completed for various reasons.

One major reason is the project timeline and pressure to reach the implementation phase, where the physical model is necessary. This causes the completion of conceptual and logical models to be abandoned and often leaves key business concepts or definitions incomplete, causing business-term issues to emerge later that must be resolved by data governance.

Understanding vendor-provided data models, how they can be extended and customized to support specific requirements, and how to model multiple domains and their relationships is critical to success. A data architect is needed to review and approve the data models. Remember to consider nonfunctional requirements, such as security, scalability, and performance, as well. Data models are important no matter what MDM style is chosen. What varies is just how models are rendered. In the registry style, the data model is virtual and resolved dynamically via metadata definitions. In transaction or hybrid styles, the multi-domain MDM hub is looking to encompass a large number of master data elements, and the data model needs to take that in consideration.

In addition, global companies need to consider local versus global data models and their ensuing internalization and localization requirements, as well as centralized versus distributed operations and how they can affect data model designs.

Data Integration

Data need to be integrated before a single version is created. The integration can be virtual, such as in the registry/federated MDM style, or physical, such as in the transactional or hybrid style. Physical data integration requires a data migration effort where data is copied or moved from existing systems to the MDM hub. Virtual data integration does not require data migration, but it remains necessary to define how two or more attributes from multiple systems represent the same thing.

From a multi-domain perspective, all domains will not necessarily need to be integrated in the same way. Other factors need to be considered, such as the number of sources containing master data, the quality of the data at those sources, how data needs to be synchronized and propagated, and how master entities are related to each other.

Another very important aspect when doing physical integration is the frequency of data movement. Does it need to be in real time or not? For certain companies, batches created daily are perfectly adequate to integrate data from multiple sources into an MDM hub; others might require real-time integration and harmonization of their operational data. As already stated, this requirement might vary depending on the domain being mastered. An extreme example is a large, global company implementing a distributed, multi-domain MDM with multiple hubs. For regional use, some domains are integrated in real time with local systems, and other domains are integrated in batches. For global use, a master hub is integrated with distributed hubs in batch mode.

Consider your integration requirements carefully and remember that the quality of your existing data can influence that decision as well. Profile your data fully before committing to a solution.

Entity Resolution

Obviously, the capability of a multi-domain MDM entity resolution engine is directly tied to proper vendor selection. But the less obvious element is how that capability can influence what MDM style is chosen, as well as how data stewardship practices will be conducted. The reverse is also true: How a company plans to practice data stewardship and the quality of its existing data can dictate what style and entity resolution engines work best.

Understanding the impact of false positives and false negatives is essential. False positives are distinct records, incorrectly identified as matches, while false negatives are similar records incorrectly unidentified as matches.

Let's use some examples to clarify. In a registry-style MDM, entity resolution is happening dynamically. As such, a tool that yields either too many false positives or too many false negatives damages the overall quality of the golden record generated. But false positives and false negatives are also directly related to the quality of the existing data. If the quality of the existing data is low, a registry-style MDM should be selected only if a powerful entity resolution engine can circumvent existing issues. On the other hand, if the entity resolution engine is less powerful or appropriate for the existing level of data quality, data stewards will need to intervene to manually correct exiting data. If the correction can happen at the sources, a registry-style MDM is still acceptable. But if data stewardship needs to be centralized, either a transactional or hybrid MDM would be more appropriate.

If the quality of the existing data is relatively good, and most of the resolution can be done automatically, data stewardship intervention is less necessary. On the other hand, if existing data quality is bad, data stewardship practices need to be elevated. Those factors will influence vendor selection and MDM style. In summary, it is not only about evaluating vendors, it is also about evaluating your own data first.

Another typical point of contention is which data-matching algorithm should be used: probabilistic or deterministic. Some tools will include both, but some will have one or the other. As usual, there is no simple answer. Probabilistic methods use statistical techniques to determine the probability that two or more records are the same. Deterministic methods use rules and patterns to transform data and allow two or more similar records to match. The similarity between records depends on the algorithm used. For example, one algorithm might consider the letters *y* and *i* equivalent, making *Bryan* and *Brian* match. It is wise to conduct a proof of concept to evaluate how well a vendor algorithm will perform against your company's data.

As expected, matching techniques and consequent false positives and false negatives are specific for each domain. That means a tool that is strong in *Customer* entity resolution, is not necessarily strong for *Product, Account,* or any other domain. Data analysis and proof of concept should be carried out on a domain basis. Remember that false positives and false negatives will never be reduced to zero. It is about finding a level that is comfortable and making sure that data is fit for usage. Some business cases will tolerate more false positives than false negatives or vice versa. Find the proper balance by analyzing your data.

Data Synchronization or Propagation

Data from the multi-domain MDM hub will certainly be consumed by multiple sources. That is the whole purpose of MDM: to serve as the single source of truth for master domain data. The more sources use data from the MDM hub, the better.

However, how data is consumed will vary depending on the MDM style. Simply stated, if multiple copies of master data exist, the data need to be synchronized. If a single version exists, either physically or virtually, data only need to be propagated. Therefore, in a registry-style MDM, since there is one single virtual version of master data, no synchronization is necessary. Data is simply consumed on demand by sources in need of trusted information. In a transactional MDM, there are no multiple copies either. A single physical version exists, and synchronization is not necessary. In a hybrid style, some attributes are copied, so synchronization is needed.

The technology for integration, synchronization, or propagation will not be included automatically as part of a vendor-provided multi-domain MDM solution. It might be necessary to acquire technology to integrate and synchronize or propagate data from a different vendor. For example, an MDM hub could be as simple as a physical data model with the logic to carry out entity resolution. To get data in and out of the hub, it might be necessary to use database tools, operating system scripts, SOA, ESB, or a combination of those.

Consider your synchronization requirements carefully. Solutions will become more complex as more systems need to remain synchronized. Minimize two-way synchronization as much as possible, as they are intricate and prone to error. Understand whether real-time synchronization is required or if batch synchronization done on a regular basis is sufficient. It is possible that these requirements will vary per domain and need to be implemented differently. When copies exist and multiple systems can potentially change data associated with the same entity, inconsistencies may arise due to latency issues. Understand what type of controls a vendor can provide to prevent these problems.

Finally, if copies of master data exist across multiple systems and proper mechanisms are indeed in place to maintain synchronized data according to the required frequency, errors still can occur. For example, chances are that data might get out of sync due to bugs or unforeseen scenarios. To address those cases, a data-quality process should be implemented to measure the consistency of master data across multiple sources. This information can be critical to helping data architects and data stewards address potential problems. Multi-domain MDM vendors will not necessarily provide out-of-the-box capabilities to measure those unexpected inconsistencies.

Technical Considerations to Other Major Functions

Up to this point, this chapter has mostly covered technologies and architecture directly related to integrating a multi-domain MDM hub into an IT infrastructure. But there are more technical considerations related to the other multi-domain MDM functions of data quality, metadata management, data governance, and data stewardship.

A lot of data-quality competencies are expected to already exist as part of a well-designed MDM hub solution. Since one of the primary functions of an MDM hub is to cleanse, standardize, and consolidate domain data, it is obviously expected that those data-quality capabilities would already be included with a vendor solution. However, data quality is needed in other areas. Data profiling, for example, is extremely important, and it cannot be stressed enough how critical it is to carefully analyze and understand existing data before an MDM solution is sought. In another example, data-quality metrics and dashboards are fundamental to data governance and stewardship activities. In the end, data-quality profiling, metrics, and improvements should be ongoing within any company looking to fully leverage data as an asset and truly adopt a data-driven mantra. With that in mind, it might be necessary to invest in additional data-quality tools to supplement what is missing from a multi-domain MDM vendor product.

Some metadata functions are included in the registry-style MDM, but that is primarily to build a data federation system to join multiple sources virtually. However, metadata management is needed in many other areas (as will be discussed in Chapter 10), and a more robust tool is highly recommended. Metadata management tools are offered either stand-alone or integrated with other data-related solutions. For example, some enterprise data warehouse (EDW) vendors might offer metadata capabilities with their data models and maintenance tools. Extract, transform, and load (ETL) vendors might also offer capabilities to automatically capture data lineage and transformations linked to their products. However, metadata management tools are also available as separate applications, agnostic to underlying vendor products, which are targets for metadata documentation. Proper decisions must consider how well the metadata solution will integrate with other technologies and processes. Keep in mind that the goal of metadata management is to be an enterprisewide practice. Carefully consider the implications of adopting a potentially specialized and localized tool that might not scale properly to the required enterprise levels of governance.

The function of data stewards is to methodically prevent and correct data issues based on business and legal requirements, data quality defect reports, and compliance with data governance policies and standards. Data stewards require great expertise in the subject matter associated with the domain they manage. In addition to business and legal requirements and data governance policies and procedures, data stewards rely heavily on data-quality reports and dashboards and glossaries defining business terms. From a technical point of view, data stewards can benefit from the following:

- Metadata tools with a comprehensive data dictionary, data lineage, data transformation rules, business rules, and a business glossary to facilitate understanding about the data and the business expectations.
- Data-quality reporting tools that can monitor and expose anomalies.
- Workflow applications to help them manage scope of work, assignments, and approval processes.
- Depending on the multi-domain MDM solution, some type of data-quality remediation tool might be included, but most of the corrections are performed using regular system applications.
- Tools that can support data corrections in bulk. The majority of data corrections are performed one by one using applications' user interfaces. But depending on the issue, data stewards can benefit a great deal from bulk updates. Needless to say, compliance issues and other risks must be considered when performing bulk updates.

Last, but certainly not least, is data governance. From a technology support perspective, data governance shares some similarities with data stewardship regarding some underlying tools. Data governance needs metadata management tools to capture a glossary of business terms and rules, data-quality expectations, ownership, data life-cycle management, and impact analysis when changes occur. Data governance also requires substantial data-quality functions, particularly data-quality reports and dashboards. Finally, data governance needs workflow applications to facilitate tracking their work related to capturing business definitions, rules, policies, and procedures and to capturing proposed changes, required approvals, and audits.

Vendors obviously understand these dependencies. Therefore, they add functionality to their existing offerings to complement other areas. For example, a data-quality vendor might add workflow functionality that is tied to their dashboards to facilitate stewardship and governance operations; or a metadata vendor might embed approval and audit processes to its tool to enhance governance capabilities. Of course, this approach has pros and cons. An obvious advantage is that there is no need for other tools to perform new functions. One of the disadvantages is that these solutions could remain fragmented and not scale well to an enterprise level because they were just an afterthought, added to increase a vendor's market penetration. Before you start looking for additional technology to purchase, understand what you can use in tools you already have and see if that meets your needs.

Let's use a hypothetical example. Say that a company adopts a particular tool because it is truly the best at creating required data-quality dashboards for the business and data governance. This tool wasn't chosen for anything other than its data-quality capabilities. Nonetheless, the vendor develops the product, adding some metadata functionality to tie business rule definitions to data elements being monitored. It also adds certain workflow functionalities to trigger email notifications when certain attributes reach undesired values. This is obviously all to the good, but from a tool perspective, data quality metrics are practically the foundation for everything else, and if the company's data governance is still in the process of collecting business definitions and rules, obtaining approvals, and so on, the newly changed tool might not suit it. Metadata and workflow functions might be needed before the actual metric is completely defined. In this case, using this data-quality tool for anything other than data quality might not work. Using what is already available has many advantages, but be aware about how much you are willing to compromise.

Don't analyze tools in isolation. Carefully consider options and requirements. Also, look to use what might already be available inside your own company before adding more technology.

What About Big Data?

Big data is certainly getting a lot of attention lately. But how does it relate to MDM and data governance?

Big data has the following characteristics in large scale: volume, velocity, and variety, also known as the *3 Vs*. Other *Vs,* such as *veracity* and *value,* have been added to this list as the definition of big data continues to evolve. Social media is seen as the largest data farm out there, and it certainly meets the 3 V characteristics. Companies are increasingly looking for opportunities to tap into social media to add value to their strategies. From purchase patterns to customer complaints, the possibilities are also great. But social media is not the only source of big data. Any data meeting the 3 V characteristics should be handled as big data. For example, sensors frequently collecting information will certainly have high volume, high velocity, and potentially high variety.

Technology to efficiently handle volume, velocity, and variety is still evolving. Furthermore, the challenge is dealing not only with the 3 Vs, but also unstructured data. Big data mostly consists of unstructured data, and technology to handle unstructured data is also maturing. Nonetheless, big data is still data, and as such, it needs governance. Data governance must manage expectations, policies, and procedures regarding big data, while at the same time mediating potential opportunities created by big data projects. Data governance is highly dependent on data-quality dashboards and metadata definitions, and those will offer additional challenges. Data-quality parameters on big data might be hard to quantify, as it is very dependent on tools being able to correctly assess unstructured data against key performance indicators. In addition, unstructured data offers very little, if any, metadata information.

On the other hand, the MDM hub primarily consists of structured master data, and it is integrated from other structured or semistructured sources in the company, such as databases and spreadsheets. Granted, master data does exist in the company in unstructured or semistructured forms, such as emails, correspondence, and markup languages, but they are not the typical sources used to create an MDM hub.

Since big data is mostly unstructured, the link between master data and big data is very similar to how master data is linked to unstructured data. Master data can be used as a basis of big data analysis, such as context, search criteria, and classification. Technology is still evolving, as already stated, but one of the keys is to be able to apply certain MDM functions, such as fuzzy and probabilistic matching, to high-volume and high-velocity unstructured data.

At this point, big data is very loosely coupled to multi-domain MDM, so it is not covered in detail in this book.

Conclusion

Technology is not the only piece of the puzzle of multi-domain MDM, but it is certainly one of the most critical ones. We'll say it again: There is no single product that will address all the necessary capabilities of multi-domain MDM. Vendor solutions have improved and continue to mature, but MDM is very specific to each company, which complicates out-of-the-box solutions. In addition, potential differences about how each master data domain needs to be handled increase the complexity of architectures and implementations.

This chapter covered general guidelines on key aspects that should be considered when planning an enterprisewide technological landscape that can sustain a scalable, multi-domain MDM solution. Adding multi-domain MDM is more than just adding applications. It is about adding capabilities that affect the most important data elements across all existing systems.

MDM technology is very complex in terms of how it affects multiple organizations across the company. Perform a thorough vendor selection process, and hire expert consultants to guide you through it.

CHAPTER 4

Program Management Office Implementation

This chapter discusses the planning and structure needed for creating a Program Management Office (PMO) to oversee the Master Data Management (MDM) program, including its roles and responsibilities in relation to resources, budgets, tools, and change management processes. It provides examples of PMO structure and process flows and the cross-functional alignment needed between program, information technology (IT), and governance functions, as well as how the MDM PMO fits into that dynamic.

As a company grows, it needs to expand MDM and data governance initiatives across the business model and data architecture. Implementing MDM across multiple domains naturally creates the need to examine how to best coordinate and prioritize multi-domain activities, particularly with regard to technology needs, quality improvement priorities, and the demand for budget and IT resources. An MDM plan needs to start by creating a distinct PMO and an associated core team to establish the foundation needed to move the program forward.

In Chapter 1, Figure 1.1 provided a high-level example of a cross-domain program model, showing the relationship between program office, data governance, data domains, and the key components that need to be supported. Along with the overall MDM program charter and scope, each domain will have a specific scope, objectives, responsibilities, and resources, similar to how individual projects within a program will have project-specific plans and deliverables in support of the overall program strategy and goals.

A multi-domain MDM program will not succeed if it tries to adopt too much of a cookie-cutter approach to the planning and support of each domain. The PMO needs to look at the orchestration of MDM from both an enterprisewide perspective, to ensure that there is a common program framework across the domain structure, and a domain perspective, to ensure that domain-specific objectives and priorities can be recognized and supported. A well-conceived PMO should always be cognizant of how to continually help enable the various domain objectives and avoid overmanaging where control and conformance are not necessary.

Depending on a company's business model and MDM strategy, the role and responsibility mix between the PMO and domain charters can vary, but in general, there should be a clear separation of duties conducive to a collaborative and supportive relationship. Because many aspects of quality management, governance, and stewardship focus are unique within each domain, these aspects should not be impeded by excessive PMO control. If the PMO charter is too broad, overly controlling, and attempts to create too much of a homogeneous multi-domain model, it can start overshooting its value if it takes authority and empowerment from the domain-specific teams. A PMO needs to cultivate an environment where a maturing MDM domain team can lead by example, developing best practices that other domain teams can use to accelerate their maturity. A leading domain implementation needs extra attention so that the business foundation that it creates for data governance, stewardship, quality management, metadata management, data integration, and technology usage can create repeatable or adaptable practices to help prime the startup of other domain implementations. This is critical for driving sustainability across the overall MDM model. Using the knowledge, practices, and experience from a leading MDM practice should be a key strategy in developing a multi-domain plan.

There are many IT-oriented services and resources needed to support MDM practices. In a multi-domain model, this can cause competing demand from the domains for these elements. As a multi-domain plan is being defined and executed, the PMO needs to work closely with IT on the technical requirements, services, and resources needed to execute MDM with each domain in scope. Launching too many MDM initiatives side by side, along with poor capacity planning by IT, will quickly lead to IT overload and bottleneck scenarios, causing program deliverables to be delayed.

Here are some important IT-related considerations that the PMO should review:

* How much capacity will business and IT organizations need to support their requirements and demands with a multi-domain plan?
* How rigid is the IT engagement process and the support practices? Can these processes sufficiently adjust to provide more flexibility and collaborative support across business-driven MDM programs?
* Will new technology actually help enable or hinder MDM efficiency and return on investment (ROI)?

The MDM PMO should be careful about creating too many critical path dependencies on new technology because of the higher potential for delays and functionality issues. Chapter 3 discussed both the value points and the challenges associated with technology in an MDM program. There are many aspects of data governance, data stewardship, business analysis, process improvement, and overall program management that do not depend on technology, so be sure that these type activities and tasks are sufficiently identified in the program plan and can still move forward while other technology issues are being addressed.

Business and IT Alignment Considerations

Business and IT alignment issues can affect the ability to execute enterprise data management programs like MDM. Companies can struggle with achieving their data management and quality management objectives because of fundamental organization and process alignment issues, such as:

- Data ownership is unclear.
- MDM and data governance programs are not aligned well with IT governance, project governance, or other key decision-making bodies that can affect master data.
- Organizational changes can slow momentum or break the governance and quality management focus of a company.
- The organization fails to work collectively to correct the root causes of data issues and instead apply point fixes randomly.
- Different groups have different systems of record (SORs) or use different reporting and analytic solutions.

From the Best Practices Report "Next-Generation Master Data Management," released by the Data Warehouse Initiative (TDWI) in 2012, among the top responses from users surveyed regarding their challenges to MDM success were:

- Lack of cross-functional cooperation
- Coordination with other disciplines (Data Integration, Data Quality)
- Poor data quality

Much of this is the result of failure to align a data governance program with other governance bodies within a company. For example, it would not be uncommon for IT governance and project governance bodies to make strategic and tactical decisions about master data without involving a data governance team. Projects are frequently launched without master data or data governance requirements and then encounter issues related to data quality management, data definition, or policies and standards that will require data governance later. This happens because data governance is not often recognized as an important component during project planning, which can cause project teams and IT functions to be unprepared to handle large-scope data quality and integrity issues when they emerge.

Alignment issues often underlie the inability to conduct sufficient root-cause analysis and implement permanent fixes to problems. For example, a data warehousing support team may identify a data quality and consistency issue across multiple source systems, but because of alignment issues between IT support and the various business process teams, a permanent fix cannot be fully implemented causing point fixes within the warehouse and notices sent to downstream user groups regarding how they will need to work around the data problem.

Another common alignment issue is where there are no cross-functional standards regarding the use of reference data, such as country codes, product codes, service codes, reason codes, language codes, or other code sets. Without enterprise standards and sufficient code set registration policies, local applications and new projects will often just find or create the reference data they need to meet their requirements without regard to other existing code sets. This will cause more duplication or overlap of reference data across the enterprise.

Building Cross-Functional Alignment

Identifying ownership and maintenance responsibilities for master data is a topic that needs to be addressed right up front between the MDM PMO and data governance. Because of the cross-functional nature of master data, identifying master data ownership and maintenance responsibilities will likely span various IT and business roles within each data domain. Reviewing the master data life cycle and completing a create-read-update-delete (CRUD) analysis, as discussed in Chapter 2, will help identify these ownership and maintenance roles. Data governance should have the authority to define or confirm these roles and responsibilities, as well as the associated policies governing the master data. The MDM PMO should have a seat on the governance team and be prepared to help support the services and alignment needs required for these roles and responsibilities. Chapter 6 will cover this in more detail from a data governance perspective, but for the MDM PMO, there are two basic questions that affect data governance:

- How does the responsibility for creating and maintaining master data need to be coordinated across IT and the line of business functions?
- What additional resources and services are needed to help support MDM as a consistent, enterprisewide program?

Each data domain may have different answers to these questions, which is why the MDM PMO office needs to be cognizant of how support needs can differ between domains. An objective examination of these questions for each domain will likely identify existing business and IT alignment issues, which will need to be mutually addressed by the MDM PMO and data governance. Figure 4.1 provides a simple illustration of a well-aligned model.

There are a number of key points to consider when building this cross-functional alignment:

- Work with data governance, IT governance, project governance, and other key steering committee bodies to define clear charters, roles, and engagement rules for how to handle issues and decisions related to master data.
- Identify how enterprisewide communications should be coordinated regarding master data issues, topics, changes, governance policies, and standards.
- Leverage cross-functional collaboration where it already exists in projects and programs.

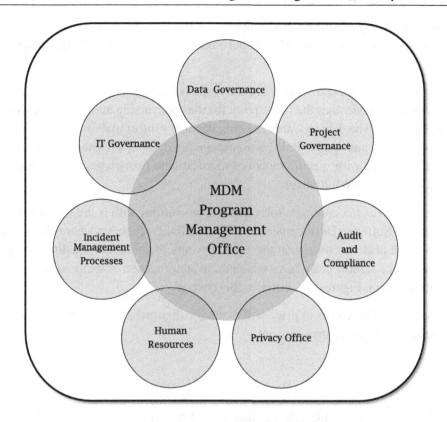

Figure 4.1: Functional alignments with the MDM PMO

- Bring attention to where good governance and quality management practices are occurring. Build from best practices.
- Be persistent, be opportunistic, but have patience.

Such an alignment can occur through various relationships. To best accommodate this, a data governance domain team should have members representing various projects and initiatives within that domain so that issues and data quality management needs can be reviewed and coordinated between the data governance and project teams.

Coordination of MDM Roles and Responsibilities

With each domain, the roles and responsibilities that need to support the master data need to be recognized early in the MDM strategy and program process. Spelling this out and planning how these roles coordinate with other business and IT roles will take any conflicts or jurisdictional issues out of the debate and enable MDM governance and data steward functions to be formally recognized and supported in the company's ecosystem. Figure 4.2 illustrates how these relationships and roles become the partnerships and supporting dynamic for master data.

A well-defined and coordinated set of roles and responsibilities between the data governance and data steward roles becomes the focus point for the sponsorship and ongoing execution of the MDM process. The data stewards not only become subject matter experts who have sufficient tools, skills, and responsibilities to manage the domain's master data across domains, but also work with specific functions to assist with many types of data analysis, standardization, or cleanup initiatives.

Another important area to coordinate roles and responsibilities with is the solution design process, such as a Software Development Life Cycle (SDLC) process, where checkpoints or gates can be put in place to ensure that there are appropriate guidelines, quality management, and data governance signoff procedures where there are proposed or required changes or impacts to master data. Figure 4.3 illustrates this concept.

Having these types of protocols in place will maintain alignment between project governance, data governance, and quality management.

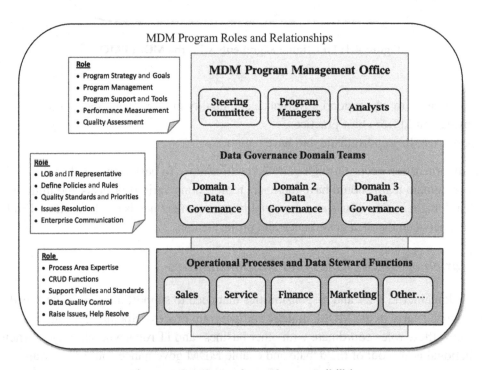

Figure 4.2: MDM roles and responsibilities

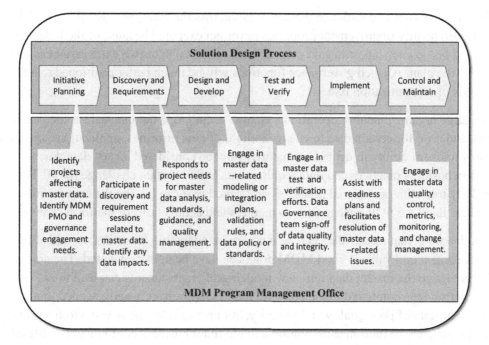

Figure 4.3: MDM PMO engagement in the solution design SDLC process

Handling Organization Change

Most companies go through some fairly substantial organizational or strategic changes, which can really slow the momentum of an MDM initiative. Whether due to market shift, mergers or acquisitions, corporate restructure, or infrastructure changes, in the corporate world, change is a regular occurrence. Quite often, structural changes in the organization cause a splintering effect that can be very disruptive, requiring various program or project groundwork and plans to be revisited or recalibrated.

The MDM PMO needs to recognize this and utilize change management and impact analysis approaches such as a Strength, Weakness, Opportunity, and Threat (SWOT) analysis to help define effective strategies for identifying and managing change.

Change Impacts

The degree of business impact from organizational change will depend on how well cross-functional alignment to the changes is managed. If there are broad corporate strategies and well managed plans to transition from legacy processes and applications to enterprise solutions, then the realignment of existing programs and processes is likely to be a natural bi-product of that strategy. If good cross-functional alignment has already been established, it will be much easier to coordinate these changes across the enterprise. Keep in mind that many needed quality improvement proposals never get executed because of the failure to established task ownership or to gain commitment for just one or two extra resources needed to execute the plan. Aligned governance functions will be much better positioned to address these types of reorganization issues.

When a large organizational or operational change occurs, it is not unusual for the value, context, and need for certain data to change in light of new priorities, applications, ownership, or simply a loss of ability to maintain what may now be considered legacy data. Such changes in business practices and data requirements are a constant challenge for IT. This is particularly true with operational processes and data, but it can also be the case for master data, where there are SOR changes due to mergers and acquisitions or platform changes.

The good news is that master data can be much more adaptable, transferable, and able to retain its context and value if good MDM practices have been implemented. The ability to quickly integrate the master data into new models and environments can lead to not only a large cost savings compared to the cost of a much larger effort usually needed to align and integrate data of poor quality and integrity, but also enables the new environment or acquiring company to minimize disruption and maintain business continuity. The MDM PMO needs to recognize the potential for such changes and highlight how the good MDM practices are an asset.

Having a good MDM PMO will help keep MDM practices highly adaptive to organizational change. Because organizational change can often be very disruptive—particularly when associated with mergers and acquisitions—and is usually expected to be completed under a specific plan within a fixed time frame, the quality and execution of a data migration effort can suffer due to time constraints. Master data that have been poorly translated and mapped into new models can cause significant issues with operational processes and customer transactions later. During major organizational and system changes involving the migration or integration of master data, engaging the MDM PMO and data governance teams early during the project and change management planning phases can help define specific data-quality requirements and quality acceptance criteria during the transition of the master data.

During organizational and operational change, IT typically has the responsibility to transition the systems and the data; however, subject matter experts on the business side who are intimately familiar with the business processes and context of the data are often transitioned quickly into new organization structures and environments, or possibly even leave the company (whether voluntarily or not). This often results in poorly migrated and mapped data, which can degrade overall data quality and create many operational issues until the situation can be corrected. An existing MDM PMO and data governance team involved in the transition plans can help avoid these knowledge and resources gaps.

PMO Tools and Processes

As mentioned in Chapter 3, there are various MDM products and tools on the market that, if being considered by the MDM PMO, will need a close examination to determine their strengths and weaknesses in relation to program needs and whether they will be a good investment. With an increasing number of vendor software solutions targeted across the MDM, data governance, data quality, data integration, and enterprise data management (EDM) markets, there are many overlapping features and capabilities that can be confusing and difficult to sort out or differentiate by a PMO when trying to find complementary and cost-effective solutions to use across an MDM program. A company is likely to already have some existing solutions that support data quality, data integration, and metadata management needs. The PMO office needs to take inventory of what solutions already exist internally and evaluate the ability to leverage these internal solutions for MDM needs. Then it should determine what other vendor solutions may be needed. As also mentioned in Chapter 3, the MDM PMO should consider the value of using an experienced consulting firm to help assess tool and vendor solution needs.

Program Communication

As is typical with any program (or project), the MDM PMO will have program communications needs with the program team members as well as with stakeholders and other audiences. Assuming that the MDM PMO has established a strong alignment and partnership with the data governance program, most external communications of the MDM program can be channeled via data governance communication processes. As discussed in Chapter 2, the domain data governance team structure includes members who represent the applications, business processes, and analytic areas, and who are creators and consumers of the master data for that domain. And assuming the data governance team has established a RACI matrix (see Chapter 6, Figure 6.5) for its communication needs, the MDM program can leverage this matrix and associated process for its outward communication needs. Using the data governance RACI matrix for the MDM program's outbound communication needs is not only good practice to avoid confusion or overlapping that can occur if these communications are not well coordinated, but it also visibly demonstrates a strong relationship between the MDM program and data governance. Chapter 6 provides more detail regarding the data governance role, as well as examples of a RACI matrix.

Program Value

There is no single recipe for fully expressing the value proposition or an ROI for MDM. Attempts to try to calculate and project a programwide ROI can be complex and highly speculative. Too much emphasis on a hard ROI can miss the central point that MDM is really a critical data management practice needed to better manage and control a company's most important data—it does not always immediately translate to a monetary benefit. A multi-domain MDM program involves many data management disciplines that need coordination across business and IT functions. This dynamic cannot be put into fixed-time and fixed-cost outcomes that can be clearly calculated up front.

If anything, the longer-term value of MDM can be truly measured only in real time, as cohesive data management and sound governance decisions are made based on ongoing business needs and strategic plans. However, there can and should be ROIs calculated for investment decisions related to vendor solutions and incremental resources that the program needs. ROIs for these type investments may be required, so the MDM PMO needs to be prepared to address the ROI question when required. But overall, the MDM program should be recognized as a developing internal core competency and a necessary investment area for improving data management practices across the company. As such, MDM should be positioned in the company so that the program can mature and realize its long-term value.

Consider what this book has identified as the fundamentals of MDM—data governance, data stewardship, data integration, data quality management, and metadata management. These are data management and quality management process investment areas that should be justifiable based on any number of existing business problems and data issues. Companies first need to recognize their most critical business needs for MDM initiatives and build the business case around them. Next, they should estimate how much they are losing by not realizing all the benefits of a having a timely, accurate, and consistent set of master data delivered to the various business functions in the company. This is sometimes referred to as *activity-based costing (ABC)*. Often, the best way to measure the potential benefit of MDM involves determining the amount of money that a company spends with reactive activities in place to compensate for a suboptimal set of processes and tools.

Program value should also be demonstrated continually once MDM domains are launched, by using a consistent communication and performance measurement approach that reports MDM program activity, performance against targets, and key program achievements. Performance measurement will be covered in more detail in Chapter 11.

Issue Management and Resolution

Ownership and change control of master data should have clear lines of sight, but because MDM issues can be associated with people, processes, and technology, issue and incident resolution needs to be effectively coordinated across the MDM program office, data governance, IT support, and project teams. As with any incident resolution process, there are three fundamental functions that need to be coordinated well:

- Reporting the problem
- Assigning and escalating the problem
- Tracking and closing the problem

Reporting the Problem

Master data issues can be discovered virtually anywhere in the operating and analytical processes. Often, data issues in the analytic areas are not discovered until far downstream. The master data landscape is further complicated by the fact that the creation and introduction of various master data occur in many processes across lines of business (LOBs) that can have different quality management and defect management priorities. Therefore, it is extremely important that master data issues are identifiable, reported, and quickly evaluated to avoid or minimize business impacts.

If a company has implemented enterprise standard incident resolution and defect management processes, it will be much easier or the MDM PMO office to work with these process teams to establish rules, attributes, and reports that can flag significant master data issues as they are being reported and progressing through the processes. If the PMO and data governance have examined master data life cycles and CRUD dynamics, it should be easy to recognize and communicate with the business process areas and the incident resolution processes where master data related issues can emerge.

Assigning and Escalating the Problem

When a master data issue does emerge, clear guidelines for handling, prioritizing, and routing the issue are needed. Most effective help desks and call centers will have such guidelines and operating procedures, but unfortunately, they typically do not include any formal engagement practices or escalation protocols with an MDM PMO or data governance program. Similar to how an MDM PMO needs to establish engagement rules with a solution design process area (see Figure 4.3), the PMO should also build relationships with incident resolution processes that can involve master data. And as those processes assign an issue to a support area, the agents and support groups should be aware of the MDM PMO and data governance as functioning bodies that can or should become engaged based on engagement rules that have been predetermined.

Often, an issue related to a systemic data quality problem (e.g., missing data, garbage data, incorrectly formatted data, or duplicate data) is reported as a trouble ticket, incident report, or defect by an operational or analytic team. A help-desk process will not typically be able to resolve such problems and will need to escalate them to a data governance or data quality support function where more extensive root cause analysis, impact assessment, and remediation can occur. Having solid relationships between the MDM PMO, data governance, and the incident resolution processes will make it straightforward for the support teams to be able to reach out or formally escalate master data issues to the MDM PMO or data governance bodies per established engagement rules.

Tracking and Closing the Problem

With having established good relationships and engagement rules, the MDM PMO can work with the incident resolution process areas to be able to monitor and track the master data issues submitted through these processes. Tracking that data and recognizing the local user areas and processes that are submitting these issues will provide very valuable, real-time usage information and insight to augment knowledge gained from examination of the master data life cycle and CRUD dynamics. From this insight and the ongoing tracking of this, the MDM PMO will start becoming increasingly familiar with the types and nature of MDM issues, where the issues are emerging, and who is affected by the issues, and therefore it can raise visibility and support solutions to permanently fix recurring problems.

The MDM PMO should also review the closure procedures related to the incident resolution and defect management processes. It is important that master data issues are not spuriously closed or left in aging backlogs that are going nowhere. If an incident resolution and defect management process does not have resources or pathways to address certain types of master data issues, the MDM PMO should examine this problem, determine if these issues need to be addressed with data governance or reassigned, or at least assist the incident resolution and defect management processes by examining and justifying the closure of aging master data issues. Premature closure of master data issues or moving them to an inactive aging state usually results from a lack of sufficient knowledge, guidelines, and reassignment paths for how these issues should be handled. The MDM PMO and data governance can assist these incident resolution and defect management processes with creating more end-to-end guidelines and examples to help support teams triage, position, and close MDM issues.

Conclusion

This chapter discussed the planning and structure needed for creating a MDM Program Management Office, including the roles and responsibilities of the PMO in relation to program resources, budgets, tools, and alignment with other key functions and incident resolution processes.

Simply stated, a MDM PMO with a multi-domain scope can expect to encounter a lot of variables, so do the math and complete the necessary analysis to identify what program and domain execution challenges there are likely to be. A successful MDM strategy and program plan will need to be prepared to address the variances, challenges, and obstacles that will apply across the domains. Gear your PMO office to help facilitate the common and unique elements, while also driving the domain programs to stay in the scope of the overall enterprise MDM model and objectives. A PMO must ensure that there is good alignment between itself, data governance, and IT governance.

CHAPTER 5

Defining a Cross-Domain Maturity Model

This chapter covers the need to establish a Master Data Management (MDM) maturity model, how to define the right maturity model, and how to apply maturity measurement consistently across a multi-domain model. It also provides examples of various maturity milestones that should be tracked.

Common to any MDM domain strategy is the need to transition master data from an insufficiently managed state to a highly managed and controlled state necessary to achieve goals identified in the MDM program plan. Achieving MDM goals requires a well-orchestrated set of milestones involving various disciplines, practices, capabilities, and quality improvement. Capturing the essence of this as a high-level, measureable roadmap over time is the purpose of a maturity model and the reason that it provides an important tool to track program progress. A multi-domain maturity model is the ability to consistently define and track progress across all MDM domains in the program scope. Let's break this down further, and then provide an example of a maturity model.

Maturity States

MDM and data governance maturity models tend to reflect either a behavioral or a functional approach for measuring states of maturity:

- **Behavioral:** Expressing maturity from a behavioral perspective using maturity phase descriptions such as Unaware, Undisciplined, Reactive, Disciplined, Effective, Proactive, and Advanced
- **Functional:** Expressing maturity from a functional perspective using maturity phase descriptions such as Unstructured, Structured, Foundational, Managed, Repeatable, and Optimized

The actual number of maturity phases in either approach can vary, although four or five is the most common. Both type of approaches have merit and eventually tend to conceptually align at the advanced states, where end-state maturity is commonly expressed as being an advanced or optimized model and process. It is the ability to rationalize and measure the milestones in the earlier stages of the maturity model that differ within each approach.

From a multi-domain program perspective, the functional approach is most effective for measuring the initiation and maturity of MDM practices and capabilities across the domains as the program plan progresses. This approach assumes that behavioral conditions such as *reactive* and *proactive* will continue to exist throughout the functional phases and across domains. In reality, there never is a purely proactive state without reactive situations, which is the reason that using the behavioral approach for measuring multi-domain maturity does not provide a truly comprehensive and progressive measurement. Unplanned or unpredictable conditions will always exist, creating reactive situations that must be addressed at any point in an MDM program even when it has reached a highly managed and optimized state. However, as the MDM program and domain areas increase their functional capabilities, there should be shifts to more proactive behavior and less reactive behavior.

How and Where Can Maturity Be Measured?

Figure 5.1 is a simple, high-level example of a multi-domain maturity model using the functional approach. This example illustrates the need to gauge maturity across data governance, data stewardship, data integration, data quality management, and metadata management. Defining and measuring the milestones for these practices and capabilities not only help differentiate where the focus, progress, and issues exist across the multi-domain model, but can serve as an excellent overall program dashboard for review with a data governance board or an executive steering committee. The actual maturity phases chosen for use in the model can be different than what is shown in Figure 5.1. No matter which phases are chosen, they should reflect maturity states and milestones that are relevant to the program goals and objectives, are consistent and measureable across multiple domains, and will be meaningful to the intended audiences.

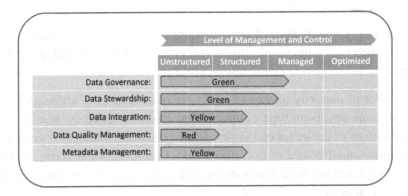

Figure 5.1: MDM program maturity model dashboard example

Measuring maturity from a functional perspective should not be interpreted as just measuring from a technical or application capability perspective. This is often the case, and that approach would overlook important MDM capabilities that are driven from a business perspective, such as data governance, stewardship, and quality management at the business-process level. MDM maturity should be understood and measured from both a technical and business capability point of view. As shown in Figure 5.1 and later in this chapter in Figure 5.2, measuring maturity at the program and domain levels should reflect milestones that are achieved by improving people, process, and technology capabilities that all contribute to better quality and control of master data.

The dashboard in Figure 5.1 indicates the following conditions:

- The data governance component of the MDM model has been firmly established across the domains in scope, is being well managed and functioning as planned, is achieving its targeted milestones regarding MDM, continues to gain visibility and momentum across the business and information technology (IT) landscapes, and is influential with improving the level of control and data management focus needed for master data.
- The data stewardship discipline and assignments are moving into place well, although a few additional resources still need to be identified or recruited to fill needs for some domain area support roles. The company has recognized the need for establishing formal data steward job roles and is on target for fulfilling these positions.
- In some domains, the plans, architecture, and capability for master data integration is on track and progressing well. In other domains, the master data integration plans are lagging due to delays in the implementation of new enterprise architecture, systems, and transition plans.
- Important data quality profiling and improvement projects are on hold while the IT organization is renegotiating the application licenses and consulting services contracts with its data quality tool vendor.
- With data governance and data stewardship practices firmly established, good headway is being made with some metadata management objectives, but because plans for data integration and data quality improvement capabilities are lagging behind, this has impacted progress with the metadata management plans.

Data Governance Maturity

The maturity of MDM is highly dependent on the ability of data governance to reach a sufficiently mature state so that it can influence and drive the maturity of the other MDM disciplines and capabilities that this book has been discussing. When and how data governance reaches a mature state will basically come down to a few key elements:

- When ownership, partnership, and cross-functional collaboration are established and continually work well

- When the governance council can repeatedly make timely, actionable decisions
- How effective the governance process is at turning the dials left or right to control its data domain, which involves having control from both a reactive and proactive perspective

The most important part of the MDM process is the ability to recognize and effectively manage business risk and operational issues. This can be accomplished by having established a mature, domain-based data governance dynamic where engagement, review, and decision making are well orchestrated in a timely and fluid process. Domain-based data governance teams aligned with MDM domains will provide timely and effective decision making to support the ongoing MDM goals, objectives, and priorities. Because a domain's data governance charter can span master data, transactional data, reference data, and metadata, there needs to be clear recognition of the master data and representation from the MDM program office with each domain governance team.

Examples of key MDM milestones for data governance maturity include the following:

- Domain-based data governance charters, owners, teams, and the decision authority have been identified.
- The master data associated to the domains have been identified and approved by data governance from an owning and using perspective.
- Data management policies and standards have been defined and implemented.
- Measurements and dashboards are in place to measure and drive master data quality and control.

Data Stewardship Maturity

For data stewardship to be effective, the concept and practice of data stewardship needs to be clearly imbedded in the key junction points between the entry and management of the master data. It is at these junctions where governance control and quality control can best be influenced through the use of committed and well-focused data stewards.

Probably the most difficult challenge with data stewardship is getting a sufficiently broad and consistent commitment for the data steward roles. Chapter 7 will cover this topic in more detail. If this challenge isn't well recognized and addressed early in the MDM and data governance planning stages, the MDM initiative is likely to be slowed. Late emergence of these types of underlying issues can be very disruptive. The concept and expectations for data stewardship must be agreed upon early and applied consistently for MDM practices to be well executed because data stewards will play a large role in the actions associated with MDM.

The ability for data stewardship to reach a mature state requires that the data steward model is well executed and functioning cohesively in alignment with the data governance process.

Many milestones targeted in the data governance maturity model need to be executed through the responsibilities and action plans assigned to the data stewards.

Similar to data governance, maturity of data stewardship is gauged by the extent to which this discipline can be orchestrated in a timely and fluid manner, but also by how successfully and consistently the data stewards address these actions. A mature data stewardship model should have a visible, closed-loop process that tracks the major action items and mitigation plans that involve the data stewards. Not having clear or consistent closure from data stewards regarding global and local initiatives usually suggests a problem with accountability or priority and signals that the MDM practice may be too focused on meetings and not focused enough on action.

Examples of key MDM milestones for data stewardship maturity include the following:

- A data steward model has been identified with processes, tools, and training needs defined for the data steward roles.
- MDM control points and practices have been defined within each domain.
- Data stewards have been identified and assigned to data quality and metadata management control areas.
- Data stewards are engaged, are meeting quality control requirements, and provide regular status updates to their data governance teams.

Data Integration Maturity

As noted in Chapter 1, achieving a single version of the truth (i.e., a golden record) is a primary objective of MDM. While this may not always be entirely possible for all data entities or records due to system or operational reasons, MDM practices should at least minimize occurrences of data duplication or variation by introducing control processes that meet an acceptable level of quality and integrity defined by data governance. Achieving a single version of the truth or minimizing occurrences involves data integration and rules-based entity resolution, as has already been discussed in Chapter 3.

Many master data quality and integrity issues can be traced to data integration activities that lack sufficient standards and rules during integration, or insufficient user inspection and acceptance criteria. The result is that poor data quality is introduced into systems and business operations, which later creates downstream user frustration, process errors, analytical issues, and back-end correction needs—all of which are classic reactions to poorly integrated data. Much of this can be prevented with more upfront data governance engagement, enforcement of quality control standards, and more effective user acceptance requirements. The data governance and data quality teams must be engaged in data integration plans to review and approve the integration standards, rules, results, and acceptance thresholds. The maturity model should include some key milestones that reflect this need.

Examples of key MDM milestones for data integration maturity include the following:

- Data integration projects that affect master data are reviewed by the domain data governance teams.
- Data stewards are assigned to participate in data integration project teams involving master data.
- IT and data governance teams have agreed on the extract, transform, and load (ETL) rules and quality acceptance requirements associated to data integration projects affecting master data.
- Consistent, reusable quality rules and standards are applied to master data integration projects to ensure that data quality is maintained.

Data Quality Maturity

A single version of the truth and data quality management practices go hand in hand. A single version of the truth implies that the available information is unambiguous, accurate, and can be trusted. Those attributes all require that good data quality management practices are occurring. If this is occurring, this is an indication that there is a quality culture within the company. Establishing this throughout the enterprise is mandatory for achieving maximum benefit from the enterprise data. Data quality is everyone's responsibility, but that requires organizations to establish the proper foundation through continuous training, clear quality improvement objectives, effective collaboration, and an efficiently adaptive model that can continue to deliver quality results quickly despite constant changes.

To achieve a quality culture and management, there are many programs, mechanisms, roles, and relationships that need to work in harmony. Using the dashboard example presented earlier in Figure 5.1, data quality management cannot reach a mature state unless the data governance, data stewardship, and data integration practices are all enabled, functioning well, and can support data quality requirements. That shouldn't be a surprise, though, because a quality culture needs people, process, and technology that are all in sync with the recognition, management, and mitigation of quality issues.

Determining the level of cross-functional collaboration for quality management is the first factor in gauging data quality maturity. That collaboration is first established through the maturation of data governance, and then should translate into creating a foundation to drive and mature data quality management. Reaching maturity in data governance should mean that less effort will be needed with data quality management since better governed data needs less correction.

Another key factor in gauging maturity is how well the quality of the data is serving the analytics community. Data quality and integrity issues are the primary cause of the conflict and divide between operational and analytical practices. Solving this gap starts by creating more awareness and connection between data creators and consumers, but ultimately it is about improving the quality, consistency, and context of the master data. Value of the data needs to be measured by how well it is servicing both the operational and analytical process. How valuable the master data is or needs to become should be a well-recognized factor and a key driver in a highly functioning and mature MDM domain model.

Data quality maturity essentially means having reached a state where an acceptable level of quality management and control and a shared view about data value exist between operations and analytics. Reaching this state of acceptability and harmony is, of course, a very tall order. Making significant strides with quality improvement will require time and building out from well-coordinated efforts that are orchestrated from the data governance and data quality forums. This is exactly why MDM and data governance need to be approached as long-term commitments and become well entrenched as priorities in the operational and analytical functions of a company.

Examples of key MDM milestones for data quality maturity include the following:

- A data quality team or cross-functional forum is working in alignment with data governance.
- In each domain, there has been analysis and prioritization of key data quality issues affecting operational and analytical functions.
- Data improvement is occurring, supported by data quality management policies and standards.
- Data quality is being monitored and maintained within governance-approved control targets.

Metadata Management Maturity

Quality management is often discussed in the context of the quality requirements and measurement of the actual data entities and data elements. However, quality of master data assets should include the quality and control of the associated business metadata. Managing quality and control of metadata can be as complex and difficult as the quality and control of the actual data elements. This is because, like the data itself, there are various types and sources of the metadata associated with the data element that can make consistent control of the metadata very difficult across data domains and models.

Therefore, master data needs to have a metadata management plan that identifies what metadata will be in scope, how it will be managed, and what tools and repositories will be involved. Chapter 2 discussed how metadata needs to be inventoried as part of the domain's master data plan, and Chapter 10 will provide a deeper exploration of the discipline and practice of metadata management in a multi-domain program. Because many actions are needed to define the metadata plan, organize and execute the control process, and ensure that data governance is involved in this, a few key milestones should be summarized in the maturity model.

Examples of key MDM milestones for metadata maturity include the following:

- The key business metadata associated with a domain's master data has been identified for quality review.
- Quality management objectives and priorities for the metadata has been established and approved through data governance.
- Enterprise policies and standards for metadata management are in place and being enforced by data governance.
- Key data definitions are distinct, with data steward control processes in place to manage the change control of these definitions

Domain Maturity Measurement Views

Figure 5.2 provides an example of maturity milestone tracking for each domain in scope. Using this format, many more milestones can be identified and tracked as needed. The achievement of the milestones can be also be indicated by using dates and references to the evidence, which can be useful for auditing purposes.

Milestones	Maturity State	Domain 1	Domain 2	Domain 3	Domain 4
Data Governance					
Governance team and charter have been identified	Structured	X	X	X	X
Master data have been identified	Structured	X	X	X	X
Data management policies and standards are enforced	Managed	X			
Metrics and dashboards are driving master data control	Optimized	X			
Data Stewardship					
Processes, tools, and training needs are defined	Structured	X	X	X	X
Master data control points and practices are defined	Structured	X	X	X	
Data stewards are identified and assigned to MDM practices	Managed	X		X	
Data stewards are meeting quality control requirements	Optimized				
Data Integration					
Data integration projects reviewed by data governance	Structured	X		X	
Data stewards engaged in data integration project teams	Structured	X		X	
Agreement on ETL rules and data acceptance criteria	Managed	X		X	
Integration and quality rules are standardized and reusable	Optimized				
Data Quality					
The data quality team is aligned with data governance	Structured	X	X	X	X
Analysis of key data quality issues has occurred	Structured	X	X	X	
Data quality management policies and standards are enforced	Managed	X		X	
Data quality is maintained within control targets	Optimized				
Metadata Management					
Metadata management scope and approach identified	Structured	X	X	X	
Metadata management priorities have been established	Structured	X	X	X	
Metadata management policies and standards are enforced	Managed	X			
Key data definitions are distinct with data steward control	Optimized	X			

Figure 5.2: Maturity milestone tracking by domain

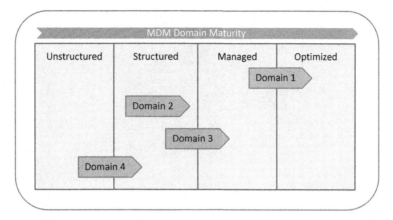

Figure 5.3: Current maturity status by domain

Figure 5.3 expresses the maturity model positioning of each domain based on the milestone tracking and achievements indicated in Figure 5.2. Each maturity level column in Figure 5.3 can be annotated further to show its key milestones as background context for where the domains are being positioned.

Conclusion

Although reaching a mature state of MDM may not be stated explicitly as a goal or objective in strategy and planning, it certainly is implied in the concept of MDM. In other words, reaching maturity is needed to achieve a successful state result from MDM. It is often overlooked in the MDM planning stages that as much focus needs to go into institutionalizing and maturing these practices as goes into initiating them. First, it is necessary to determine what constitutes a mature MDM model and how this can be gauged.

In this chapter, a methodology has been presented for defining and measuring the overall maturity of the multi-domain MDM model by gauging maturity more discretely across the five key disciplines. Each discipline area needs to develop in relationship to and in coordination with the other areas, with data governance and data stewardship having the most influence.

Getting to a mature state of MDM can be a slow, deliberate process that requires some adjustments and out-of-the-box thinking. Take the time to consider what constitutes a mature MDM model and how this can be measured. This will enable an effective tracking approach that will provide valuable guidance during your investment in MDM.

PART II

Implementing the Multi-Domain Model

CHAPTER 6

Establishing Multi-Domain Data Governance

This chapter covers the discipline and practice of data governance in a multi-domain model, including the relationships and focus needed between data governance and the Master Data Management (MDM) program management office, business areas, and information technology (IT). In addition, it will provide strategies and examples of how to establish a consistent, transparent governance model across MDM domains.

Throughout Part 1 of this book, we have emphasized the relationship needed between MDM and data governance. In this book's preface, we described MDM as "the application of discipline and control over master data in order to achieve a consistent, trusted, and shared representation of the master data."

Now, let's also consider the definition of data governance provided by the DAMA Data Management Body of Knowledge (DMBOK 2010):

> *Data governance is the exercise of authority and control (planning, monitoring, and enforcement) over the management of data assets.*

The words *discipline, authority, control*, and *data assets* used in these definitions convey the common objectives of MDM and data governance.

Chapter 1 mentioned that as much as data governance does not require MDM, the opposite is not true, especially in an inherently complex, multi-domain MDM. Whether the MDM model is top-down, middle-out, agile, or hybrid, an MDM program requires strong data governance support at many points. As MDM is expanded into more domains that cover an increasing amount of master data, the need for data governance becomes even more critical because the data management activities, decisions, prioritization of work, and user base naturally increase as well. And as MDM focus expands across more operational and analytical groups, each of these groups can have different or competing data management practices, data definitions, views, metrics, and quality requirements for the master data that it uses.

The challenge for data governance and the MDM Program Management Office (PMO) becomes how to move domain master data from a fragmented state into a more conformed state and, ultimately, into a more integrated state. Figure 6.1 illustrates this concept. As master data moves into a more integrated state, the data governance focus will shift more toward the enterprise management and quality control of the data. As the MDM program

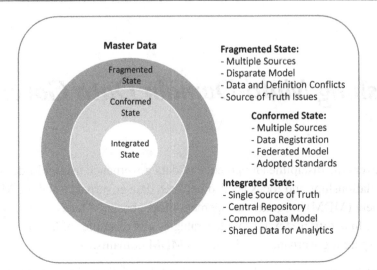

Figure 6.1: Fragmented, conformed, and integrated states

and data governance processes mature, the management and quality control of master data become more embedded in the day-to-day business operations and IT functions, largely through data stewardship roles and quality monitoring processes.

The extent of how much a domain can achieve a conformed state or integrated state depends on the information model and systems architecture within each domain area. For example, a domain with a data hub architecture and operational data store (ODS) will be positioned well to support a highly integrated state, whereas a more federated architecture may only be able to achieve a conformed state through the implementation and enforcement of common standards across various source systems and process areas. But in either case, without a data governance process to define and drive the necessary policies, standards, and rules to support conformed and integrated states, the individual business or analytical groups will make decisions that best serve their own interests, but those may not necessarily be sound enterprise decisions. This will only perpetuate a fragmented state. Therefore, the MDM PMO and data governance need to develop a strong partnership to ensure that decisions related to master data are fully vetted and support enterprise strategies, policies, and standards.

The Data Governance Role and Relationship with MDM

The MDM PMO, like most program and project teams, focuses primarily on the planning and implementation of MDM objectives, infrastructure, and deliverables. During the planning and implementation phases, many issues and conflicts regarding usage, definition, and alignment of master data will be revealed that exist across the business process areas. Chapter 2 described how these cross-functional differences are revealed when examining the sources and use cases of master data.

The ability to resolve many of these cross-functional issues exceed the scope of the MDM PMO and require an authoritative data governance process to be engaged. In a multi-domain MDM strategy, the MDM program will need data governance to help establish priorities, make domain selections and data ownership decisions, and address various issue/resolution needs that will emerge from the MDM PMO and business process areas. If such a data governance process is not already available for the MDM program to use, the strategy and execution plan for MDM will need to identify data governance as a critical path dependency, and the MDM program itself will need to become the driving force for the implementation of a data governance process.

Figure 4.2 in Chapter 4 provided a high-level illustration of the roles and relationship between the MDM program, data governance, and operational process areas where data stewards need to be engaged. Now let's take a closer look at those roles indicated for data governance and how they relate to the MDM program.

Domain Jurisdiction and Line of Business (LOB) Representation

As is often pointed out, data governance should be primarily a business-driven process, but defining the governance model and aligning business functions to specific data domains and associated governance bodies may not always be straightforward. It can require some deeper assessment to align business representation with the domain structures and their jurisdictions. Some business models, such as a Health Care model that has line of business (LOB) areas such as Member, Provider, Contracts, Claims, and Care Management, will have their data domains and subject areas described in a similar way thus enabling alignment between business functions and data domains. However, within a product- and manufacturing-oriented business model with LOB areas such as Marketing, Sales, Operations, Service, and Finance, there will not be clear functional alignment with data domains such as Customer, Product, Partner, Supplier, and Materials (the typical data domains in this type of business model).

Organizational structures and the hierarchies within them will not typically provide obvious alignments to a data domain. Organizationally, business units are more vertical, whereas data domains will typically have a more horizontal alignment across various business units that use the data. Figure 6.2 provides an example of these vertical and horizontal relationships and shows where business functions intersect with data domains. Examining these relationships and how these functions interact with data will reveal the type of representation and interests that the functional area should have with a data domain, particularly as it applies to the management and control of master data.

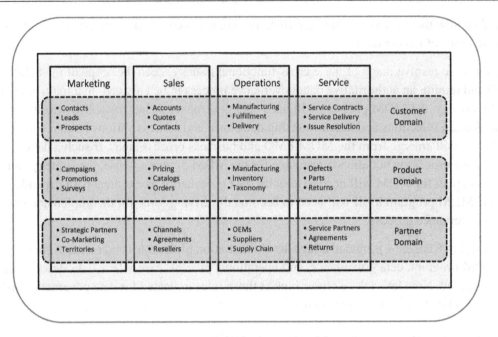

Figure 6.2: Alignment of business functions with data domains

Figure 6.2 also suggests why the governance of master data in a multi-domain model will require a federated data governance approach. If an existing data governance process has been operating with a centralized approach—that is, one committee or council that has a singular authority for data governance decisions, policies, and standards across the business and IT functions—the planning and implementation of a multi-domain MDM strategy require the governance process to take on a federated approach. This is needed create more specific data governance and quality management focus for each domain, but still operate within a common overall enterprise data governance framework with oversight from an executive steering committee.

Federated Data Governance

A federated data governance model is a structure that supports decisions, policies, standards, and information sharing between <u>multiple</u> semiautonomous entities, such as data domains, committees, business and IT functions, and projects. A federated data governance model is typically used in a complex business model to ensure that decisions made within or across these semiautonomous bodies represent outcomes that are consistent with or support enterprisewide standards and strategies. A federated model will usually have a steering committee that oversees the governance process and addresses issues or needs that can't be addressed at the domain level. Figure 6.3 provides an example of a federated data governance model.

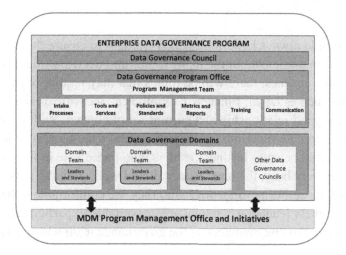

Figure 6.3: Federated data governance model

Data Governance Team Resources

More often than not, staffing a data governance team sufficiently will become a continual challenge in a multi-domain model. Conceptually, most data governance team structures aim to have a multitier team structure involving an executive sponsor layer, a decision-making layer, a data steward layer, and they may also include some IT support roles, such as business analyst, data analyst, or data architect. In practice, however, it may be difficult to fully enlist all these team members because these people will usually have other full-time roles and responsibilities that can create commitment conflicts. Most business areas and their leadership teams will acknowledge the needs and benefits of data governance but be reluctant to commit their time and sponsorship if they don't have an immediate stake in the game or they don't see a direct connection between data governance objectives and their business goals or revenue numbers for the year.

A reasonable approach is to have a data governance process work with business areas to identify various services and facilitation support to help implement a foundational level of data governance structure that can start demonstrating value. Over time, as the value proposition and visibility of this data governance process grows, so will the level of participation and support. In other words, be prepared for data governance to begin as a lean program that needs to apply data governance disciplines in project areas that are very receptive to and require data governance. Build governance value and recognition through those opportunities and use those attributes to continue to build a broader business case for expanding data governance. A MDM initiative should have these data governance requirements and provide the foundation for data governance to mature as the MDM program expands across more domains.

Bench Strength

Data governance should always have good bench strength to ensure that subject matter experts are available to participate in the many topics and decisions that need to be covered. For example, at times, there will be topics that may require representation from corporate functions such as Legal, Finance, Compliance, Security, or Human Resources (HR). Maintaining a good relationship and current set of contacts with personnel representing these corporate functions can greatly enhance the timeliness and effectiveness of data governance. And because business leaders who participate in the governance process are typically very busy, the team leader should work with the governance team members who have the authority to identify who they are comfortable to have act as proxies for these business leaders when they are unavailable to participate. Ideally, these people would be other existing members of the governance team who are familiar with the process and topics.

Define Policies and Rules

Master data is largely a fixed asset, with only a limited amount of ability to maintain, change, enrich, or cleanse it. Therefore, the value of master data is highly dependent on how accurately they are captured and how relevant they are in the context of their usage. The responsibility for developing master data, therefore, falls primarily on the data entry and operational processes. These data entry and operational processes are where the MDM program and data governance need to have sufficient influence and policies to ensure that data standards and quality control expectations are visible and actively enforced during the processes.

The ability to accurately capture master data often depends on how and where the data is entered and to what degree this data entry is subject to quality and integrity control conditions, such as format control, validation rules, reference data, user guidelines, and so on. Local data entry is typically influenced by the requirements and limitations associated with the particular application and business process being used. These types of data-entry conditions can vary by system, application, region, country, or any combination of these.

The net result is that the aggregate quality and consistency of this data from these various entry processes will undoubtedly be poor unless common policies, rules, and standards have been applied to these data entry and operational processes by a data governance process. This is where data governance influence matters the most to master data. The extent that data governance policies, rules, standards, and monitoring capability can directly influence master data entry practices and operational processes—but without undue burden that could negatively affect transactional performance—reflect how effectively data governance is operational within a company. Policies, rules, and standards will have little impact if they are not appropriately positioned and effectively enforced.

There needs to be a good balance, with the ability to execute and enforce policies, not just create and post them. A policy without the ability to execute and enforce it is of little value. Keep in mind that in most programs and projects, the resources needed for execution are always in short supply; therefore, any manager will typically assign resources based on execution needs rather than policy needs. This is an area where the MDM PMO or data governance team can help provide services to address policy needs without affecting project deliverables.

Quality Standards and Priorities

Chapter 5 presented examples of several data governance–related milestones that are important to the maturity of a multi-domain MDM model. Two of those milestones suggest the need for data governance to establish policies, standards, and priorities related to master data quality management and measurement:

- Data management policies and standards have been defined and implemented.
- Measurements and dashboards are in place to measure and drive master data quality and control.

Let's take a closer look at these items to more fully describe how data governance–driven quality standards and priorities for master data are critical factors for an MDM program.

Data management policies and standards have been defined and implemented

For a multi-domain MDM program, being able to define and implement such policies, standards, and priorities across the master data requires a mature, cross-functional governance model with an executive steering committee to work through them. Considering that at various times in a multi-domain model, each MDM domain implementation will likely be at a different point in the MDM maturity model (as shown in Figures 5.2 and 5.3 in Chapter 5), the prioritization and execution of MDM policies and standards will be influenced by the maturity of these domains.

A mature MDM domain that has identified its master data assets, the sources and processes involved, the data touch points, and has established an accountable and responsive data governance process, will be ready to define and implement the quality policies and standards necessary to drive more quality control of the master data. Whereas a domain still in the early stages of its MDM plan and still in the process of identifying its MDM assets and touch points will not be ready to clearly understand what quality management policies and standards are needed and where they will need to be positioned.

An existing data governance program may already have some broad policies and standards defined that may apply to all domains. For example, there may be standard change control policies, data integration rules, or quality measurement standards and rules that each domain will need to adopt. Execution of these enterprise policies and standards within the MDM program should be coordinated by the MDM PMO and the data governance program.

As more MDM domains are implemented, expect the need for additional quality policies and standards to emerge. As the MDM scope expands, more reference data and business term conflicts are likely to be discovered. As these conflicts or overlaps are discovered, these cases should be brought into the data governance process, where enterprisewide standards can be determined for adoption and enforcement.

Measurements and dashboards are in place to measure and monitor master data quality and control

In a multi-domain model, data governance needs to examine data quality measurement needs, any existing practices, and the ability to achieve a standard, common approach to measure and monitor data quality. If prior to implementation of MDM practices, a particular business area or data warehouse environment already has high-quality measurement and dashboard practices, such as reuse of various quality profiling rules, quality dimension definitions (e.g., how quality dimensions such as completeness, consistency, accuracy, and validity are defined) and quality scorecard formats, those practices may be good candidates for enterprisewide adoption. The data governance process should review existing data quality measurement practices, agree if any existing practices can serve an enterprise's best practices, and determine the policies and the adoption needed to ensure that this will become standard operating procedure in the enterprise. Having such standards in place enables an MDM program to quickly absorb these standards and move forward.

Unfortunately, such enterprisewide quality standards that are ready for multi-domain adoption and use will not generally exist in a company. Similar to the previous discussion about reference data and business terms, various organizations and functions are more likely to have their own versions of quality measurement and reporting practices. In this scenario, the MDM PMO and data governance process will need to examine the variations and their requirements to propose and gain agreement on a standard approach for enterprise data quality measurement and reporting formats. Chapters 9 and 11 will provide further detail on more specific quality and performance measurement.

Issue Resolution

Chapter 4 mentioned that having clear charters and good working relationships between the data management support teams, MDM PMO, and data governance process will make

Issue	Incident Resolution Role	Data Governance Role	MDM PMO Role
Master data definition conflicts across various data models	Route issue to data governance	Engage data stewards to resolve conflicts and define standard	Define plan to update data models and metadata repository
Who owns this master data?	Route issue to data governance	Identify owner or review with MDM PMO if not in scope	If not in MDM scope, review owning need against MDM plans
Source system data quality issue	Log and track issue to closure.	Engage if the corrective action needs data governance review	Work with source system to position and execute the corrective action.
System error due to incorrect master data values	Log and track issue to closure.	Engage if need to review business rules and standards	Work with IT and system to position and execute the corrective action.
Change request to a master data field (e.g., Name, Address, Status)	Log and track issue to closure. Make change if standard procedure	Engage if an exception to a policy or business rule	Engage if there may be process or downstream impacts

Figure 6.4: Common issues and engagement roles

it straightforward for support teams to be able to reach out to, or formally escalate master data issues to, the MDM PMO or data governance bodies per established engagement roles and responsibilities. Formally defining these engagement guidelines will help identify the type of items or issues that should be in scope across these relationships and how and when the data governance process should be engaged. A data governance team should also be aware of the other support and decision-making channels to ensure that any items not within the data governance scope that are being submitted by a person or team can be routed to the correct support group, hence avoiding any further misdirection or significant process delays.

Figure 6.4 provides an example of a common set of issues and how these should be coordinated between the support teams, MDM PMO, and data governance process. The engagement rules between these groups can vary depending on the actual agreements and functional roles, but this type of matrix will be very helpful for communication and training purposes across the MDM program.

A governance process should also provide clear guidance and good templates where needed to assist the submitting person or group with providing governance-ready information for the governance team to evaluate and act on. These details should include sufficient information, including the following.

The data governance program overview should clearly describe:

- The data governance charter, purpose, and value statements
- Key guiding principles and program objectives
- The data governance framework and management structure
- The functional model, intake process, key processes, and deliverables
- Operating governance teams and future roadmap
- Location of the program website and additional reference material and program websites

The data governance engagement guidelines should have the following elements:

- Guidelines for how and when to engage data governance
- Examples of in-scope and out-of-scope items or issues
- Who to contact if there are any scope or engagement questions

Item/issue submission, tracking, and presenting should include:

- A submission template indicating all required information
- An accessible log for tracking status and details from open to close
- A template for presenting material to the governance team

When an item submitted to data governance gets returned to the submitter, that most often occurs because it lacks sufficient detail or clarity for the data governance team to act on it. And this is usually due to insufficient background, context, or clarity as to what is being asked of the governance team. Gathering more information or clarifying the open questions usually results in getting the item accepted into the data governance process. If the approval and implementation of the submitted item require any further development, research, processes, or other specific task activity, the submitting party may need to be prepared to offer the funding necessary for this additional work to be executed.

Data governance groups often can only review and approve the concepts, proposals, solution approaches, policies, and standards or guidelines associated with the data item. They don't have the scope or ability to assign resources for implementing many types of corrective action. Here are some examples of actions that typically are beyond the scope of data governance:

- Application fixes or enhancements
- Operational process improvements
- Data-quality corrections at the source
- Process area user guides and training

A well-established data governance process will frequently be engaged in the review, approval, and prioritization of these type of items, but implementing the corrective action typically needs to be addressed by the MDM PMO, project teams, IT functions, or business process areas that actually own the applications or processes needing correction. These application or process areas are likely to have a change control process to address the corrective action request, and depending on the impact and level of effort involved, there may need to be funding required from the requesting party to implement the correction. The application or business process area may have the budget in place for planned improvements and may also have some discretionary funding set aside for handling other low- to medium-effort corrections, but otherwise, funding may be required from the area requesting the change.

Therefore, as data governance items are submitted and reviewed, the submitting party and the data governance team need to know that a decision made supporting a corrective action could be subject to funding requirements in order for the action to be executed. A mature data governance process should be aware of these types of cases and set expectations accordingly to help the requesting party consider its funding responsibilities should such arrangements be necessary. Similar to the discussion in Chapter 4 regarding the importance of building cross-functional alignment, the data governance scope should be clear and appropriate engagement guidelines established with other functional areas. This will distinguish the data governance scope, function, and capabilities from other IT, project, or process management functions that own the actual change control and implementation processes for the applications and business processes.

All significant items or issues that data governance accepts and addresses should be formally entered into an issue/item tracking process that will capture sufficient detail regarding the nature of the requesting person and group, the nature of the request, supporting details, summaries of discussions and decisions or other outcome details, what governance members or teams were involved, and any other information that provides clarity and acceptable detail from an auditing perspective. Data governance always needs to clearly track how, where, and why decisions were made. In a multi-domain MDM model, the data governance intake and closure process should also be able to clearly identify and record what data domains the issue/item is associated with. During the intake process, this can trigger an alert with the MDM PMO and domain team leads, who then can determine if they or other people will need to be involved in solving the problem, and on the closure side, this can trigger closure communication with the interested parties.

Enterprise Communication

A standard artifact of any data governance process should be a RACI chart to identify what roles are responsible or accountable for, or consulted or informed about various decision events. A RACI chart can and often will be customized to best suit the decision process and communication model dynamics, but however it takes shape, the RACI concept is important to a high-functioning governance process. This RACI chart provides a vehicle where master

Roles Communication Item	Steering Committee	Governance Council	Lead Data Stewards	Business Area Data Stewards	Technical Leads
Sponsorship and Charter	R	A	C	C	I
Data Ownership	C	R	A	A	I
Policies and Standards	C	R	A	A	I
Business Rules and Guidelines	I	R	A	A	C
Data Quality Issues, Reports and Metrics	I	R	A	A	A
Data Models and Data Dictionaries	I	A	C	C	R
Processes and Procedures	I	R	A	A	C

R - Responsible; A - Accountable; C - Consulted; I - Informed

Figure 6.5: Data governance RACI chart

data decisions can be leveraged to ensure that there is clear engagement and communication for these decisions. Figure 6.5 provides an example of a RACI chart.

In general, the tracking and management of key communication items as they relate to master data should be managed closely by the MDM PMO using the data governance RACI chart as a communication tool. Although these audiences on the RACI chart will also be interested in other data governance–related communications, they should always be kept informed about any major policies, standards, rules, changes, events, and other important items involving master data.

Conclusion

This chapter covered the discipline and practice of data governance in a multi-domain model, including the relationships and focus needed between data governance and the MDM PMO, business areas, and IT. The discussion provided strategies and examples for how to establish a consistent, transparent governance model across MDM domains, with an emphasis on developing a federated approach where master data issue tracking, decision making, communication, policies and standards, and corrective action can best be addressed in a cross-functional manner. As MDM expands into more domains covering a larger amount of master data, the need for data governance becomes even more critical because the data management activities, stewardship needs, and prioritization of work efforts become inherently more complex, resulting in the need for more governance authority, policies, and standards to help manage this.

Because master data has many touch points and consumers, data governance needs to ensure that the data domain structure and business functions are aligned across the business model. This will enable the MDM PMO to effectively leverage the data governance model for support with communications, issues, decisions, and corrective action needs that require cross-functional engagement across a diverse application and business process landscape.

CHAPTER 7

Data Stewardship

In this chapter, we will discuss many opportunities where data steward roles can be applied, but it will be up to the MDM PMO and the data governance council to clearly understand their company's business model, the ebb and flow of their master data, and how and where to most effectively position data stewards so that the practice of data stewardship has a broad foothold for support across a multi-domain MDM model. In a MDM model, data stewards cannot just be agents for data governance policy and standards; they also need to be closely aligned to the touch points and consumers of the master data where data entry, usage, management, and quality control can be influenced most.

Throughout this book, there is frequent discussion of the importance of the data steward role. Whether this role exists within a company from employees with formal data steward job titles, or from employees with other job titles but which provide data steward–type functions, the most important point is that these roles will truly support the concept and practice of data stewardship as an underlying discipline and success factor for MDM. Here is the definition of data stewardship provided by the DAMA Data Management Body of Knowledge (DMBOK 2010):

The formal accountability for business responsibilities ensuring effective control and use of data assets. Some of the responsibilities are data governance responsibilities, but there are significant data stewardship responsibilities within each of the other data management functions.

Data stewardship should run deep through all of MDM, but the data steward focus and requirements can vary with each domain. Therefore, a multi-domain plan needs to closely examine the data steward needs for each domain in scope to determine how and where data steward roles can be best positioned and how the right resources can be identified and engaged. Once the MDM data steward model is defined and aligned with data governance, the successful execution and practice of data stewardship will then come down to how effectively the data steward processes and supporting technologies are able to repeatedly address and control data quality needs over time.

To begin defining the right data steward model and approach for maximum support of master data, several fundamental factors need to be examined:

- What is the current state of data governance?
- Should "data steward" be a formal job role and job title?

- What is the right data steward approach within each MDM domain?
- How to engage data stewards in data access control processes?
- What processes and technologies are needed to support data steward roles?

Let's take a deeper look at each of these important points.

What Is the Current State of Data Governance?

For a multi-domain MDM program to succeed, data governance and data stewardship practices need to be closely orchestrated. This effort needs to start with an effective data governance process aligned with the MDM strategy and implementation plan. Chapter 6 provided strategies and examples for how to establish a consistent, transparent governance model across MDM domains and indicated that if a sufficient data governance process and structure does not already exist for the MDM program to use, the MDM program itself will need to become the driving force behind the implementation of the necessary data governance processes. Similarly, if an appropriate data steward model does not already exist, the MDM program and data governance will need to become the driving forces behind the implementation of the data steward model. Without well-aligned data governance and data steward models, the MDM program cannot succeed.

Prior to a company having a multi-domain MDM strategy and plan, there are likely to be existing instances of data governance and data steward practices that have resulted from locally or functionally oriented data management initiatives. For example, in one functional area, a data administrator or a support engineer may be acting in a data steward role to control a specific set of master data, such as validating sources to target data loads according to certain acceptance criteria and monitoring error log activity associated with any data mapping or integration issues.

On the other hand, in another functional area, a data management team holds a broader and more highly visible responsibility for overseeing various change control processes and data quality management activities that include master data. Both are good examples of various information technology (IT) or business functions taking the initiative to implement data steward activity, but these cases are usually independently defined based on data management requirements associated with a specific functional area; they lack a broader alignment with an enterprisewide data governance strategy and plan.

As a company executes a multi-domain MDM strategy, these existing data steward functions need to be identified and aligned with the enterprise strategy. This will pull together a more cohesive network of data steward and quality controls that supports local and enterprisewide requirements. For example, a local or regional order management process requires the customer's name, address, and payment information to handle an order, but the customer's email address and telephone number is not required, even though other functions in the company, such as marketing, finance, or customer service, would benefit by having that additional information. In an enterprise MDM and data governance model that has well-positioned data stewards, it will be much easier to identify these data capture needs to satisfy the broader enterprise requirements and demands for this data. A well-structured data governance process aligned with the MDM program model and data architecture strategy will greatly aid in determining the master data priorities and control points where data steward roles can be most effective.

Should "Data Steward" Be a Formal Job Role and Job Title?

If your company is serious about data governance and data quality management, it must get serious about creating formal data steward job titles and roles. As with almost any job, a person with a specific job role and set of responsibilities should have a job title and career path associated with that role and those responsibilities. The purpose and function of data stewards are vital to maintaining the high-quality data that a healthy company needs. If data is in fact one of the most important strategic assets within a company, then data steward roles should be highly valued and formally recognized. This is important from a number of perspectives:

- From a cultural perspective, it is critical to indicate that a company truly values and formally recognizes the data steward function as a necessary component for establishing a high-quality culture.
- From a career development perspective, there is a growing focus in the data management industry on the data steward role and career path. This can be observed through job postings, industry training, and certification offerings, as well as the fact that data steward–oriented topics are often featured at many annual data governance and data management conferences.
- From a management and HR perspective, there is a need to statistically track how and where data steward roles are positioned and performing within a company.

Unfortunately, reaching a situation where the data steward job role and job title are formally recognized in a company can take a long time and be an evolving factor in the maturity of MDM and data governance. Companies will not typically have data stewards until there is a strong internal initiative and business justification that can drive the need and creation of this job role by Human Resources (HR). In the meantime, however, the concept and practice of data stewardship can be addressed without having formal job titles in place. Working cross-functionally, the MDM PMO and data governance process should examine all the options needed to implement data steward roles by leveraging other existing IT and business roles. In parallel, the MDM and data governance programs should build the justification and foundation to get formal data steward job roles and titles established in the company as part of the strategic roadmap.

Consider that the data steward role typically involves one or more of these responsibilities, skill sets, and knowledge areas:

- Training and enforcement of data policy and standards
- Process area expertise regarding data use, flow, and touch points
- Subject matter expertise in data governance activities and decisions
- Process analysis and development of the data management process
- Familiarity with certain data models and data infrastructure
- Data analysis and research
- Monitoring of data quality and error conditions
- Correcting data error conditions
- Supporting specific data management, change control, or maintenance tasks
- Data access management

Many of these responsibilities and areas of expertise already exist in one form or another in job roles in various other IT and business areas. Therefore, there certainly are opportunities early in the MDM program plan to define and begin initiating some data steward practices by leveraging support from these existing roles, discussed in the next section.

Leveraging IT and Business Support

In a typical IT engagement model, there are specific resource request processes that allow projects to identify and secure IT resources on a fixed time and budget basis provided that the resources and funding are available. In this scenario, an MDM or data governance project initiative can plan for and gain certain IT assistance, such as with data mining, profiling and analysis, and application support, or address certain data integration, administration, or corrective action needs that fit into the IT services portfolio. Fixed time and project support arrangements with IT can certainly provide much value for many needs that MDM and data governance programs will have as these programs expand and mature, but this type of IT support will usually only be able to address technical and infrastructure-oriented requirements. Thus, IT support can play an important role, but it cannot be a substitute for creating an ongoing data steward model. In an MDM program, the roles and responsibilities for data stewards reach beyond technical support needs and must penetrate deeply into the business process areas.

And while there are opportunities to leverage IT support for specific technical support needs, the ability to leverage existing business resources and expertise for business support can be far more challenging and will not usually have a specific resource request process that exists in the IT model. Therefore, during the planning and initiation of the MDM program, it is critical that the business areas are engaged, aligned properly, and can help with supporting the build-out of the data steward models needed by the MDM domains in scope.

Otherwise, if the requirements for data stewards were not sufficiently planned for and emerge later—as they will—getting the resources and time commitments needed from the business side at that point will be very difficult. These people may be unavailable (or only partially available) to participate as subject matter experts in data governance teams and often unable to take on tasks outside their current job responsibilities. Business functions or projects that are most affected by master data issues may try to offer some resources on a short-term or part-time basis. In other situations, the use of contractors may have to be considered, but often the cost associated with that has not been planned in any budget. Having only limited business support and trying to use contractors to fill the gap will not be a sufficient or sustainable approach to address the longer-term needs for data steward support across a multi-domain MDM program. Without a more dedicated data steward model in place, it will be difficult to get master data management and quality improvement projects underway or fully completed.

Now contrast that with a scenario where a more focused enterprise data management model and quality culture exists in the company and where an effective data steward model has been implemented. Having recognized data stewards who are sufficiently skilled, empowered, and well-positioned in key functional and regional areas can immediately help support the projects and priorities determined through the MDM and data governance roadmaps. Having well-positioned data stewards demonstrates that there is a commitment within the business to data management and quality improvement. There are some key factors that will drive the more proactive approach described previously:

- Ensure that early in their planning, MDM and data governance programs call out data steward budget and resource needs as being critical to MDM success.
- Work with the data governance council to define enterprise policies to ensure that project development and solution design processes have requirements for data steward and quality management support where master data is involved in the deliverables.
- MDM and data governance programs should initiate efforts with HR to justify the formal creation of data steward job roles within the company if they don't already exist.
- Minimize the use of IT and consulting help as substitutes for real data stewards.

Too often, projects developing and delivering data models and applications that involve new assets, such as additional master data and reference data, do this without planning sufficiently for quality control and ongoing data management of these assets. This leads to data ownership and stewardship gaps that later can become unwanted wrestling matches between business, IT, and data governance teams as a result of data quality or maintenance problems, information protection issues, internal audits, and other issues. Again, early planning and having project requirements to account for data management and stewardship roles will significantly reduce the occurrence of data ownership and accountability problems.

What is the Right Data Steward Approach Within Each MDM Domain?

It's important to recognize that how and where data stewards can be most effectively engaged in a multi-domain model will be highly dependent on the data architecture and master data flow within each domain. Throughout Part 1 of this book, while discussing the planning aspects of MDM, it was pointed out that implementing a successful MDM initiative starts with choosing the right approach—one that will drive the proper fitting of the MDM practices to an enterprise architecture and business model. A company's enterprise architecture and business model will consist of many specific functions, processes, teams, and job roles that already interact with the master data. By examining the usage and flow of master data in a particular domain (also see Chapter 2), you can determine critical points where the practice of data stewardship can be effectively applied. This may involve master data entry points, data integration points, or other downstream processes where the master data quality and consistency need to be controlled.

This may also require data monitoring to alert the data steward of conditions that will need attention. For example, in a customer data hub environment, there may be rules that require certain types of customers to have certain types of account setups and profiles. A company can have various types of business relationships with its customers that require the use of different types of accounts, contracts, and pricing details to define them. End user customers who interact on a retail basis with a company may have an end user type of account setup, but typically they will not have any special contract or pricing relationships with the company. On the other hand, customers who are wholesale purchasers or product resellers will have specific account, contract, pricing, credit, and payment details associated with that relationship. In each case, it is important that customer account types are correctly identified and set up by the process area responsible for managing the accounts. This doesn't always happen correctly due to administrative oversight, incorrect customer information, or data integration issues. For instance, in a data merge process involving customer records, the merge logic can create a false-positive or false-negative condition that produces the wrong merge result, leading to an incorrect customer master record.

Using another example, in the health care industry, there needs to be consistent business definitions, rules, and data attributes that defines health care providers at the institutional level (e.g., a provider organization such as a hospital, medical group, pharmacy group, clinic, or emergency care center) and the individual level (e.g., a doctor, pharmacist, nurse, therapist, psychologist, or chiropractor). These definitions and distinctions are critical not only to how contracts, claims, payments, and networks are handled between health insurance companies and service providers, but also to presenting accurate information to health plan members and potential members regarding what services and providers are included in in-network or out-of-network coverage for any given health plan. Therefore, the accuracy and consistency of provider data, definitions, and rules are vital to the success of any health care company and to the industry as a whole. The accuracy and consistency of this data will hinge on having effective data governance standards and steward practices in place to manage the quality and integrity of this data across the many entry and consumption points this data can have.

Scenarios like this are examples of where checks and balances are needed with master data. These checks and balances should be brought to the attention of data stewards who are asked to ensure that the master data is correct and that the usage is consistent with the policies, standards, rules, business requirements, and operational guidelines. It is also important to have data stewards clearly engaged in the applications and data repositories associated with the metadata, reference data, and any external vendor-provided data involved in master data. These additional areas play important roles in the overall consistency, maintenance, and standardization of master data. These aspects are explored further in the next chapters, which cover data integration, data quality management, and metadata.

Chapter 6 mentioned that a multi-domain MDM program will likely require a federated data governance model that can support centralized and decentralized system and data architecture. This also means that different data steward approaches need to be considered and applied in order to address centralized and decentralized architectures in a multi-domain MDM model. Each domain will likely have different architecture and processes that the master data is subject to; therefore, as part of an MDM and data governance execution plan, each domain scenario should be examined to determine the right data steward model and approach. Let's examine this task from a centralized data hub architecture perspective and a decentralized architecture perspective.

Data Stewardship in a Centralized Data Hub Architecture

In a domain with data hub architecture, there should be great focus on the quality management of the data coming into and out of the data hub. A data hub will typically have multiple internal systems connected as spoke systems and may have one or more sources of external data (such as vendor data) used in the data hub. These inbound and outbound flows of data are all key areas where data stewards should be assigned. These data stewards should be very familiar with the data and the transactional or vendor processes that are connect to the hub. For example, customer and product domains may each have a data hub that interacts with multiple transactional systems involved with sales, quoting, shipping, and customer service processes, and is likely to also use data from one or more external vendors. Data stewards should be positioned to oversee these inbound and outbound interactions, as well as the data quality. Figure 7.1 provides an example of this concept.

This type of data steward model ensures that there is monitoring and data quality control with the master data flow. As any data flow or quality issues emerge, data stewards can quickly address them through the data governance and quality management processes in that domain or, if needed, with other domains if cross-domain impacts are related to the root cause and correction of the issue.

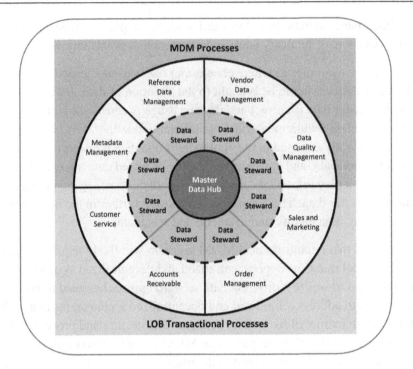

Figure 7.1: Data steward in a data hub model

Data Stewardship in a Decentralized Model

Contrast the scenario involving a data hub architecture with a situation with a data domain that has a more decentralized operational architecture where sales, orders, distribution, and customer services are handled through processes and systems on a regional basis. Each regional system's transactional data may or may not be consolidated into a central data warehouse, and there can be various quality and consistency issues with the data from each source system. Obviously, this creates a more challenging footprint for data governance and stewardship practices. In this decentralized model, much more mapping and normalization of data are required at various points, such as by extract, transform, and load (ETL) processes, entity resolution processes, checks and balances, and other data quality management processes. This will translate to more data stewards that need to be engaged across source systems, data warehouse, data marts, and other environments.

For example, in this type of model, data stewards should be positioned across various transactional and analytical processes and system areas and with the vendor data entry points. Together, these data stewards can work as a collective community aligned with the data governance process to address master data issues, common standards, business rules, business term definitions, reference data, and data quality management needs. In a decentralized model, this network of data stewards will provide tremendous value with their ability to

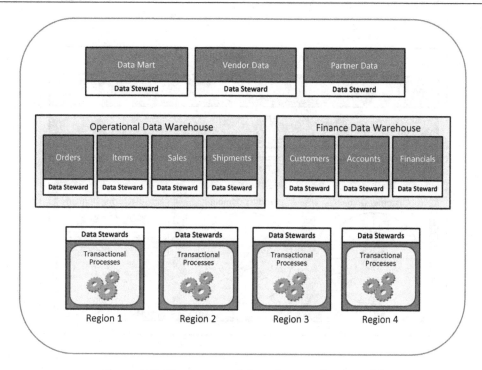

Figure 7.2: Data stewards in a decentralized model

proactively or reactively address emerging data quality and data governance issues or needs. Figure 7.2 provides an example of this concept.

Without this network of data stewards, data issues in the source systems or data warehouses will be much harder to address in a timely fashion due to delays when trying to assign resources to do the root-cause analysis and address corrective action needs where data ownership and accountability issues exist. These type of issues can be largely avoided or more easily handled with a well-positioned network of data stewards.

Data Stewardship Across a Federated Data Governance Model

In a multi-domain MDM model, there is likely to be a mix of data hub and decentralized operational models across the domains, meaning that in multi-domain MDM, there can be many layers of complexity and cross-functional involvement that need flexible data governance and data steward approaches. This is why the federated data governance model described in Chapter 6 will typically be needed within a multi-domain MDM program to coordinate data governance and data steward focus across various domain structures. Figure 7.3 provides an example of this concept.

As these models and layers become better understood and reveal the coordination needed to successfully drive data quality improvement initiatives, companies begin to realize that the

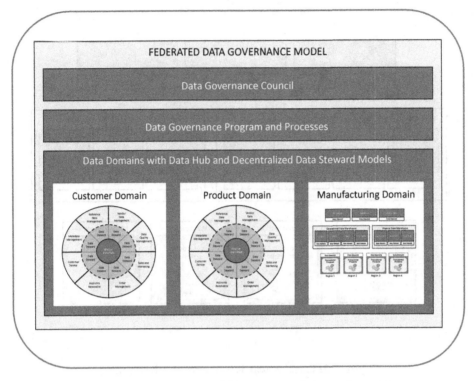

Figure 7.3: Data stewardship across a federated model

analysis of a significant data quality issue and the implementation of the action plan to correct that issue will require a number of orchestrated tasks from a number of committed resources from across the business and IT functions. The data stewards will make the difference between poor and successful execution of these initiatives.

How to Engage Data Stewards in Data Access Control Processes?

Many companies today require employees to complete internal training related to information protection and business conduct. In these courses, there are usually various real-life examples cited where fraud, theft, inside trading, information privacy issues, and other types of accidents, violations, or misconduct have occurred in relation to company data and proprietary information. Many of these cases involve employees in business roles who are knowing or unknowing participants in the incident. These cases are used in training to help emphasize how damaging the lack of information protection and control can be.

As MDM practices mature, more and more applications and users are being migrated to increasingly integrated platforms and shared environments where the common use of tools, interfaces, and master data exists. What had been independently controlled applications and groups of users now collectively become a much larger pool of users interacting with a common environment. The user, application, and data separation that physically existed before does not exist any longer. Maintaining information protection and user access control to master data now requires closer examination of and accurate information about employee identification, job roles, data usage intent, and monitoring of cross-functional process interactions with data, to the extent that a simple systems administrator approach for managing access control is no longer adequate.

In data hub or data warehouse environments, there can be a complex variety of process interactions and data access needs from various user groups involving different combinations of data. Because of this, the access management methodology and master data control practices for these types of environments need to be more rigorous and should involve a data steward role acting in an access control gatekeeper function associated with an MDM domain and the data governance process. The primary purpose of this gatekeeper function is to define and manage a more business process–oriented set of checks, controls, and monitoring focus that is needed to augment existing access management and authorization processes in order to more precisely recognize and control who has the authority to access the master data for any given domain. The data steward–oriented gatekeeper process can be an additional function and process layer integrated with an existing access control model, as shown in Figure 7.4.

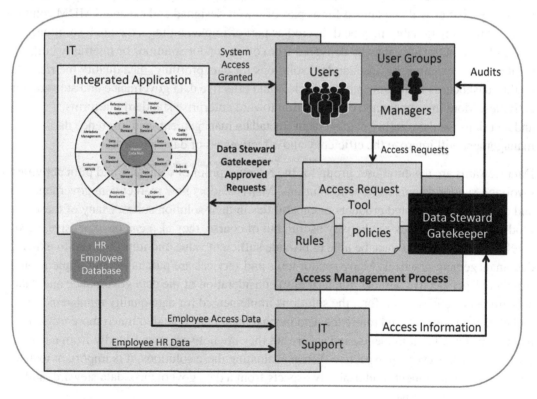

Figure 7.4: Data steward role in the data access management process

This is all about information protection and the ability to more tightly manage compliance and other risk factors associated with uncontrolled events or any misconduct involving master data. Master data access control can be greatly enhanced if data stewards can be included in a gatekeeper role during the planning and implementation of data access management. This will enable more business involvement and accountability in the process.

What Processes and Technologies Are Needed to Support Data Steward Roles?

Similar to data governance practices, data steward practices are primarily people- and process-driven activities that need to be specially fitted within business models and data architectures. There are no business applications or vendor solutions that can deliver a comprehensive data steward model and process. Data stewards, however, can be greatly enabled and work much more effectively when they have training and access to common tools, applications, and reports that allow them to understand the use and flow of data, as well as to analyze, control, and monitor data quality in the areas for which they are accountable.

Chapter 3 mentioned that a certain amount of data quality management capability is expected to already exist or will be planned for as part of a well-designed and executed MDM solution. Some of this functionality may be delivered as part of implementing a data hub solution, while other functionality may be delivered from other vendor solutions or internally built solutions. For example, having standard solutions for data profiling, data quality metrics, and quality dashboards is fundamental to efficient and effective data governance and stewardship activities. More investment and consolidation toward enterprise standard platforms and solutions for data quality management, metadata management, and reference data management will improve the efficiency and effectiveness of data stewards.

Data stewards are a natural user group for the reviews, proof of concepts, and pilot activities involving vendor data management solutions. Many vendors now market data governance– and data steward–oriented products or capabilities in their solution suites. Many of these products and capabilities can be very useful, but of course, they also can be expensive, need careful assessment, and must be able to provide sufficient value and improvement to existing data management practices. Many vendor tools and services are purchased and implemented from an IT perspective without much (if any) consideration of the data governance and data steward perspectives. Therefore, the solutions implemented for data quality management, metadata management, and reference data management can be geared much more toward meeting technical requirements, and as a result they are not very user-friendly from a data governance and steward perspective. When evaluating these solutions, it is important to also consider the requirements and usability aspects from a data governance, data steward, and business user perspective.

Conclusion

This chapter covered the role of data stewardship in a multi-domain MDM program and stressed that data stewards cannot just be agents for data governance policy and standards. Rather, they need to be closely aligned to the touch points and consumers of the master data, where data entry, usage, and quality control can be most influenced.

There is an implicit relationship between data quality management, data governance, and data stewardship. For a multi-domain MDM program to succeed, these practices need to be closely orchestrated. Data stewardship should run deep through all of MDM, so a multi-domain plan needs to develop a firm concept of how a data steward model will look and function, where the data steward roles will be best positioned, and how the right resources can be identified and engaged. This chapter pointed out that a multi-domain MDM model can have a lot of layers of complexity, requiring a great deal of cross-functional involvement and support, and that as the layers become better understood and reveal the coordination needed to successfully drive the quality and control of master data quality, the data stewards will make the difference between poor and successful execution of these initiatives.

Ideally, there should be formal job titles for data stewards to demonstrate the value and importance this role has in a company, especially in relation to establishing a high-quality culture. But creating those job titles and developing a quality culture are often the result of reaching many prior milestones within the MDM and data governance maturity models. Until such time that formal data steward roles are in place, the concept and practice of data stewardship as an underlying discipline and success factor for MDM will still need to be supported through IT and the business resources that have the knowledge, skills, and focus needed to support and control master data.

It is important that data stewardship quickly starts proving its value and worth. Therefore, choose high value and visible points to position data steward roles, but also expect that the ability to expand the data steward footprint across the enterprise landscape can be a slow process that will compete with other internal growth and investment areas for resource and budget allocation.

CHAPTER 8

Data Integration

This chapter covers the discipline and practice of data integration in a multi-domain model. It discusses the need to establish consistent techniques for data profiling, quality assessment, data validation, and standards when integrating data into a Master Data Management (MDM) environment. It also covers the need to appropriately engage data governance teams and data stakeholder/consuming groups to help fully evaluate requirements and impacts associated with data integration projects. Data integration can be a very complex and time-consuming process. It can have multiple components depending on the solution implemented. For example, it might involve a one-time data migration and ongoing synchronization across multiple sources, or it might involve regular data extractions via batch or real-time interfaces, or it could be virtual data integration with ongoing metadata rule management. To be successful, data integration must be approached methodically and engage business, information technology (IT), and data governance.

Why Is Data Integration Necessary?

Multi-domain MDM solutions address an issue that most companies have: silos of master data throughout the enterprise. To resolve that problem, it is necessary to look at the data as a whole to identify duplicates, resolve inconsistencies and fragmentations, create relationships, build intelligence, control access, and consequently minimize maintenance costs and maximize governance and stewardship effectiveness. Therefore, either physically or virtually integrating data becomes a needed activity in any MDM program. In addition, if master data continue to physically reside in multiple locations, they must be maintained in a synchronized manner to truly address the MDM fundamental goal of avoiding discrepant information.

In an MDM initiative, data integration is a critical component to enable the interpretation and identification of records across multiple sources that are associated with the same entity. This process, also known as *entity resolution,* involves identifying the many occurrences of master data across disparate systems; cleansing, standardizing, matching, and enriching them; and finally ending up with a single version, which is often called the *golden record.* This record is a unique set of master data elements related to a single instance of an entity. A single instance of an entity means one person, or one company, or one patient, or one account, or one product, and so on, in spite of how many data records exist for each of them. The golden record is,

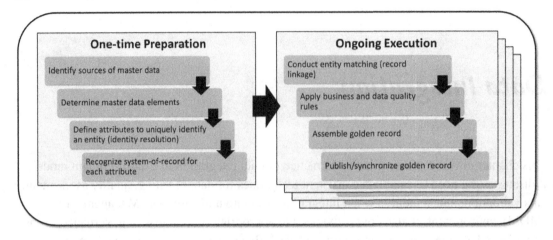

Figure 8.1: Entity resolution process

in essence, the sole version of the truth for a given entity occurrence. Entity resolution can be effectively performed only when data is properly integrated. Figure 8.1 depicts the entity resolution process. Each step is described in more detail later in this chapter. The actual data integration life cycle is also described later in this chapter, but understanding the steps behind entity resolution is important to eventually connect the why, what, how, who, and when of data integration.

Typically, entity resolution has a one-time preparation to profile data, properly recognize sources and data elements, and define the identity attributes and system-of-record (SOR) for each data element. After preparation, ongoing execution takes place to regularly maintain linked data, apply business and data quality rules, and finally create a golden record and publish or synchronize it with consuming sources. Obviously, much of what happens as part of entity resolution also depends on the MDM style chosen. For example, with a registry style, record linkage happens virtually, while with a hybrid style, record linkage is physical and data movement is required. Therefore, it is important to understand the concepts explained here, but adjust them accordingly to your needs.

In a multi-domain environment, entity resolution is conceptually the same for the different domains, but implementation might vary quite a bit depending on requirements, data profiling analysis, sources of data, business and data quality rules, golden record survivorship rules, and publishing or synchronization of data. As such, make sure to track each domain independently, but capture the impact on the overall data model when integrating multiple domains at once.

Let's cover each step of the entity resolution process in more detail next. Remember that entity resolution is just one part of data integration. Data integration will have additional requirements, as described later in this chapter.

Identify Sources of Master Data and Determine Master Data Elements

Chapter 2 covered defining and prioritizing master data. The first two steps related to entity resolution were explored in detail in that chapter since it is indeed very important to define and prioritize what domains and master attributes to manage. Any artifacts generated as a result of defining and prioritizing master data should be used as a starting point to the entity resolution process. Those artifacts shall be enriched with more detailed information as new findings and more data profiling lead to more relevant information.

After these two steps are completed, sources of master data and master attributes for each domain should be clearly stated. All data sources should be considered to keep any important master data from being left out. All master data elements in scope for MDM should be listed as well. Remember, as described previously in Chapter 2, not all master attributes will necessarily be in scope for the MDM hub. Recall that an MDM hub is primarily the repository for enterprise master data elements, which are generic and applicable to most lines of business (LOBs). LOB-specific information can remain distributed at each local source as applicable. To balance what is enterprise data element versus what is not is challenging. The more enterprise attributes there are, the more complete the golden record is. However, it will require more coordination, agreement, and overall governance across LOBs.

Define Attributes to Uniquely Identify an Entity (Identity Resolution)

Master elements were identified in the previous step of the process, but the question now is: What set of information from multiple sources, or even within a single source, belongs to the same entity? First, there is intersystem data duplication, where certain attributes are duplicated across sources. Second, there is intrasystem duplication, where attributes are duplicated within the same source. Third, information for the same entity is segmented across many sources, where one piece of information is in one source while another piece is in another source. Finally, there is inconsistency, with the same attribute in multiple sources, but carrying different content.

Before all those discrepancies can be resolved, it is necessary to find a way to link those entities within and across the many sources. Each system will have a uniquely generated key, but each of those keys doesn't truly define an entity. They are simply assigned to make records unique in each system for data normalization purposes. Therefore, it is necessary to find a set of attributes that can be used to uniquely identify an entity so that proper record linkage can occur.

What data elements do you use to uniquely represent a given entity? That question has no definite answer, which complicates commercial off-the-shelf solutions. They are obviously different for each domain, but even in a given domain, they vary among industries, companies, LOBs, different regions in a global company, and within contexts in a single organization.

One of the critical goals of MDM is to enable a single version of the truth. Therefore, the definition of what attribute or attributes to use to uniquely identify an entity has to be consensual at the enterprise level. Creating this key, which usually is a combination of multiple attributes, is fundamental and will drive many future decisions. However, since each LOB might have its own definition, it becomes a challenge to come up with a single designation that meets everybody's needs. This is certainly a business function because an entity worth mastering has a tremendous business value behind it. As discussed in Chapter 6, data governance can facilitate the process of reaching consensus among the multiple LOBs involved. There is a technical implication as well, since the chosen identity has to be practical to implement according to existing technologies.

Defining the identity of an entity is a lot more difficult than companies realize. The complication arises from trying to represent in computing terms a real-life individual, organization, object, place or thing, as well as their many contexts. Another challenge comes from having fragmented information. Normally, the key will be defined by no more than the lowest common denominator of the many attributes that are associated with that entity in its many different versions across the company.

For instance, in a health services company such as a hospital group, a *Patient* entity might have the following attributes in the Finance department (just a potential subset is shown in these examples):

- *First Name*, *Last Name*, Social Security Number (SSN), *Data Of Birth (DOB)*, *Address*, Payment History, Health Plan Insurer, and Health Plan ID.

However, in the Care Management department, the attributes available might be the following:

- *First Name*, *Last Name*, *DOB*, *Address*, Primary Physician, Physician Type, and Treatment History.

The italic attributes in these examples are the lowest common denominator. It makes sense that the key would come from one of those elements. If an attribute that doesn't exist in one of the systems (such as SSN in this example) is used to create a unique identity, it becomes difficult to establish the relationship between the entities in the two systems. It is obviously all right if something other than the lowest common denominator is used, though. Concluding the example, the following attributes could be used as keys:

- First Name, Last Name, and DOB

Those attributes are likely sufficient to uniquely identify a patient. But let's take a look at the consequences surrounding this decision:

- *Nicknames:* For example, is Bob Smith born on 03/15/1962 the same patient as Robert Smith born on 03/15/1962?

- *Name changes:* For example, Mary Johnson marries, and changes her name to Mary Williams.
- *Duplicate information:* What if you have the same SSN associated with multiple patients with different First Name, Last Name, and DOB combinations? Is it a bad data entry, fraud, or an honest mistake by the patient?
- *Different information:* What if the address associated with that patient in Finance is different from the address associated with that same patient in Services? Which system is the SOR for this information?

In this example, there are one domain, two systems, and eight total attributes, and there are at least four critical questions to answer. Imagine what happens when the number of domains, systems, attributes, and business rules and processes is much larger. Complexity will certainly increase in such a scenario.

An obvious side effect of going through this exercise is controversy. Each LOB will argue that its data is better and its business rules are more important to dictate the identity of an entity. Again, data governance becomes a critical function to help facilitate the process.

Using the automotive finance industry and the vehicle domain as another example, services may maintain that a vehicle can be defined simply by its make, model, and year. But originations may determine that trim is also needed, since pricing must be done at the trim level. Another possibility is the actual key will differ depending on the stage of the process. The annual percentage rate (APR) for financing a vehicle may depend on make, model, year, and trim. However, once a vehicle is financed, a vehicle identification number (VIN) becomes available, and at that point, the VIN could become the only key needed since all other attributes can be derived from it. The actual MDM of vehicle data could be a combination of pre- and post-financing. During pre-financing, vehicle master data would be a VIN-independent catalog based on the make/model/year/trim, while during post-financing, the vehicle master data would be VIN-based and associated with account information.

Recognize SOR for Each Master Data Element

At this point, all sources of master data should have been identified. Master attributes in those sources should have been profiled and properly classified as being in or out of scope, which means whether or not to include them as part of that entity's golden record. The next question is: What happens when the same attribute exists in multiple sources? Which one should be used? In essence, it is necessary to identify the SOR for each data element. The SOR is the authoritative data source for a given data element. Obviously, if an attribute exists in only one source, there is no dispute. On the other hand, if it exists in more than once place, that can cause controversy.

This step clearly highlights the need and consequential benefit of a data governance program. Data governance becomes critical to facilitate the resolution of the many disputes that are sure to arise when deciding which source is best for a given data element. Each LOB will say that its data is better and will want its information to take precedence. Having a mediator with overall interest at the enterprise level is vital to resolve any disputes.

The data governance Project Management Office (PMO) should lead the exercise, which culminates in a final decision on the authoritative source for each data element or piece of information. Evidently, this process of determining what data should be the trustworthy source starts by understanding the business purpose of the data, and the procedures of the LOB. Understanding the create-read-update-delete (CRUD) management steps for each data element within an LOB's associated business processes might give a good indication about what source has the latest information and likely would be the best candidate for SOR. For example, the enterprise resource planning (ERP) system might be the only official system where vendor information should be updated, while other sources are simply consumers of that information. However, companies have a tendency to create exceptions that are never formally communicated and eventually become the norm. Let's say that vendor information that flows from ERP to customer relationship management (CRM) might end up being updated in CRM without a properly captured business process. In this case, it is possible that CRM has the best information.

With that said, the final decision should also take into account in-depth data analysis. It cannot be stressed enough how important it is to conduct an exhaustive and systematic data profiling. Data profiling will be covered in more detail later in this chapter, as part of a discussion of the data integration life cycle. Nonetheless, it is important to note a few things about this topic at this point.

Not all data profiles are created equal. When defining in-scope attributes, it is necessary to understand the degree of completeness of a certain data element. Data completeness, which means the level of data that are missing or unusable, is indeed a fundamental characteristic and valuable for many purposes. But when identifying the SOR for a certain data element, completeness alone may not be sufficient. Other data quality dimensions, such as validity, consistency, accuracy, and timeliness, will play a bigger role. You want to use the source with the highest possible quality for each data element. Data quality dimensions are covered in detail in Chapter 9.

Data quality practices, therefore, play a fundamental role in entity resolution and MDM as an overall discipline. It is obvious that developing high-quality data suitable for use by the business should be the ultimate strategic goal for an enterprise. As a component of entity resolution, data quality must be applied tactically, both to understand the fitness for use of the existing data and to make it fit. What does that mean in this particular step? All data elements across the many sources must be evaluated fully from a quality standpoint to identify their degree of eligibility as an authoritative source. It is not sufficient to attend to each LOB, its processes, and its reasons why its data are vital to the company. Of course, there is some truth to this, but the problem is, a lot of times, the personnel in a company don't know what they don't know. Having real metrics backing up their statements is required.

Reference data sources become an effective and essential resource as well. Sometimes it is difficult to assess certain data-quality dimensions without using some sort of comparative method. For example, multiple data sources might have address information, and the addresses in all sources might be fairly complete, meaning that they are mostly populated. But are they valid? External references can be used to validate addresses, which can assist with deciding about what source is best.

Consistency of data across multiple sources is a great metric. First, if all sources agree on a particular related data set, this indicates that the data is up to date from an enterprise point of view. Second, if they all agree, there is no one source that is better than the other for that single piece of data. However, the fact that the information is consistent does not mean that it is accurate. It could be that it was at some point, but now it is outdated. For example, a partner may have been acquired by another company, and information about that has not been captured yet in any of the company's systems. This situation is clearly a data-quality issue, but it is irrelevant for now since the current goal is simply to determine the best source. If they are all the same, there is no dispute. Thus, there is value in looking for consistency across multiple sources to assist in SOR identification. Consistency analysis can also establish that the formalized CRUD process is being followed.

Another important aspect when defining a SOR is to correctly group related data elements together and associate them with the same source to avoid a "Frankenstein effect." For example, when working with a location, you shouldn't use the Street Number and Name from one source, combined with the City and State from another source, even if they are all associated with the same patient entity. All components of an address should be from the same source to avoid a badly composed set of information. That's why certain data elements cannot be evaluated independently. To cite another example, let's say that a company tracks financial account–related attributes as a group, such as a set of flags related to government-required customer privacy preferences. It is possible that there is interdependency within multiple flags, depending on how they were implemented in some of the sources. If that is the case, all the flags should come from the same source. If there is a question about the quality of those flags, the issue should be addressed apart from defining the SOR.

Finally, data from a preestablished SOR will not necessarily be used in every single instance. For example, an email address might be present in multiple sources, and a certain source will have priority over another and consequently designated as the SOR. But if an email address is missing in the SOR, then the email address from another source should be used. Furthermore, besides content, it is also important to evaluate the meaning of source attributes. Some attributes might have generic names but specialized meanings. For example, an address field could contain billing address, home address, email address, and so on.

Typically, one data source is established as the SOR, and most of the time, the data from that source will trump other systems. But, in certain instances where information is not available in that location, or if data quality is better in another source, the SOR can be overridden. A priority should be established, with clear business rules when one data source should trump another for each data element. Again, data governance plays a key role in leading the effort to collect those business rules.

To summarize, this section covered the following points:

- Data governance is essential to ensure that the proper SOR is chosen with the best interest of the enterprise in mind. A suitable data governance body is the best-equipped organization to mediate disputes that are sure to arise.
- Documenting CRUD for each data element per source can assist with the determination about what sources are eligible for the SOR role. Remember to confirm the expectations with proper data analysis.
- Data quality management practices are critical to establish the truth about the quality of the existing data.
  - Data profiling is the foundation of this whole process. Always keep in mind the dimensions of data quality, such as completeness, conformity, consistency, accuracy, uniqueness, integrity, and timeliness. Understanding those aspects of the data is a must.
  - Reference data usage can be extremely efficient. If a data set can be properly certified against a trusted source, the level of confidence rises significantly.
  - Consistency of information across multiple sources is valuable information as well. It can be used to validate the expected business process were implemented and followed accordingly.
  - Group data elements appropriately. Do not combine related data elements from mixed sources. Do not mix and match separate fields from multiple sources.
  - Establish one SOR for every data element or related data element. Clearly define any rules that should be followed to override the information from the SOR with the information from another source, if applicable. For example, a simple rule could be: CRM is the SOR for Customer Email data, but if email doesn't exist in CRM for a given customer, use the information collected from recently collected marketing materials instead if it is reliable.

Conduct Entity Matching (Record Linkage)

Once the identity of an entity is properly defined, it is possible to move on to the next step, which is to use that identity to link the multiple records associated with the same entity. Remember that those records could be in multiple sources due to intersystem duplication, or within the same source due to intrasystem duplication. Record linkage is the realization of identity resolution where multiple records with the same identity are considered to belong to the same entity.

This step will reveal the level of fragmentation and inconsistency of information across sources. Once two or more records associated with the same entity are compared side by side, it will reveal what attributes exist in one source and not the other, as well as, if the attribute does exist in multiple sources, how they agree with each other. Record linkage happens either virtually or physically, depending on the MDM style chosen.

In a registry-style MDM, attributes from multiple sources are linked to each other by their identities, which are kept in the hub along with a reference back to the original system. In a transaction-style MDM, the hub becomes the new SOR. Record linkage is a one-time operation to centralize and consolidate all records into the hub. After that, records are added and modified directly into the hub and published to other sources. In a hybrid-style MDM, record linkage is applied to data that are initially migrated into the hub, and afterward, as an ongoing process, when new data are added to sources and flowed into the hub.

Apply Business and Data-Quality Rules

Data collected from multiple sources will have very different levels of quality. However, master data records will need to meet certain standards to even be considered contributors to the final golden record. Business and data-quality rule requirements should have been captured previously and applied properly to records clustered together through record linkage.

Different data domains will have distinct business rules and data-quality standards. Subject area experts from multiple organizations will need to be consulted when compiling a list of all those rules and standards. Once more, data governance is a critical element of facilitating the process and ensuring that formal steps are taken and proper approvals are issued.

Another big consideration for this step is how data stewardship will operate. Depending on the MDM style chosen, data stewardship will have certain constraints. For example, on a registry-style MDM, business and data-quality rules have to be completely automated and are applied to virtually connected data. This limits the options for data steward teams, as they cannot manually intervene during record linkage. Analysis will occur after the fact, and corrections will be done at the source or the automated logic will have to be adjusted. On a hybrid-style MDM, processes can be added to allow data stewards to manually intervene and correct data before they are added to the MDM hub and propagated to other sources.

Reference data sources should be used whenever possible to help improve the quality of the existing data. Reference data are very specific to each domain. Specialized vendors in different industries will provide a large variety of offers, along with multiple ways to technologically integrate their solutions.

Assembling a Golden Record (Survivorship)

Master data from multiple sources has been integrated, records belonging to the same entity have been matched up, and raw data from original sources have been cleansed, standardized, and enriched. Now it is time to decide which data element from each of those contributors is the best suited to survive in the golden record.

It is obviously a big challenge to automate the decision on what data source to use on each situation. We have already discussed the rules to implement when prioritizing what source to use when there is a dispute. The automation of those rules is critical, as the MDM hub will likely need to meet strict requirements related to the delivery of timely information.

Figure 8.2 depicts a potential decision-making flowchart to resolve what data to use to assemble the golden record. That logic needs to be followed for each dependent set of data attributes. Most of the time, a data element is a single attribute, but sometimes it is a set of attributes. For example, an address is a combination of several attributes: street number,

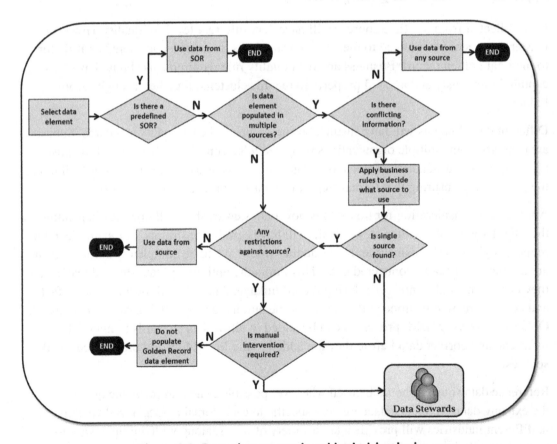

Figure 8.2: Data element survivorship decision logic

street name, city, county, state, ZIP code, and country. Remember that when putting together an attribute, do not survive pieces from different sources. When surviving the address, for example, take all attributes from the same source: do not mix sources.

Not every domain, MDM style, or organization will allow manual intervention by data stewards during the assembly of a golden record. Most of the time, full automation is required. In those cases, a safety-net type of logic is created to decide what source or data content to use when all other conditions fail. Later, data-quality metrics can be added to check whether certain automated decisions are erroneous and need correction.

In some cases, due to the enormous volume of information, manual intervention by data stewards alone might not be effective. The concept of crowdsourcing for data stewardship can be a viable approach. *Crowdsourcing* is the process of obtaining content from a large group of people, each person working on a specific area but adding a small portion to the greater result. For example, salespeople could update and review the addresses of their specific customers once they are changed.

Publish and Synchronize the Golden Record

Once the golden record is created, maintained, and available in the MDM hub, it can be published or synchronized to other sources as applicable. Data is either published or synchronized depending on the MDM style. In a registry-style MDM, there is one single virtual version of master data; therefore, publication is only needed and consumed by downstream systems. In a transactional-style MDM, there are no multiple copies either: a single physical version exists, and only propagation is sufficient. In a hybrid-style MDM, some attributes are copied; consequently, synchronization is necessary.

Data Integration Life Cycle

Entity resolution is just one part of data integration. Other requirements related to data integration exist in addition to what is needed for entity resolution. There are many flavors of data integration and synchronization, which depend on the multi-domain MDM style and architecture (as described in Chapter 3). However, the overall process and steps to evaluate and implement data integration in a multi-domain MDM program can be generalized. Figure 8.3 depicts the data integration life cycle, and each step is described in detail in the following sections.

Gather Requirements

The requirements for data integration are just one part of the overall requirements of a multi-domain MDM program. Nonetheless, they are critical to establish a solid technical foundation to proper support business functions, data stewardship, and data governance. All standard practices required for sound requirement analysis are obviously applicable here.

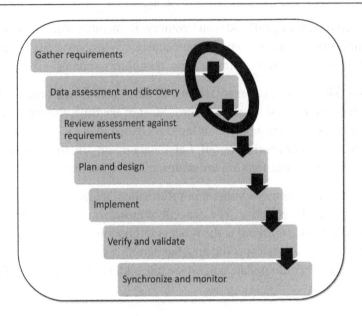

Figure 8.3: Data integration life cycle

Among other things, requirement analysis involves identifying, understanding, and documenting business needs. Clearly, a multi-domain MDM program should also have a strong business focus. However, remember that there are requirements to govern and maintain the integrated information, especially when seeking high data-quality standards. Those requirements will not necessarily be spelled out by the business. Business teams automatically expect high-quality information delivered in a timely manner, but they don't necessarily understand what it takes to achieve that. That is when solid data governance and stewardship plans are critical, and the requirements to meet those plans should be captured as early as possible because they can have a tremendous impact on the implementation of the final solution.

How is data integration in the context of MDM different from other data integration projects? Let's dwell on this question for a moment. Companies are constantly undergoing data integration projects. A typical one is data migration (i.e., permanently moving data from one system into another when replacing obsolete applications). Another is the ongoing extraction of data from upstream systems into downstream systems, such as in a data warehouse project. Others include one-time or regular data transfers between systems, either in batch or real-time interfaces. All those integration efforts can encounter a range of challenges related to different semantics across many heterogeneous sources, which can conflict by structure, context, value, or any combination.

Different MDM styles will need different levels of data integration. Depending on the integration type selected, these requirements will include the elements that other data integration projects need; however, a multi-domain MDM program will have additional requirements as well. The reason for that is that a well-implemented MDM needs the foundation to proper govern, monitor, and act upon the data. For example, a company implementing a hybrid-style MDM will certainly need to perform a one-time data migration to initially populate the MDM hub. Furthermore, the hub will need to remain synchronized with other sources of data, but that synchronization might be affected by how data stewardship activities are structured and data quality is applied. This could change if one-way or two-way synchronization is necessary, depending on where the data is corrected.

Another consideration is if the data integration project is part of an MDM implementation, or if a particular data integration project is being leveraged to apply MDM to a new domain. We have already discussed the fact that a company may implement domains in phases. Let's say, for example, that a company has implemented MDM to the customer domain and went through data integration specifically for that purpose. Later, the same company is going through a data migration effort to upgrade an obsolete application, and it decides to implement MDM to additional domains at the same time. That is normal, but it is important to capture the integration requirements for the MDM piece along with the other requirements that are already in place for the data conversion.

Generally, businesses will be interested mostly in functional requirements, but nonfunctional requirements play an important role in data quality and governance. Data integrity, security, availability, and interoperability are just a few of the nonfunctional requirements that are sure to strongly influence certain design decisions. In the end, remember to consider data governance, data stewardship, and data-quality requirements as well as any other standard requirements.

A multi-domain MDM hub can be implemented either as real-time or batch interfaces. This may even vary by domain within a single hub. Certain domains might have different data timeliness requirements than others. For example, consider an MDM hub hosting customer, product, and vendor data. This hub might not be the SOR for all three domains. Furthermore, the volume and frequency of data might vary for each domain. Let's assume that the hub is the SOR for customer and vendor data, but not the product data, and that there is a high volume and frequency of customer and product data changes, but less so about vendors. Therefore, one company might decide to implement data change in real time for the customer domain because it is high-volume and the hub is the SOR for it, decide to implement product in batches because the MDM hub is not the SOR for it, and implement the vendor domain in batches due to the low volume and low frequency of changes. All these considerations are important when writing the multi-domain MDM integration requirements.

Discover and Assess Data

In any data project, requirements alone are not sufficient. Data must be analyzed to confirm or challenge any existing expectations. Much of the time, a business has a completely distorted view about the quality of the data or it completely ignores certain characteristics of the data. Therefore, data profiling is essential to provide further evidence that the requirements are solid and can indeed be met. Data profiling is important to understand how to model the MDM domains and their entities and relationships.

Figure 8.4 depicts an illustration in quadrants representing the idea that both business understanding and data profiling are necessary to minimize any risk of incorrect assumptions about the data's fitness for use or about how the data serve the business.

In a multi-domain MDM program, data profiling is required at multiple stages of the process. It is needed to evaluate and prioritize data domains. Business teams may have a perceived idea of what data domains are more important to apply MDM based on the value those domains bring to them, but that opinion may not necessarily be based on the data itself. For example, an auto-finance company is highly dependent on dealers. As such, the business might prioritize the *Dealer* domain very highly. However, an extensive data-profiling analysis might show that the existing systems do a great job maintaining dealer information through robust CRUD management, practically no data redundancy, very little inconsistency, and most important, proper fitness for use. Therefore, MDM for the Dealer domain is less important.

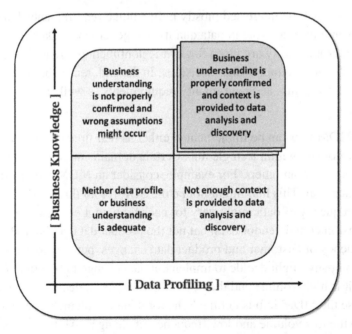

Figure 8.4: Properly supported data profiling

Once domains are properly evaluated and prioritized, data profiling is critical to determine what master data elements for given domains should be considered worth managing. Structure, content, and relationships, along with completeness, uniqueness, consistency, validity, and accuracy of information, will influence the assessment. Data profiling at this stage is also critical to confirm, dispute, and catalog enterprise metadata information. This becomes the foundation to create a sound data model to store multi-domain master data.

When data needs to be migrated or integrated into a multi-domain MDM hub, data profiling is again critical to complement this information with the current expected quality of information and business usage suitability. The MDM hub is only as good as the data in it. "Garbage in, garbage out" is a well-known saying, and the truth of it is only amplified with MDM. An enterprise multi-domain MDM hub is built to function as the ultimate reference for delivering master data to the entire company. If low-quality data from original sources is brought into the hub, the compound effect will have disastrous consequences. Previously, independent organizations had to deal only with their local data issues and had preestablished workarounds to deal with them. The moment that an MDM hub might distribute issues from one organization to another, the worse the situation will get. It is important to use data profiling to understand those issues and correct them before migrating or copying them into a centralized hub.

As part of the entity resolution process, data profiling is essential to defining what data elements to use to uniquely identify an entity, what operations are required to transform data into a minimum required standard of quality, how to cluster similar records together, and finally, how to assemble a golden record. Without data profiling, those activities could completely miss the mark by performing operations based on incorrect assumptions or incorrect enterprise metadata.

The bottom line is that data profiling is multifaceted and a lot more complex than people realize. It is easy to understand the categories and metrics of data profiling, but there are several challenges, such as the following:

- Understanding when to apply a specific technique
- Interpreting results correctly and properly adjusting subsequent steps
- Using existing metadata, if available, but utilizing profiling results to confirm or challenge current definitions
- Using profiling results to help correctly derive metadata if it does not already exist

Figure 8.5 illustrates the principle that data profiling is not a two-dimensional discipline. It is not only about applying a technique and interpreting the metrics and results. It is also about understanding where you are in a third dimension: enterprise metadata or the business's expected meaning. Notice the word *expected*. Many times, what is documented or assumed is not really what is expected. Consequently, data-profiling techniques and the resulting metrics

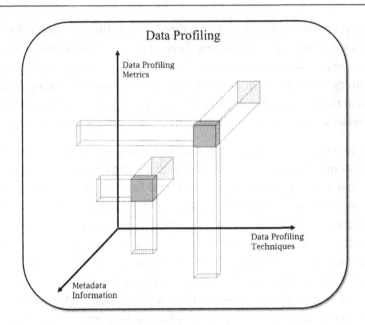

Figure 8.5: Data profiling as a function of metadata

need to be revised according to actual metadata exposed by real usage of the data, not what is listed on paper. Think of it as adjusting data profiling in a three-dimensional plane.

Examples of data profiling techniques include frequency distribution, pattern analysis, domain analysis, type identification, interdependency verification, redundancy analysis, primary and foreign key determination, and many other statistical measurements. A multi-domain MDM vendor solution might not necessarily include a robust data profiling functionality. It is possible to use database languages, reporting tools, or both to profile information, but specialized tools offer a greater level of sophistication and are highly recommended.

Review Assessment Against Requirements

The nature of data profiling itself is iterative. Moreover, data profiling results must be used to assess if the provided data integration requirements can be properly supported and met. Granted, requirements are mostly listed to request functionalities to attend business needs, which can be quite strict. However, using the results of the data analysis to dissect the requirements is invaluable.

As mentioned previously, business teams may have a distorted view about the data, and this misunderstanding can lead to misguided requirements. There is nothing like real data to shed light on business problems, and it is not uncommon for requirements to change completely once the supported metrics are presented. In addition, a clear understanding of the data can help you institute a much better approach to solving any issues.

Requirement gathering, data assessment, and ensuing review should happen as many times as necessary until there is high confidence that the requirements are based on a solid understanding of current state. This cyclical process is represented by the circular arrow around the first three steps shown in Figure 8.3.

Plan and Design

Once the requirements are completely validated, it is possible to move to the planning and design phase. Notice that the data profiling analysis described previously is not only useful to validate requirements, it is also extremely useful when designing the final solution.

When planning the integration of multiple domains, it is important to recognize the priority and complexity of each one of them. Certain domains will have a much higher volume of information than others. Volume is an important factor to consider because it will have a direct effect on the effort to integrate data. The higher the volume, the higher the probability that more duplication and inconsistencies exist. Therefore, integrating high-volume data into an MDM hub will be more time-consuming and present greater risk of improper entity resolution.

Data profiling results will give a good indication of the volume of information and level of data quality. Use those results to estimate how much of the integration effort can be automated and how much will require manual intervention. With data projects in general, chances are that a certain amount of data correction can be automated, while a portion of it will have to be manually fixed. It is important to categorize your data and find ways to fix each of the categories. Focus on the categories with the highest volume of data and look for automated alternatives for them.

Data stewards must be involved in the process of evaluating data profiling and data quality results and also participate in the planning. One important element is to determine how data will be improved to satisfy initial data integration. Another is to plan data quality maintenance on a regular basis during ongoing integration and synchronization. Data stewards are primarily responsible for guaranteeing that data are fit for use by the business teams. Therefore, they need to be involved in the decision process. Understanding the quality of the existing data is essential to anticipating future issues and deciding the best process to either prevent or correct them.

Obviously, data governance also needs to participate in overseeing the planning process and evaluating whether the proposed design meets existing policies, procedures, and standards. The need for additional policies, procedures, and standards will arise, depending on the level of maturity of an existing data governance program, if any. Therefore, these elements must be captured and documented properly. Data governance should also ensure that all teams are properly represented to review and approve the final design.

Depending on its style, a multi-domain MDM solution will have varying levels of impact on existing processes. More intrusive MDM styles, such as transaction and hybrid, can certainly affect existing processes deeply. More intrusive MDM styles are sure to have high demands of data integration. As such, to properly plan for highly invasive data integration projects, it is important to understand current and future business processes and communicate all changes properly.

A solid change management program should already exist as part of the overall multi-domain MDM implementation. Details related to the data integration planning and design must be added and properly communicated via channels established by the change management team. The impact of the integration on the existing business must be communicated in a timely and effective manner. Do not underestimate the need to communicate changes to both the technical and business teams for two primary purposes: to validate what is being done and to prepare for any changes caused by the actions in question.

Implement

As discussed previously, it is very common to implement a multi-domain MDM in phases. Most of the time, the phased approach is related to how data is integrated. Multiple sources are gradually integrated, multiple domains are gradually integrated, or both. There is no single recipe concerning what order or how domains and sources should be integrated. Choosing what domains and sources to integrate first are directly related to their business value, volume, volatility, reusability, and complexity.

Business value is typically the biggest driving factor. In essence, if there is enough business interest, the costs and risks associated with addressing high volume and high complexity are well justified. Reusability can be an additional factor to consider when prioritizing domains or sources to integrate. For example, if a certain domain has already been successfully integrated into an MDM hub, another domain might be easier to add if the two domains are similar enough in terms of requirements and integration logic. This reusability aspect can be used to favor the MDM of a certain domain over another. In the end, however, the key criterion is business value.

Obviously, technical aspects are highly relevant because of the cost-benefit equation. Even if there is a high business value in integrating certain sources and domains, costs and risks can be limiting factors when calculating return on investment (ROI). Integrating data will have technical challenges, as well as compliance and regulation risks. Data integration technology is more advanced for certain domains than others. The key is mostly the technology to facilitate automation. Entity resolution, which is a vital aspect of data integration, is more advanced in some subject areas than others. For example, the *Customer* domain is generally easier to master than the *Product* domain because the technology for recognizing matching entities is more mature with regard to people and company names.

Therefore, mastering other domains that involve people or company names will be easier to master than domains with other taxonomies.

Except for the registry style, other MDM solutions will require data migration of master data from the original sources to the MDM hub. This migration can be done in phases, with data from distinct sources gradually introduced into the MDM hub. The main point is to identify the impact to business operations. Certain business processes may suffer if only certain data sources are migrated, while other business processes will be more affected as the number of combined sources increases. This outcome is a consequence of how much the MDM implementation will affect existing systems and accompanying processes. Needless to say, the more intrusive the MDM style and the more sources are involved, the greater the impact is.

The actual implementation of data integration hinges on proper planning and execution. But it is not only about the planning and execution of data integration; it is about planning and executing the other associated parts: data governance, data stewardship, and change management. Data governance is important to oversee the process, engage process business teams as needed, and ensure compliance to policies, procedures, and standards. Data stewards are critical because as data experts, they need to ensure that data are migrated according to business expectations, meet high quality standards, and can be properly maintained for the future. Change management is essential to communicating how data integration will affect the current state and setting proper expectations. Since projects rarely go completely as planned, it is important to keep stakeholders informed about any deviations from the original plans.

Verify and Validate

Like any other software implementation, newly developed logic must be properly tested. The challenge with data projects is to make sure to compile a comprehensive list of data scenarios, evaluate data integrity throughout their life cycles, and make maintenance as easy as possible. Usually, software testing focuses on validating functional requirements, and not necessarily other data management aspects. Granted, functional testing will require looking at many data scenarios, which are sure to test many of the aspects pertaining to data. But how the integrity of the information will be validated, how data will stay consistent with time, and how data quality is maintained are often left untested. This particular issue can cause degradation over time.

To address these issues, develop a data-driven approach. It was explained earlier in this chapter how a solid data model is fundamental to creating a scalable, high-quality, and easily maintained data system. Make sure to test those aspects of the integrated domains. This challenge increases as more domains are added. Data models become more complex when modeling relationships across multiple domains and when multiple business teams are using the master data. As data are integrated into the multi-domain MDM model, many aspects of such integration must be validated.

Verification and validation of data integration projects must be done from a technical point of view, as well as from the standpoint of business usage of data. As always, the question concerns data's fitness for use. But data can be fit for use when they are initially migrated but become less so as time passes. If the model doesn't preserve data integrity properly over time, or if error prevention is not a focus during data entry, data quality can easily decline and affect the data's fitness for use. Unit, integration, and acceptance testing will not necessarily uncover those issues. Data architects, data modelers, and data stewards need to work together to test for those scenarios and methods for maintaining high-quality data.

Synchronize and Monitor

The need for data synchronization depends on the MDM style. If copies of master data are maintained at other sources as well as the MDM hub, they must be synchronized on a regular basis. Certain domains might require real-time synchronization, while others can be satisfied by batch updates. One key factor is which system is the SOR for master data in that particular domain. Remember that there are MDM styles where the MDM hub becomes the SOR for a given domain master data, while in other styles, the MDM hub is simply a system of reference.

When the MDM becomes the SOR for a particular domain, chances are that it will be required to have the most up-to-date information in real time. However, if the MDM is only a system of reference, keeping the MDM hub up to date in real time may not be required. That will depend on the systems that use the MDM hub as a reference and their underlying business processes. Therefore, updating the MDM hub with data from the actual SOR may be done every night in some situations.

Real-time interfaces are more complex than batch interfaces. Be sure to consider carefully the decision of whether they are really required, and base your deliberations on each specific domain. Obviously, a single MDM hub can be used for multiple domains. However, not all domains must follow the same synchronization scheme. Also, the MDM hub might be the SOR for one domain while serving only as a system of reference for another. Having multiple mechanisms to synchronize master data into the hub can be confusing and makes maintenance more difficult. On the other hand, requiring real-time synchronization of very low volume of data can be overkill. Make sure to balance the complexity. Having a single architecture to uniformly synchronize all domains might be desirable, but if that single architecture is real-time, two-way, and consequently complex, it might be too costly to use for low-volume, low-complex, and low-business-value domains.

In the end, despite the synchronization approach taken, the actual consistency of data across systems must be monitored and maintained. Even if a solid design is in place, certain implementations can lead to mismatches due to bugs or unforeseen circumstances. Automating a report to monitor eventual discrepancies can be a wise decision, depending on the criticality of the domain and its accuracy to business processes. Customer retention, competitive advantage, and regulatory compliance may be heavily dependent on timely, high-quality information.

Data stewards exercise a bigger role in this particular step. Ultimately, they will be responsible for keeping the data accurate and available. Prevention of data issues is the primary goal, but this may not always be possible. Therefore, establishing processes for data stewards to quickly intervene and remediate any data issues is sure to reap huge benefits. This can involve adopting a system to be used exclusively by data stewards to correct data following proper compliance, having data stewards use existing systems to update incorrect information, or a combination of both approaches. Understand whether what is offered by MDM vendors is sufficient to meet your needs. In general, MDM solutions will have a strong focus on data integration, but not necessarily the rigorous data-quality support that is necessary to detect and correct anomalies.

Entity Resolution Within the Data Integration Life Cycle

Data integration is concerned about more than entity resolution, but entity resolution is an important component. Figure 8.6 shows the entity resolution process executed within the data integration life cycle.

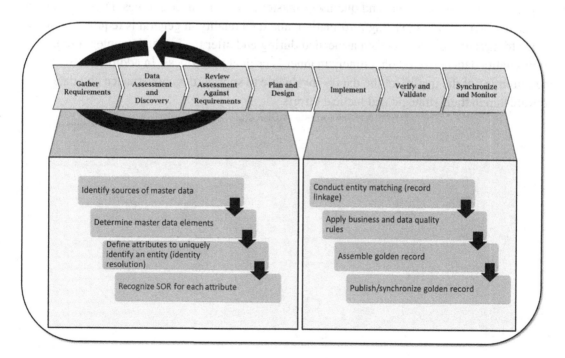

Figure 8.6: Entity resolution within the data integration life cycle

Conclusion

Data integration is clearly a complex exercise, with multiple details and business and technical challenges. In addition, it is not a one time-project. Certainly, the initial data integration effort will be either a one-time project or a phased approach, but synchronization and monitoring is part of an ongoing program, supported by business, IT, data governance, data stewardship, data quality, and metadata management. The data-driven nature of these types of projects requires rigorous disciplines of data management.

Notice how integrating data from multiple domains and sources will have more than just a technical impact. Business definitions previously contained within their own business functions are now spread and shared among multiple organizations due to its data-sharing nature. Data integration requires more collaboration but facilitates more formal processes to document who, where, when, and how data are created, used, modified, and deleted. Metadata management is the centerpiece to properly capturing, confirming, and disseminating data definitions, usage, and impact when changes occur. It is a fundamental practice to support correct decisions by business and technical teams, data governance, and data stewardship. Metadata should be captured throughout the data integration life cycle when fundamental decisions are taking place.

A successful data integration project requires a solid understanding of the many domains in scope, sources of master data, and quality of master data from those sources. Data profiling is a must in order to assess existing information, and data quality in general is required at many points to measure and correct data as needed during and after the initial data integration. High-quality data delivered on a timely manner is critical to business. In addition, a true measurement of the quality of the data is invaluable to support data governance and data stewardship in their strategic and tactical efforts.

CHAPTER 9

Data Quality Management

This chapter covers the discipline and practice of Data Quality Management (DQM) in a multi-domain Master Data Management (MDM) framework. It discusses how to define and apply a DQM model consistently across a multi-domain environment, and how to expand the practice of DQM to an enterprise level. This chapter starts by presenting how DQM fits into a multi-domain MDM environment and how important it is to manage DQM strategies, decisions, and execution. It continues by introducing a DQM model that is critical to supporting and scaling the discipline beyond MDM. Finally, it covers a data-quality improvement life cycle, with the required steps and activities to analyze, plan, execute, and monitor data quality projects effectively and efficiently.

DQM in a Multi-domain MDM Environment

Trusted data delivered in a timely manner is any company's ultimate objective. No company will ever question the need for high-quality information. The major challenge is to establish a model that can both minimize bad data from being introduced and efficiently correct any existing bad data. Data quality requires both strategic and tactical focuses in addition to strong business and information technology (IT) collaboration. Strategically, a company needs to start by establishing a culture of quality. Data quality is everyone's job, but it's up to management to communicate that view, and most important, establish the proper foundation and channels to help people succeed. Tactically, organizations need to identify and assess areas in need of data-quality improvement, and conduct data-quality projects to both fix issues and prevent them from happening in the future.

Let's discuss data quality in the context of a multi-domain MDM implementation. One of the selling points of MDM is that it helps improve the quality of data. But why is MDM so conducive to data-quality improvement? The answer is simple: first, MDM requires data to be consistent across multiple sources so that proper linkage is established; second, MDM fosters the assembly of fragmented information across disparate sources; and third, MDM becomes a central point to maintain, improve, measure, and govern the quality of master data. All those three points have a data-quality focus, which forces companies to dig deep into their data by performing meticulous analysis, and once issues are identified, to perform the proper correction.

Companies will have to address data-quality concerns during an MDM implementation due to the intrinsic problem that MDM addresses. It is important, post-MDM implementation, not to lose that momentum and use it to establish a solid foundation to continue a sound data-quality program even after one or more domains are completely integrated into an MDM hub. Furthermore, it is typical to gradually master different domains in multiple phases. As such, there is a clear advantage in increasing the maturity of DQM to shorten future phases. Even a single domain can be implemented in multiple phases due to a large number of sources to integrate. Any data-quality methodology established and knowledge acquired should be clearly documented for future reference and reuse.

DQM is very broad and deep. Certain aspects of DQM can easily be re-used across many different domains, but others not so much. For example, validating customer data can be quite different from validating product data. Still, many techniques of data profiling and data cleansing can be applied similarly across multiple domains. Solid leadership and expertise in DQM are required to differentiate when to generalize and when to specialize data-quality components, processes, and methodologies for multiple domains.

A Data-Quality Model

There are many factors influencing how a company will address data quality, such as the multi-domain MDM approach being implemented; how multiple lines of business (LOBs) interact with each other; the level of collaboration between business and IT; the maturity level of data governance, data stewardship, and metadata management; the degree of high-level management engagement and sponsorship; technological resources; and personnel skills.

Data-quality efforts cannot be isolated into a corner or managed like a software development team. Data-quality specialists must be engaged into other activities within the company, and be actively involved into data-related decision making subjects. Data-quality experts should be assigned to projects, working side by side with data architects, data designers, system integrators, software developers, data stewards, and so on.

Data quality can be managed within its own Project Management Office (PMO), as a function of the data governance PMO, or as a function of the MDM PMO. Still, these practices need tight strategic alignment to avoid charter and priority conflicts. Furthermore, in spite of the specific model chosen, the data governance PMO should be highly engaged to DQM for proper strategic directions and oversight. Figure 9.1 depicts a model for DQM. Notice how it shows a separate DQ PMO, but it also indicates the need for alignment with the data governance and the multi-domain MDM PMOs. The separate DQ PMO is presented to allow for explanation on specific DQM activities and functions.

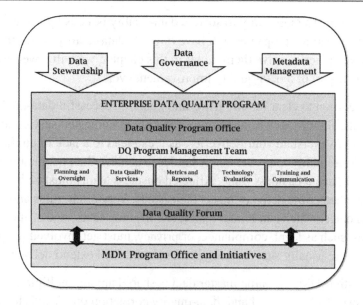

Figure 9.1: A DQM model

Planning and Oversight

A data-quality program is ongoing. There will be many data-quality improvement projects, but the overall goal is to have a strategically sustainable office to direct and foment initiatives. Strong data-quality leadership needs to work closely with a data governance office to align business needs and continuing prioritization of efforts. A data-driven company needs to encourage everyone to detect issues and propose data-quality improvements. Of course, any proposed initiative will have to be analyzed, reviewed, and prioritized. A data quality office can oversee the analysis of data issues, evaluate the impact that it has on the business, propose solutions to cleanse existing data, and either mitigate or prevent future occurrences.

In multi-domain MDM, it is natural to have certain data-quality requirements and activities already presumed since they are intrinsic to consolidating and synchronizing master data, as explained earlier in this chapter. Therefore, the data-quality roadmap is somewhat embedded to the overall MDM roadmap. Although MDM provides the opportunity to start a data-quality practice, DQM needs to be built as a strong practice with well-supported capabilities and leadership. To be sure, they need to be collaborating functions. But if companies do not already have a data-quality program, they need to take this opportunity to start one and expand the role of data quality beyond master data.

Data-Quality Services

Data-quality services are the primary reason for the existence of a data-quality program: the delivery of actual data-quality improvements and a constant drive toward a more mature and proactive organization. The ideal way to solve a data-quality issue is by avoiding it from occurring. But even mature companies will have ongoing data-quality issues that require reactive processes in place to solve them. Later in this chapter, we will cover data-quality activities in detail as part of a data-quality improvement cycle.

In any event, in addition to clear requirements and goals, a successful data-quality program also needs to set the right expectations through a well-communicated service-level agreement (SLA). Be sure not to overstate your deliveries, as it can lead to a lack of confidence on the entire program. Data-quality improvement is harder to achieve than people imagine, because it is both a technical and a business issue. Affected business teams must be involved at all times to evaluate whether the delivery meets their needs. Very often, rules and regulations may limit data updates, which can hinder data fixes. In some cases, one or more corporate regulatory offices, such as legal, compliance, or privacy, must get involved in approving corrections. These are usually slow-moving processes that will extend delivery time.

Remember that with MDM, the same master data is shared among multiple LOBs. That is a double-edged sword. On the one hand, data-quality correction only needs to occur in one location, which is then propagated to other sources consistently. On the other hand, data changes must be accepted and approved by all affected business units. Data governance can facilitate the approval process, although a data quality forum is also a viable alternative to engage business liaisons along with data-quality experts to expedite analysis, testing, and acceptance of proposed modifications.

Metrics and Reports

Metrics and reports are about measuring and reporting the overall performance of the data-quality program itself, not actual metrics and reports on data-quality issues, which is considered a data-quality activity in this book, and is explained later. A data-quality program must have measurable goals with meaningful key performance indicators (KPIs) and well-established return on investment (ROI). As such, those goals must be measured and reported to demonstrate the value of the data-quality program as a whole.

As stated previously under planning and oversight, a complete data-quality roadmap may or may not be included in the overall MDM roadmap. It is more advantageous for a company to expand the scope of data quality beyond MDM. Programs and projects can have various forms and levels of DQ metrics, either within MDM or not. Still, DQM standards should be approved by data governance to insure proper reporting alignment and use across multiple programs.

Technology Evaluation

Tools for data quality are constantly evolving. In addition, do not expect a vendor-provided MDM solution to have all the technology needed for a comprehensive DQM program.

They will usually provide what is required for MDM-related data quality, which is just one portion of all data-quality activities. There are many facets to data quality, which may require multiple tools and multiple skills. The many activities around data quality are covered in the next section. The data-quality program office should spend a reasonable amount of time evaluating new technologies and staying abreast of new capabilities that can help prevent data issues and improve competencies to profile data and expedite data-cleansing initiatives.

Furthermore, using reference data to either verify or correct other data is typically a good strategy. If a trusted source exists for a particular subject, it should be explored as part of a data-quality effort. Therefore, it is important that reference data management and DQM collaborate as part of an overall data management organization. In the context of multi-domain MDM, certain domains will offer more or less options for reference data depending on how general the domains are. For example, depending on how specific a product is, it can be much more difficult to find reference data related to the *Product* domain than to the *Customer* domain.

Training and Communication

Data quality is everyone's responsibility, and that message must be communicated clearly in a truly data-driven enterprise. Just about everyone in the company will recognize data-quality issues do exist; however, no one person or business group will typically understand the extent of those issues, their cost, how the issues affect their current decisions, and how to fix them. Therefore, simply communicating how important it is to have high-quality information is not sufficient. It is necessary to present tangible information and techniques that can be converted to actions to detect, assess, and improve the overall quality of the data.

Data issues are typically identified on a singular basis. A certain user notices an issue to a certain record while interacting with a customer or partner, or while performing a given business process. The instinctive action is to correct that one record and move on. A truly proactive company should have mechanisms for this user to report the problem, which is analyzed to identify whether it is indeed a single occurrence or it is a systemic problem that must be addressed. This certainly requires proper infrastructure, but awareness and proper training are key elements to make it successful.

Technology alone is not enough to prevent and correct issues. It requires people to be sensitive to issues and how their actions have the potential to negatively affect downstream systems and processes. This is as much of a business issue as it is an IT issue. It is a business issue because data is mostly entered and maintained by business teams. It is an IT issue as well because, as custodians of the data, IT teams are responsible for providing a solid infrastructure that minimizes data anomalies according to how data is used.

In a multi-domain MDM environment, bad data can be magnified. MDM is about eliminating data siloes by bringing disparate sources together, eliminating inconsistencies and fragmentation, and finally distributing golden records throughout. That is obviously fine, so long as data coming into an MDM hub are either good, or just bad enough that they can be fixed. However, if the data are of such low quality that cannot be fixed at all, or its low quality can't be automatically detected, the MDM hub will distribute the bad information to the enterprise. That is why the functions of stewardship, quality, and governance are even more important. The consequences of bad data entered into what was previously a siloed system are now exacerbated, making the need for proper training and communication even more relevant to avoiding negative consequences.

Continuous training, both formal and informal, is essential to achieve everyone's participation and strengthen a culture of focus on data quality. Actually, several studies have shown that informal learning can be more effective than formal learning. With that in mind, companies need to find creative ways to disseminate DQM information, such as with mentoring and coaching programs, brown-bag sessions, reviews of lessons learned, and so on. Technology should be leveraged to increase collaboration. Social media still has a long way to go in the workplace, but that channel needs to be considered as a mechanism to increase collaboration and promote information sharing. There are multiple categories of social media applications, such as blogs, microblogging, social networking, wikis, webcasts, podcasts, and more. Balancing what resources to use and to what extent is a challenge. Companies in certain industries may have less difficulty in adopting some of those applications. As an example, it is likely that high-tech companies are more prepared than healthcare companies to embrace and spread the use of social media in general. When defining what will be most effective in a company, it is necessary to take into consideration the company culture, computer resources, and human resources and skills.

Data-Quality Improvement Cycle and Activities

There are many aspects of DQM, including the source of bad data, as well as the actual definition of what bad data really is and its associated representation. Let's take a look at a couple of examples to illustrate this further:

- There is no contention about what the two acceptable values are for the gender attribute. However, one system may represent it as M/F, another with 1/0, another with Male/Female/MALE/FEMALE, and yet another without any validation whatsoever—with a multitude of manually entered values that could be missing, correct, or incorrect. Furthermore, it is possible to have a correct gender value improperly assigned to a given person. In the end, this information can be critical to companies selling gender-specific products. Others, however, may not be affected as much as if a direct-mail letter is incorrectly labeled Mr. instead of Mrs.
- Some data elements may not even have an obvious definition, or its definition depends on another element. An expiration date, for example, has to be a valid date in the calendar, as well as a "later than" effective date.

- In another scenario, some customers are eligible for a certain service discount only if they have a gold account.

These examples show just one facet of data quality or lack of it. Data suffers from multiple problems, including fragmentation, duplication, business rule violation, lack of standardization, incompleteness, categorization, cataloging, synchronization, missing lineage, and deficient metadata documentation.

One may wonder why companies get in such a mess. Difficult situations usually are caused by a multitude of factors, some potentially more avoidable than others. Certain companies grow at an incredible and sometimes unpredictable pace. Mergers and acquisitions are very common vehicles to increase market share or to tap into new business endeavors. Every time a new company is acquired by another, its data must be integrated. That can translate to more data-quality issues and defects being injected into the integrated environment. Companies usually do not have time to cleanse the new data coming in as part of the migration process, except when it is absolutely required to make them fit into the existing structure. "We'll cleanse the data later" is a common motto and rarely achieved.

Additionally, software applications have historically been developed to solve a particular aspect of the business problem and rarely consider the impact to other business processes or data consumers. That has led to years of multiple distributed software and business applications with disparate rules. Different systems might contain multiple instances of a customer record with different details and transactions linked to it. Because of these reasons, most companies suffer from fragmented and inconsistent data. The net effect is that companies face unnecessary and increased operational inefficiencies, inconsistent or inaccurate reporting, and ultimately incorrect business decisions.

Even enterprise applications, such as ERP and CRM, have remained silos of information, with data being constantly duplicated and laden with errors.

There is also the business process as part of the equation. It is human nature for people to look for creative ways to solve their problems. That means, when users have technical problems or run into business limitations during data entry, they will find ways to do it, even if it means breaking business rules or overriding well-defined processes. From a data-quality perspective, this is not a good thing, but should the users be blamed? After all, they may be facing a particular customer need that doesn't fit well into an existing business process or lacks sufficient business rules, or there is a system defect that is delaying a high-profit transaction requiring the user to take alternate actions that can lead to data capture issues.

Let's assume a company does have all the correct elements in place, such as data governance, data stewardship, data quality, IT support, and so on. Users are less likely to engage the proper teams if their confidence on the support process is low. They may think: "by the time I get this problem resolved through the proper mechanisms, I'll have a customer satisfaction

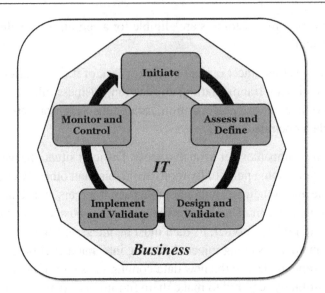

Figure 9.2: Data quality improvement cycle

issue beyond repair." Therefore, for the benefit of the company, they act with imagination and independently solve the immediate problem to their satisfaction and possibly with nonstandard solutions and non approved data entry. Making matters worse, these out-of-spec practices and associated data issues are usually difficult to monitor, detect, and correct.

With that said, the primary goal of a company should be to not only have the proper elements of a well-governed entity, but have them working effectively as well. This comes with maturity and a constant focus on process improvement. Simply improving the data entry process alone is not enough. It is necessary to improve the support process around it. Just about everything is constantly changing: business needs, business landscape, technology, people, and so on. The only hope is to have an efficiently adaptive model that in spite of all these changes can continue to deliver results quickly. The topic of continuous improvement is addressed in Chapter 12.

Figure 9.2 depicts a data quality improvement cycle, which conveys the steps to identify, correct, and control data-quality issues. Notice that the steps intersect both IT and business to emphasize the strong collaboration needed between them. Each of the steps has multiple data-quality activities embedded. Let's describe the steps and their accompanying activities next.

Initiate

A data-quality effort can be initiated in many ways. Drivers are essentially the initiators of data-quality activities and the means by which they bring data-quality issues to the attention of the proper people. A company with a mature data-quality practice should be able to support a multitude of drivers. Not only that, it should demand that everyone across the company participate in improving the overall quality of the data. After all, data quality is everyone's responsibility.

Essentially, data-quality initiatives fall into two categories: (1) reactive and (2) proactive. In general, proactive initiatives are measures established to avoid problems from happening or worsening, while reactive initiatives are measures adopted after the problem has already occurred and must be corrected. Drivers throughout the company, acting on their particular roles and driven by specific business needs, will either be reacting to data-quality problems or proactively preventing new problems from happening or existing problems from getting worse.

Users following a particular business process for data entry, for example, may detect irregularities with the data due to a system defect, a bad practice, or weak enforcement of business rules. They will not necessarily know the root cause of the problem or the best way to resolve it, and that is to be expected. But they need a mechanism for presenting the problem and requesting a correction.

Most companies will implement a type of trouble-ticket system that will allow users to communicate any problems they see. These trouble tickets are then categorized and routed to a suitable team for proper action. In this scenario, the problem entered by the user on the ticket becomes the requirement or problem statement.

The trouble ticket is just one mechanism by which a company should support requests for data-quality improvements. Special projects and certain activities commonly performed are very likely to have data management effects and should be supported with proper engagement of the data-quality team according to preestablished policies and SLAs. Here are some examples of activities that will require close data-quality participation:

- Migrating data from one system into another due to mergers and acquisitions, or simply to consolidate multiple systems and eliminate redundancy.
- Changes in system functionality, such as adding a new tax calculation engine, may require a more complete, consistent, and accurate postal code representation than before.
- Regulatory compliance, such as new financial reporting rules, the Sarbanes-Oxley Act (SOX), the U.S. PATRIOT Act, or Basel II.
- Security compliance, such as government data requiring particular access control rules.
- Bad or inaccurate data values that cause additional business costs and customer dissatisfaction, such as bad mailing addresses, inaccurate product descriptions, out of date product IDs, and more.

The drivers behind these activities will vary depending on the organizational structure. Even within a company, the same category of change could come from different organizations. For example, an IT-initiated system consolidation task may be the driver of a data migration activity, while a merger or acquisition is a business-initiated activity that could also lead to data migration. In another example, a regulatory compliance requirement can come either from a financial organization or from an enterprisewide data governance initiative.

Most important to remember in such cases is that the data-quality process supports all data-driven requests, no matter what the driver is. Remember that the goal is to create a culture of focus on data quality. If a company limits who is allowed to report data-quality issues, it will create skepticism regarding its true objectives, which could ultimately lead to a companywide DQM failure.

In the context of multi-domain MDM, the initiation of certain data-quality activities is immediate. As stated in the beginning of this chapter, one of the goals of MDM is to tackle data-quality problems. Therefore, MDM itself is a major driver for data-quality improvements.

Assess and Define

The actions of assessing and defining are what make DQM different from other solution design activities, such as application development. With typical application development, business units have a very clear understanding of the functionality required for them to perform their jobs. New requirements, although vulnerable to misinterpretation, are usually very specific and can be stated without much need for research. Also, software defects sometimes might be difficult to replicate, diagnose, and fix, but again, the functionality to be delivered is mostly clear.

With data, the landscape is a bit different. One of the mantras for data quality is fitness for purpose. That means data must have the quality required to fulfill a business need. The business is clearly the owner of the data, and data's fitness for purpose is the ultimate goal. However, there are some issues. First, the business does not know what it does not know. A lot of the time, company personnel have no idea of the extent of the problem they face when it comes to data quality or lack thereof. Second, fitness for purpose can be difficult to quantify. There are certain situations where you just want to get your data as good as possible to minimize any associated costs, but it is not clear how much they can be improved. Third, the business might not fully understand the ripple effects of a data change.

In a multi-domain MDM implementation, there are certain predefined data-quality expectations, such as the ability to link inconsistent data from disparate sources, survive the best information possible, and provide a single source of truth. Still, the current quality state is mostly unknown, which tremendously increases the challenge of scoping the work and determining the results. The business might have a goal, but achieving it can be rather difficult.

The only way to really understand what can be accomplished is to perform an extensive data-quality assessment. It cannot be stated enough how data profiling is important. To efficiently and effectively correct data problems, it is a must to clearly understand what the issue is, its extent, and its impact. To get there, data must be analyzed fully and methodically. For an extensive discussion of data profiling, consult Chapter 8.

A recommended approach to organize data-quality problems is to categorize them into dimensions. Data-quality dimensions allow complex areas of data quality to be subdivided into groups, each with its own particular way of being measured. Data-quality dimensions are distinguishable characteristics of a data element, and the actual distinction should be business-driven. Since it is possible to characterize a particular data element in many ways, there is no single definitive list of data-quality dimensions. They can be defined in many ways with slight variations or even overlapping context. The following list represents the type of dimensions and definitions generally used:

- *Completeness:* Level of data missing or unusable.
- *Conformity:* Degree of data stored in a nonstandard format.
- *Consistency:* Level of conflicting information.
- *Accuracy:* Degree of agreement with an identified source of correct information.
- *Uniqueness:* Level of nonduplicates.
- *Integrity:* Degree of data corruption.
- *Validity:* Level of data matching a reference.
- *Timeliness:* Degree to which data is current and available for use in the expected time frame.

Data-quality dimensions are also very useful when reporting data-quality metrics as part of the Monitoring and Control phase, as will be discussed later in this section.

At the end of this step, it is possible to have a clearly stated set of requirements on what needs to be accomplished for each specific data-quality activity. Remember that most of the time when the process is initiated, there is not yet enough information to produce a complete set of requirements. This step complements the initiation by adding much-needed analysis.

Design and Validate

Once requirements and data analysis are complete, the next step is to design the solution. Notice there are many types of data-quality initiatives. The most common is a reactive data-quality anomaly that must be corrected. How companies address this common issue is a strong indication of their DQM maturity. The more mature companies will take this opportunity to do the following evaluation by answering these questions:

- How is business affected by this issue?
- What is the quantity and frequency of the problem?
- Is this an application bug or a process problem?
- Can this issue be prevented in the future?
- Does this issue require proper training to be avoided in the future?
- Are there any legal implications if data is corrected or left intact?
- Have any wrong decisions been made due to this issue, and who, if anyone, should be informed about the situation?

- Is data governance aware of the issue?
- What policies and procedures affect or are affected by the problem?
- Is it necessary to monitor this problem moving forward?
- What is the cost to the company if this issue is not corrected?

The reason for most of these questions is obvious. But notice the sixth item related to legal implications. Often, there are legal aspects associated with changing the data even if the data is wrong. For example, it might be illegal to modify a certain piece of information provided by a customer without their legal consent. Similarly, the ninth item evokes the need to contemplate any policies and procedures related to the data or to changing them. With multi-domain MDM, there could be many organizations affected by the change—make sure to consider all of them. A data governance body can facilitate the process of obtaining the proper approval for a change.

Let's cover the many data-quality activities (depicted in Figure 9.3) that should be considered when designing and eventually implementing a data-quality improvement effort.

Error Prevention and Data Validation

The best way to avoid data-quality issues and their costly effects is to prevent them from occurring. Of course, this is easier said than done. Technological limitations, time constraints, business complexities, and ever-changing business rules are some of the factors preventing real-time validation at the data-entry point. In addition, there are many interconnected systems, internal and external, that make it very difficult to constantly ensure the high quality of all data flowing in and out.

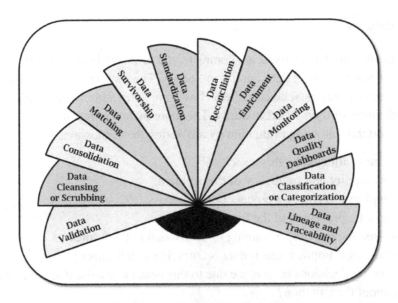

Figure 9.3: Data-quality activities

The technology behind multi-domain MDM varies from vendor to vendor, but it will typically encompass software applications, middleware, batch jobs, and databases. Therefore, data validation can be accomplished by a combination of client- and server-side techniques. Both client- and server-side validations have advantages and disadvantages.

Thin or fat clients will dictate the type of tools available for client-side validation, which will include varying levels of built-in code, along with graphical user interface (GUI) elements such as drop-down lists, check boxes, list boxes, radio buttons, and lookup tables.

The advantages of client-side validation include the following:

- Some GUI elements prevent users from entering incorrect values because they have to select from a predefined list.
- Performance is improved since there is no need to process a request/response message exchange with a remote server for further validation.
- When presented with a predefined list of options for a given attribute, users have the opportunity to choose the best one.

The disadvantages of client-side validation include the following:

- Any operation not done using the front-end interface will miss the client-side validation logic, potentially corrupting the data.
- Most GUI elements used for client-side validation are impractical when dealing with large amounts of data, adversely affecting user experience and productivity.
- Client-side validation can be maliciously bypassed and is subject to security concerns.
- Validation done via application code on the client side can be difficult to update and distribute, depending on the architecture in use.

Server-side validation can also be accomplished in multiple ways, with the most common being database referential integrity rules and software code embedded in the middleware layer or the database layer via stored procedures and batch scripts. Some products will offer database-independent solutions, with most of the server-side validation accomplished in a middleware layer, while others will be heavily database-driven.

The advantages of server-side validation include the following:

- Technology on the server side typically allows higher sophistication of validation rules.
- Validation rules developed directly into the database via referential integrity rules or triggers and stored procedures cannot be bypassed, providing the highest level of corruption prevention.
- Changes to existing rules are typically easier to make because they are centralized.

The disadvantages of server-side validation include the following:

- User response time is affected because of the additional request/response message exchange with a remote server.

- Valid options are not immediately obvious to the user.
- Software validation code embedded in the middleware or database batch scripts can still be bypassed with direct access to the database, risking data corruption.

The best approach is to combine client- and server-side validations to achieve optimal results. It is also important to minimize validation code duplication to prevent discrepancies or redundant work when rules change.

Companies also try to prevent data corruption through business process rules. However, this approach can be very ineffective depending on the size of the company, the quantity and skills of users, the level of training, and the emphasis on quality. For data-quality error prevention to be effective using business process rules, it is necessary to have constant communication and ongoing training and monitoring, coupled with incentives and rewards for high-quality data entry and maintenance.

Business rules, policies, and procedures can be dynamic. As they change, software upgrades may be required to incorporate additional data entry or maintenance validations. Those software changes can take a long time to occur due to IT resources and constraints. The business will typically opt to amend business processes to convey the new rules until the actual software change is complete. In this case, it is also critical to plan for a comprehensive data cleanup of previous data that no longer comply with the new rules. In summary, two additional activities may be required to address a business rule change:

- Making any necessary software changes to support the new rules and associated validations
- Cleaning up data that is no longer compliant or data that is temporarily entered or changed incorrectly until the change goes into effect

These two projects will need to be planned, prioritized, and executed independently according to business needs, also taking into consideration their mutual dependencies.

Unfortunately, it is difficult to totally prevent bad data from entering the system. Many data elements can be very difficult to validate in real-time, either because reference data does not exist at the level needed or because it can take a long time to search when you consider that a customer could be on the phone while data is being entered, and you do not want to make that person impatient. Mistakes happen when users are entering information into free-form fields due to incorrect interpretation of business processes, typos, or miscommunication with customers, partners, and vendors.

Fundamentally, it is important to anticipate data issues and include error prevention in the solution design. That is why a company that has instituted more proactive DQM measures will have fewer data issues affecting business and analytical operations. It requires data-quality participation from the beginning. A typical situation is the following: Data quality starts with sound data model design, making a data-quality specialist a must from the very beginning. Data quality is not maintained just for the sake of data quality. Data have to have the required level of quality to fulfill a specific business need. However, if data models can be designed to prevent data anomalies to occur in the future, unquestionably it should be implemented right away, even if the business cannot foresee their future benefits.

Let's use marital status as an example. Assume that the business did not specify that it needed strong data validation. It simply stated that it had to ascertain marital status as part of a data entry process. Assume the following implementation scenarios:

Scenario A

Marital status is implemented as a free-form entry field. The team designing the data model does not have a data-quality specialist reviewing its work, and implements the plan without any data normalization.

Scenario B

Marital status has been normalized and implemented as a reference look-up field.

Both implementations fulfill the immediate business need. As data is captured as part of the newly data entry process, let's see what happens in both scenarios.

Scenario A

In this implementation, it is possible to enter many variations of the same marital status, invalid values, or no values at all. In this case, it is possible to violate the following dimensions of data quality: completeness, validity, conformance, and accuracy.

Scenario B

Only values from a predefined list are available for selection, avoiding the violation of completeness, validity, and conformance as occurred in scenario A. Accuracy might still be an issue in case data is provided incorrectly or users mistakenly select the wrong option. However, there is no question that this scenario leads to a much better outcome from a data-quality perspective.

Imagine now that a marketing campaign using demographics is initiated, and marital status is a key element to determine how products are consumed. Of course, the quality of marital status is now critical, and here is what happens in both scenarios.

Scenario A

Data analysis to assess quality issues and the ensuing cleansing effort must be executed in order to correct issues. As indicated previously, many data-quality dimensions will have to be addressed, making it potentially difficult to fix data so that they achieve the required fitness for purpose.

Scenario B

Existing data is likely as good as it gets, no matter what. Depending on data-entry practices, it is possible that accuracy issues are large. Still, there is no question that this scenario presents a much better situation even if some analysis and cleansing are still required. It is certain that the number of issues will be much less than in scenario A.

This example with these scenarios is very basic, but it clearly shows how a simple design approach can avoid a lot of aggravation in the future. It also shows that we shouldn't expect the business to spell out every single requirement, even if that would be helpful when trying to solve a business problem,. A proactive design should be the focus of a high-quality IT organization.

In the end, companies need to be creative with their data-quality efforts and reorganize themselves to make error prevention a top priority. Data-quality specialists need to be engaged in many data-related projects to ensure that good practices are followed at all times. MDM increases the opportunity for preventing data-quality issues for master data. Before MDM, inconsistent and duplicated information was entered all across the company. A sound MDM implementation will minimize those problems, and in addition, it will provide the opportunity to cleanse, standardize, and enrich information, as will be discussed next.

Data Cleansing or Data Scrubbing

Data cleansing (aka *data scrubbing*) refers to a process to correct or improve data. This implies that the data were bad already, which means that error prevention or validation wasn't done, and now any anomalies must be corrected.

But there are many things that could be wrong with the data. In the previous section, data-quality dimensions were covered. In essence, different data-cleansing activities need to be applied depending on the dimension associated with the failed quality rule. For example, if conformance is an issue, then data standardization must be applied to the data. If inconsistency is a problem, then data reconciliation is necessary, and so on.

It is at the core of multi-domain MDM to address many of these data-quality issues. It will typically attack the following topics:

- *Completeness:* Before MDM, data are fragmented across multiple sources. By matching data among many sources, it is possible to complement data from one system with another, hence increasing the level of completeness.
- *Conformity:* Data standardization is usually a prerequisite to data matching. It is very difficult to match data when they do not follow a particular format. Granted, there is fuzzy matching. Still, one form of standardization or another will be needed to support the matching of data across multiple sources as part of MDM data integration. This will improve conformity.

- *Consistency:* The end goal of MDM is to have a single source of truth. As such, inconsistencies are not tolerated and are, expectedly, addressed by MDM.
- *Accuracy:* MDM requires a particular set of data to be the surviving information for a given master record. Usually, a certain system is picked over another due to its status of the system-of-record (SOR) for that particular set of information. Assuming that the selection is right, this will be indeed the most accurate information related to a given entity inside the company. Furthermore, MDM advocates the use of reference data to ensure a more accurate multi-domain MDM hub.
- *Uniqueness:* MDM is about establishing and tracking the various sources of master data, and one major focus is to eliminate duplicates.
- *Integrity:* There are many contexts to integrity of data. For example, it could be integrity in the context of referential integrity in a database or the level of data corruption. A good multi-domain MDM hub should deliver solid referential integrity within and across multiple domains, preventing corruption of information.
- *Validity:* Whenever possible, the usage of reference data specific to each domain is encouraged to increase the legitimacy of master data.
- *Timeliness:* Without MDM, companies would struggle to deliver a complete and accurate list of master data records on a timely manner. With a multi-domain MDM hub, this is readily available to meet the ever-growing need for rapid delivery to gain an edge on competition.

Notice how MDM is intensive about improving the quality of master data. Companies need to leverage the practice of data cleansing throughout. Remember that every cleansing effort should include two additional efforts:

- Preventing this issue in the future: root cause analysis and mechanisms to avoid the problem altogether
- Monitoring the occurrence of this problem moving forward

Data Consolidation, Matching, and Survivorship—Entity Resolution

Three data-quality activities, consolidation, matching, and survivorship, are usually applied collectively. As a matter of fact, one definition of data consolidation implies the actual deduplication of information, which implies matching and survivorship. One other definition of data consolidation, however, is simply grouping data together without any particular intelligence behind it. This latter definition is more of a system consolidation than a data consolidation. Nonetheless, it is important to clarify to what extent data are truly consolidated.

Multi-domain MDM is all about fully consolidating data by matching and deduplicating data from multiple sources. This is at the core of entity resolution, which was covered to a great extent in Chapter 8. Nevertheless, as with many other data-quality activities, companies should be looking to extend these data-quality practices outside of MDM, or even prior to starting MDM. Single systems can have lots of duplicates already. If data consolidation is started on an individual system basis even before MDM is started for that particular domain, it will tremendously help any later efforts to consolidate multiple systems.

Data Standardization

With multi-domain MDM comes a stronger need for enterprise-level data standardization. Integration of data is intrinsic to MDM, and for it to be effective, it requires the alignment of data definitions, representation, and structure. Therefore, data standardization becomes a core data-quality technique to facilitate the connectivity, consistency, and synchronization of information.

The ideal scenario would be for all matching information to conform to a unique standard in all systems across the enterprise, but that is not always feasible. Companies today have many commercial off-the-shelf (COTS) and in-house-developed applications spread across the many different organizations with different structures and models. In addition, there are many external data items from vendors and partners that reach internal systems through many interfaces. Those external systems are also structured differently with their own models. Here are some examples of how similar information can be represented very differently across systems:

- A person's name may be captured as separate fields for First, Middle, and Last names in one system, but as a single field for Full Name in another.
- An address in one system may have one single address line for street number and name, but two or more in another.
- One system might have a single field for the entire US ZIP+4 information, while another has two separate fields; and dashes may or may not be required.
- One system might store a social security number as a string, while another stores it as a number. Again, there could be multiple fields or not, and dashes or not.
- One system might capture gender as M and F, while another captures it as 0 and 1.
- One system might use a two-digit state code, while another spells out state names.

These are only a few of the many differences that can occur across multiple systems for similar data elements that are semantically the same. It is easy to see how unlikely it can be to modify all systems to conform to a single standard. From data models to data-view layers, IT systems can be very specific and expensive to change just to comply with a particular standard. Does that mean that you should give up on data standardization? Of course, the answer is no. However, the scope of data standardization is wider than usually expected.

Data standardization is not only about creating enterprise rules on what the data should look like, but also about how they need to be transformed to fit specific systems that cannot follow an enterprise-level definition. A company should strive to have a single standard, but it must be flexible enough to adapt and transform data as needed when moving information across systems with noncompliant constraints.

To understand this concept, imagine a set of enterprise standard data definitions. Not all IT systems will follow all those standards, for the reasons explained previously. However, the intent is for a multi-domain MDM hub to follow those standards because one of the reasons to implement MDM is to improve the overall quality of information. As data flows from the hub to other systems, it can be transformed as needed if downstream systems cannot conform to predefined standards. Likewise, as data flow into the hub but are not already compliant, they need to be transformed to conform to predefined standards. Therefore, MDM implementation provides the perfect opportunity to comprehensively standardize master data across the enterprise.

Let's break the standardization process down into parts to explain it better. For this example, let's assume a hybrid-style multi-domain MDM, with a publish/subscribe method to synchronize data across all sources. Figure 9.4 depicts the high-level architecture.

In the hybrid MDM hub style, master data flow into the hub from multiple sources. As they reach the hub, they typically go through a series of data-quality improvements to cleanse, standardize, consolidate, and enrich data. The focus of this section of the book is on data standardization, which is shown in Figure 9.5.

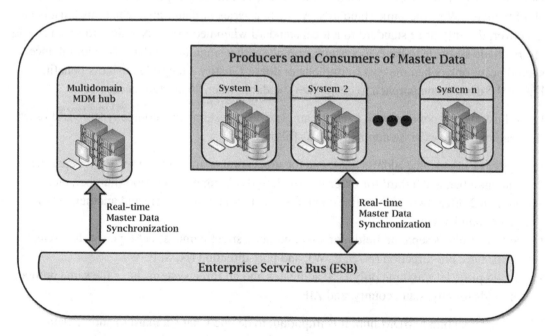

Figure 9.4: Hybrid-style multi-domain MDM with publish/subscribe synchronization

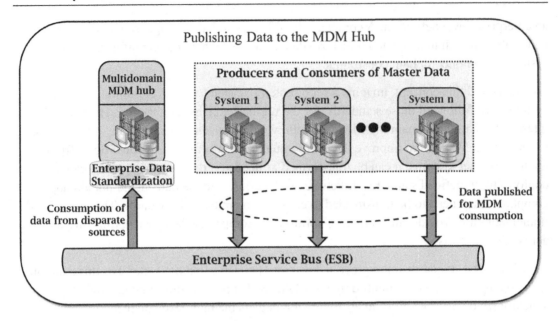

Figure 9.5: MDM consumes and standardizes data from multiple sources

Now that the data are standardized in the MDM hub along with multiple other data-quality improvements, it is obviously beneficial to propagate good data back to their original sources. However, each system will have its own idiosyncrasies, making it practically impossible for all of them to follow the same standards. As such, a series of data transformations must occur to convert the enterprise standard to a local standard when necessary. Needless to say, a strong effort should be made to have all systems comply with a singular standard. Noncompliance should occur only when the cost to implement doesn't justify a tangible business benefit. Figure 9.6 depicts an approach to customize standards when absolutely necessary.

Let's illustrate this concept with a data example. Many systems in a company store addresses. Let's assume three existing applications, as follows:

- System 1 offers three address lines: one for street number and name, a second for apartment/suite number, and a third for other information (building number, floor number, etc.).
- System 2 offers two address lines: one for street number and name and another for any other complements.
- System 3 offers separate fields for street number, street name, street type (St, Rd, Ave, Blvd, etc.), pre-direction (N, S, E, W), and post-direction (N, S, E, W).
- To simplify, let's assume only U.S. addresses and all three systems have the same number of fields for city, state, county, and ZIP.

When implementing a MDM hub, it is important to decide what standard to adopt. Data governance can drive the decision by working with the solution architects and the proper

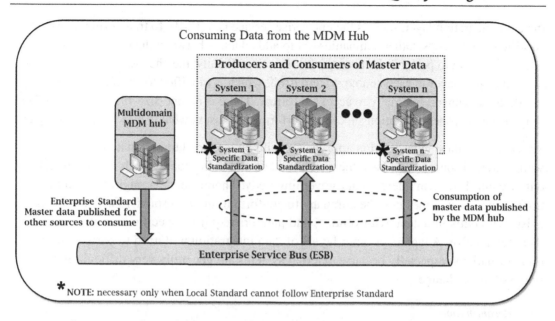

Figure 9.6: When enterprise standards are not supported by specific systems

business units. Let's assume that the enterprise standard adopted matches system 2. Therefore, when data from systems 1 and 3 are integrated into the MDM hub, they must be transformed to the enterprise standard. In addition, it is likely that all addresses coming into the hub will be cleansed, validated, and enriched by a reference source. In the end, there is a clean, valid, and standardized address in the hub. As this address is synchronized now with the original sources, there is a challenge. System 2 can simply pick up any changes and overwrite its contents since the structure is the same. However, systems 1 and 3 cannot simply take the data as they are. Assuming that system 1 has no business function relying on the third address line, it can simply start using only two lines and ignore the third one. Still, some minor transformation needs to happen to blank out address line 3 when receiving data from the hub. On the other hand, system 3 has a lot of work to do. Fitting two address lines into distinct elements for street number, name, type, pre-direction, and post-direction requires some heavy transformation. In addition, modifying system 3 to using only two lines can be very expensive since it may affect databases, user interfaces, business processes, and so on. In this example, systems 1 and 3 will require some type of customization to accommodate data consumed from the MDM hub.

The question becomes: Where should those necessary transformations occur? Enterprise standardization for data coming into the hub is typically part of a series of data-quality transformations already provisioned for as part of the multi-domain MDM hub architecture and design. The other necessary transformations for data flowing from the MDM hub to other sources can be implemented in different ways. Some companies opt to increase the role of the data integration layer, such as the enterprise service bus (ESB), to transform the data to specific system needs. Other companies opt to add adapters between the integration layer and each system to perform the necessary conversion. Finally, the change can occur directly at the interface layer in each source system itself, which is modified to accept an enterprise standard, but convert internally to accepted format. There is no one-size-fits-all solution. Due diligence and proper evaluation should be performed to assess what is best for your company.

This overall data standardization approach should be extended to external systems as well. External sources will have their own models and definitions, which are completely out of control from an internal data-governing body. Therefore, data might need to be transformed as it comes into the company to conform to internal standards. The same issue exists with outbound data, with vendors and partners requiring specific formats to data that they receive. Adapters or other layers of data integration will need to perform proper transformations, especially because external systems are generally very difficult, if not impossible, to change.

Data Reconciliation

In general, data reconciliation is about measuring and correcting inconsistencies among data sets. Multi-domain MDM as a whole can be seen as a system to reconcile master data from multiple sources. Data reconciliation is very common as an activity to ensure that the process to transform and move data went as expected. For example, data reconciliation is done as part of a data-migration effort to make sure that the data at the target system contain all the data from the source, and that all differences have been identified and justified. An ordinary technique for reconciliation is to compare results of the same metric from two different systems, such as the classic example of balancing a checkbook.

In multi-domain MDM, there can be many situations where data reconciliation is necessary. For one, if data migration is needed as part of an initial population of the MDM hub, data will need to be reconciled to ensure that they were converted properly. As new sources of data are added, regular reconciliations are needed. Ultimately, MDM is constantly reconciling master data by integrating, matching, surviving, and synchronizing data across the enterprise to maintain master data consistent. A complete MDM solution should allow for inconsistent data to be reported and a mechanism to properly address any discrepancies.

Data Enrichment

Data enrichment or augmentation is the process of enhancing existing information by supplementing missing or incomplete data. Typically, data enrichment is achieved by using external data sources, but that is not always the case.

In large companies with multiple disparate systems and fragmented information, it is not unusual to enrich the information provided by one source with data from another. This is particularly common during data migration, where customer information is fragmented among multiple systems and the data from one system are used to complement data from the other and form a more complete data record in the MDM repository.

As with any other data-quality effort, data enrichment must serve a business purpose. New requirements come along that may require data to be augmented. Here are some examples:

- A new marketing campaign requires nonexisting detail information about a set of customers, such as Standard Industry Code (SIC), annual sales information, company family information, etc.
- A new tax calculation process requires county information for all U.S. address records, or an extended format for U.S. postal code, which includes ZIP+4.
- A new legal requirement requires province information to be populated for Italian addresses.

Much of this additional information needs to come from an external reference source, such as Dun & Bradstreet or OneSource for customer data enrichment, postal code references for address augmentation, and so on.

It can be quite a challenge to enrich data. This process all starts with the quality of the existing data. If the existing information is incorrect or too incomplete, it may be impossible to match to a reference source to supplement what is missing. It can be quite expensive as well, since the majority of the reference sources will either require a subscription fee or charge by volume or specific regional data sets.

When matching data to another source, there is always the risk that the match will not be accurate. Most companies providing customer matching services with their sources will include an automated score representing their confidence level with the match. For example, a score of 90 means a confidence level of 90 percent that the match is good. Companies will need to work with their data vendors to determine what is acceptable for their business. Typically, there are three ranges:

- *Higher range:* For example, 80 percent and above, where matches are automatically accepted
- *Middle range:* For example, between 60 and 80 percent, where matches have to be manually analyzed to determine if they are good or not
- *Lower range:* For example, 60 percent and below, where matches are automatically refused

Once a match is deemed correct, the additional information provided by the reference source can be used to enrich the existing data. Address enrichment is very common, where the combination of some address elements is used to find what is missing. Examples include using postal code to figure out city and state, or using address line, city, and state to determine postal code.

The challenge comes when there is conflicting information. For example, let's say that city, state, and postal code are all populated. However, when trying to enrich county information, the postal code suggests one county, while the city and state suggest another. The final choice comes down to the confidence level of the original information. If the intent is to automate the matching process, it may be necessary to evaluate what information is usually populated more accurately according to that given system and associated business practice. If it is not possible to make that determination, a manual inspection is likely to be required for conflicting situations.

Data Classification or Categorization

Data classification is about categorizing and organizing data for better analysis and decision making. There are many ways to classify data. For example, categorizing data based on criticality to the business and frequency of use can be important to business process definitions. Classifying data based on compliance and regulations can be part of a risk management program. Data profiling is highly driven by data types and collections of data with similar content.

A particular type of data classification highly sought in a Customer MDM program is customer hierarchy. Customer hierarchy management entails managing customer data relationships to represent company organizational structures, for example. Another classification (in Product MDM, for instance), is product taxonomy, which is needed to organize products for a variety of purposes.

From a Business Intelligence (BI) perspective, hierarchical organization of data is essential. It allows a vastly superior understanding of market and industry segmentation. The volume of master data can be quite overwhelming. Classifying this data hierarchically is a critical first step to make the most sense of the information. The results can be applied to market campaigns, cross-selling, and up-selling.

From an operational perspective, hierarchy management is also critical in improving efforts to maintain master data. Some LOBs, such as sales, may have a vested interest in hierarchical organization for the purpose of territory segmentation and earning sales commissions.

It is doubtful that a single hierarchical representation for each data entity will meet the needs of all LOBs within any large company. Multiple representations are not uncommon but add to the project's cost. Maintaining a single hierarchy can be very challenging as it is. As the different perspectives grow, companies risk compromising the main reason that they engaged in an MDM project in the first place: an agreed-upon view of master data across the entire company. Finding the right balance is key.

Most likely, a multi-domain MDM repository will have relational relationships (e.g., a customer has multiple addresses or accounts, an asset is associated with a particular account, and so on). These types of relationships are inherent to the structure of the repository and are conceptually different from hierarchy management. Furthermore, your MDM repository may not support hierarchy management. That might not be an issue to your implementation, as certain companies opt to do hierarchy management outside an operational multi-domain MDM hub, and inside an analytical environment. Expert guidance is always helpful to advice on the best approach.

Data Lineage and Traceability

Data lineage states where data is coming from, where it is going, and what transformations are applied to it as it flows through multiple processes. It helps understand the data life cycle. It is one of the most critical pieces of information from a metadata management point of view, as will be described in Chapter 10.

From data-quality and data-governance perspectives, it is important to understand data lineage to ensure that existing business rules exist where expected, calculation rules and other transformations are correct, and system inputs and outputs are compatible. Data traceability is the actual exercise to track access, values, and changes to the data as they flow through their lineage. Data traceability can be used for data validation and verification as well as data auditing. In summary, data lineage is the documentation of the data life cycle, while data traceability is the process of evaluating that the data is following its life cycle as expected.

Many data-quality projects will require data traceability to track information and ensure that its usage is proper. Newly deployed or replaced interfaces might benefit from a data traceability effort to verify that their role within the life cycle is seamless or evaluate whether it affects other intermediate components. Data traceability might also be required in an auditing project to demonstrate transparency, compliance, and adherence to regulations.

Implement and Validate

Much about data-quality activities was covered in the previous section. This step is about the realization of what was previously designed. The diversity of data-quality projects should be obvious by now. Data-quality efforts could be stand-alone, such as cleansing a specific data attribute, or they could be part of some bigger activity, such as a data migration project that encompasses improving the converted data. Obviously, multi-domain MDM requires many data-quality initiatives. Depending on the MDM approach, many of the following data-quality tasks are needed:

- Data integrity constraints as part of a data model implementation
- Data validation and prevention as part of a user interface customization
- Data cleansing, standardization, consolidation, enrichment, and reconciliation as part of a data migration implementation

- Implementation of business and data-quality rules to integrate, match, and survive a golden record from master data at multiple sources
- Realization of enterprise standardization for master data
- Addition of data validation to interfaces during data synchronization
- Integration with reference data for data enrichment

Data are everywhere, and so are opportunities for improving them. But besides implementing solutions, it is also important to test them meticulously. Companies are used to functionality tests, which do include different data scenarios, but they usually underestimate what it takes to truly test data quality.

Recall from Chapter 3 that the business has a shallow and narrow view of data because operational business processes only use a subset of all entity attributes at a time (narrow view of the data), and operational business processes use only a small number of rows of information at a time (shallow view of the data). To truly test data, it is important to widen and deepen that view. Therefore, when implementing data-quality improvements, understand how data will be changing in the future and how those changes will affect data integrity. Create data scenarios simulating those situations. Do not limit yourself to functional testing only.

Monitor and Control

Data-quality metrics falls into two main categories: (1) monitoring and (2) scorecards or dashboards. Monitors are used to detect violations that usually require immediate corrective action. Scorecards or dashboards allow numbers to be associated with the quality of the data and are more snapshot-in-time reports, as opposed to real-time triggers. Notice that results of monitor reports can be included in the overall calculation of scorecards and dashboards as well.

Data-quality metrics need to be aligned with business KPIs throughout the company. Each LOB will have a list of KPIs for its particular needs, which must be collected by the data-quality forum and properly implemented into a set of monitors, scorecards, or both.

Associating KPIs to metrics is critical for two reasons:

- As discussed previously, all data-quality activities need to serve a business purpose, and data-quality metrics are no different.
- KPIs are directly related to ROI. Metrics provide the underlying mechanism for associating numbers to KPIs, and consequently ROI. They become a powerful instrument for assessing the improvement achieved through a comprehensive data-quality ongoing effort, which is key to the overall success of an MDM program.

The actual techniques for measuring the quality of the data for both monitors and scorecards are virtually the same. The differences between them are primarily related to the time necessary for the business to react. If a critical KPI is associated with a given metric, a monitor should be in place to quickly alert the business about any out-of-spec measurements.

Data-quality-level agreements (DQLAs) are an effective method to capture business requirements and establish proper expectations related to needed metrics. Well-documented requirements and well-communicated expectations can avoid undesirable situations and a stressed relationship between the data-quality team and the business and/or IT, which can be devastating to an overall companywide data-quality program.

The next two sections describe typical DQLA and report components for monitors and scorecards.

Monitors

Bad data exist in the system and are constantly being introduced by apparently inoffensive business operations that theoretically follow proper processes. Furthermore, system bugs and limitations can contribute to data-quality degradation as well.

But not all data-quality issues are equal. Some affect the business more than others. Certain issues can have a very direct business implication and need to be avoided at all costs. Monitors should be established against these sensitive attributes to alert the business about their occurrence so that proper action can be taken.

A typical DQLA between the business and the data-quality team will include the following information regarding each monitor to be implemented:

- *ID:* Data-quality monitor identification.
- *Title:* A unique title for the monitor.
- *Description:* A detailed description of what needs to be measured.
- *KPI:* The KPI associated with what is measured.
- *Data-quality dimension:* Helps organize and qualify the report into dimensions, such as completeness, accuracy, consistency, uniqueness, validity, timeliness, and so on.
- *LOB(s) affected:* A list of business areas affected by violations being monitored.
- *Measurement unit:* Specifies the expected unit of measurement, such as number or percentage of occurrences.
- *Target value:* Quality level expected.
- *Threshold:* Specifications for the lowest quality acceptable, potentially separated into ranges such as acceptable (green), warning (yellow), or critical (red).
- *Measurement frequency:* How often the monitor runs (e.g., daily or weekly).
- *Point of contact:* The primary person or group responsible for receiving the monitor report and taking any appropriate actions based on the results.
- *Root cause of the problem.* Explanation about what is causing the incident to occur (if known).

- *Whether the root cause has been addressed:* Prevention is always the best solution for data-quality problems. If a data issue can be avoided at reasonable costs, it should be pursued.

Table 9.1 describes a potential scenario in which a monitor is applicable. Notice the explanation of the root cause of the problem and the measures that are being taken to minimize the issue. Sometimes it is possible to address the root cause of the problem, and over time, eliminate the need of a monitor altogether. In these cases, monitors should be retired when they are no longer needed.

The monitor report result is best if it is presented graphically. The graph type should be picked according to the metric measured, but it is almost always relevant to include a trend analysis report to signal if the violation is getting better or worse with time.

Scorecards

Scorecards are typically useful to measure the aggregate quality of a given data set and classify it in data-quality dimensions. Numbers for a scorecard can be obtained from regularly executed data assessments. The individual scores can be organized in whatever ways are needed by the business and presented in a dashboard format.

Table 9.1: Sample Monitor DQLA

Id	DQ001
Title	Number of duplicate accounts per customer.
Description	Business rules require a single account to exist for a given customer. When duplicate accounts exist, users receive an error when trying to create or update a service contract transaction associated with one of the duplicated accounts. The probability of users running into duplicate accounts is linearly proportional to the percentage of duplicates. A 1% increase in duplicates translates into a 1% increase in the probability of running into an account error. Each account error delays the completion of the transaction by 4 h, which increases the cost by 200% per transaction. Keeping the number of duplicates at 5% helps lower the overall cost by 2%.
KPI	Lowers the overall cost of completing service contract bookings by 5% this quarter.
Dimension	Uniqueness
Affected LOBs	Services
Unit of measure	Percentage of duplicates
Target value	5%
Threshold	<= 10% is Green, between 10% and 20% is Yellow, >20% is Red
Frequency	Weekly
Contact	services_alias@company.com
Root cause	Duplicate accounts are a result of incorrect business practices, which are being addressed through proper training, communication, and appropriate business process update.
Fix in progress?	___Yes ___No _x_Mitigation ___N/A

Table 9.2 shows a sample scorecard. The objective is to obtain a score for a particular combination of context, entities, attributes, and data-quality dimension. Once the score is available, the scorecard report or dashboard can be organized in many different ways, such as the following:

- The aggregate score for a given context and entity in a certain dimension, such as 74 percent accuracy for addresses in the United States.
- The aggregate score for a given entity in a certain dimension, such as 62 percent completeness for all customer attributes.
- An overall score for a given data-quality dimension, such as 64 percent consistency.
- An overall score for all data-quality dimensions, which represents the overall score of the entire data set being measured. This associates a single number with the quality of all data measured, which becomes a reliable thermometer reflecting the data-quality efforts within the company.

The threshold should be set according to business needs. Data-quality issues represented by scores in the Red or the Yellow category should be the targets of specific data-quality projects. Furthermore, the scorecard itself will become an indicator of the improvements achieved.

The scorecard becomes a powerful tool for the following reasons:

- It assigns a number to the quality of the data, which is critical to determining if the data are getting better or suffering degradation.
- It can be used to assess the effect that a newly migrated source would have on the overall quality of the existing data.
- It clearly identifies areas that need improvement.

Table 9.2: Foundation Scores for the Data Quality Scorecard

Entities	Attributes	DQ Dimension	Score	Threshold Red	Threshold Yellow	Threshold Green
Customer	Name	Completeness	98	<=95	>95 and <98	>=98
Customer	Social Security Number or Tax Identification Number	Completeness	60	<=55	>55 and <70	>=70
Customer	Social Security Number or Tax Identification Number	Conformity	70	<=80	>80 and <95	>=95
Address (U.S.)	Postal Code	Conformity	68	<=75	>75 and <90	>=90
Customer	Name/Country	Uniqueness	80	<=70	>70 and <90	>=90
Address	Address lines 1–4:City County State Postal Code Country	Accuracy	75	<=70	>70 and <85	>=85
Account	Account Type	Uniqueness	90	<=85	>85 and <95	>=95
Account	Account Number	Integrity	85	<=85	>85 and <95	>=95
Customer	Customer Type					

Notice that the scorecard alone may not be sufficient to determine the root cause of the problem or to plan a data-quality project in detail. The scorecard will highlight the area that needs improvement, as well as measuring enhancement and deterioration, but it might still be necessary to profile the data and perform root-cause analysis to clearly state the best way to solve the problem.

The DQLA for scorecards between the business and the data-quality team can follow a format similar to Table 9.1.

Conclusion

Data-quality activities are central to a multi-domain MDM implementation. This chapter covered how MDM fundamentally tackles data-quality problems by combining fragmented and disparate data from multiple sources, and distributes a single version of the truth in a timely fashion to multiple organizations within the enterprise. In a multi-domain MDM environment, certain data-quality activities need to be tailored to specific domains, but a single controlling body should guide the overall practice of DQM for more efficient execution and coordination.

There are clear benefits to establishing a centralized data-quality organization to coordinate the overall data-quality activities in support of a multi-domain MDM implementation. As a matter of fact, a DQM office should be structured to support a variety of data-quality efforts throughout the organization, working in conjunction with data governance to properly serve the most pressing business issues.

DQM needs to be managed as an ongoing practice, bridging business and IT regarding data-quality issues. A data-quality improvement model is important to ensure that the highly technical nature of most data-quality activities are properly founded by business needs, support, and validation.

Finally, data-quality needs to be measurable. The practices of monitor and control are necessary to measure the existing level of quality, as well as keeping track of any future degradation. Mature companies need to push the envelope toward proactive DQM, as opposed to only reactive efforts.

CHAPTER 10

Metadata Management

This chapter covers the discipline of metadata management in a multi-domain Master Data Management (MDM) model. It discusses a standard approach to defining, identifying, and managing enterprise-level metadata assets such as enterprise business terms, reference data, data models, data dictionaries, and other artifacts that express the flow and life cycle of data. Well-organized and -maintained metadata is critical to the efficiency and success of multiple data management activities, especially data governance and data analysis. Metadata management is perceived as difficult to implement, tedious, and with low return on investment (ROI). Although metadata can be complex to manage, its benefits are extremely valuable. This chapter will expand on how metadata management lower costs and risks associated with manipulating data assets.

Metadata Management in the Context of Multi-Domain MDM

"Metadata is data about data." You probably have heard this definition many times before. While not incorrect, that statement is too simplistic and masks a lot of significant information about metadata. A more comprehensive definition is provided by the National Information Standards Organization (NISO):

> *Metadata is structured information that describes, explains, locates, or otherwise makes it easier to retrieve, use, or manage an information resource.*

Still, not all metadata is equal. There are many categories of metadata, and different experts will have different categorizations. Our discussion will cover the following categories, which were originally defined by Ralph Kimball, who is a respected author on the subject of data warehousing and business intelligence:

- Business metadata—Includes glossaries of business definitions and reference libraries of business rules, data qualities, and algorithms
- Technical metadata—Includes physical data structures, interfaces, data models, data lineage, and transformations
- Process or operational metadata—Includes statistics about data movement such as frequency, record counts, component by component analysis, and other pieces of information collected for quality assurance (QA) purposes

One major mistake is to handle all metadata the same way. The management of business metadata, for example, is quite different from the management of technical and operational metadata. Another mistake is to fail to prioritize metadata definitions within their proper categories. One of the reasons that metadata management projects fail is because companies try to move from having no metadata at all to documenting every single data element all at once. Metadata should be prioritized accordingly. More on managing metadata categories and prioritization will be discussed later in this chapter.

Metadata management is an important discipline in any company. Just like data governance, metadata management should be a practice employed with or without an MDM implementation. The methodologies and tools behind metadata management are invaluable to formally document data assets, their use, and their life cycle across the many data systems in a company. Proper metadata information will capture the context required to fully understand data elements and their usage. Metadata management, along with Data Quality Management (DQM), becomes a critical element to properly support data governance. Data governance without formally captured data definitions relies on a few individuals with subject matter expertise to describe those terms. This reliance on individuals instead of formal practices is vulnerable to misinterpretation and might lead to incorrect governance.

While data governance and metadata management can and should exist even without MDM, the opposite is not recommended. A multi-domain MDM implementation is about bringing many disparate systems together by combining or linking data from multiple lines of business (LOBs) into a single location. This is sure to amplify the already-existing challenges related to proper understanding and governance of data assets. LOBs are likely operating in siloes and have their own definitions, standards, and rules. The moment that data from multiple systems are combined, the chance of disputes and misunderstandings are likely to increase. MDM becomes more difficult to succeed without a formal discipline to capture definitions, data life cycles, data models, business rules, data quality standards, and data transformations. These elements are important not only to establish rules on how to master data, but also to keep data consistent with time.

The more domains and master data are managed, the greater the need for metadata management. Complexity increases at a rapid pace as more data are integrated, more data models are established, and more business functions share the same information. One may wonder if MDM is truly beneficial, considering the increased need to manage and govern data at an enterprise level. Fortunately, the answer is a resounding yes. This is a matter of allocating the appropriate level of effort at the right task. Companies today spend a lot of time and money on managing duplicated information, developing and maintaining redundant systems, and dealing with the consequences of low-quality information and the ensuing bad decision making, among many issues. Metadata management helps in two major categories:

- It proactively prevents issues by properly documenting multiple aspects about enterprise data.
- It helps to identify areas in need of improvement. Improvement not only in metadata itself, but also on governance, stewardship and quality of data.

Metadata management has many more advantages, which will be described throughout this chapter. Let's start by exploring a typical company and its data sources in a scenario where collecting metadata information would be valuable.

Metadata in a Typical Company

A typical company will have islands of metadata across the enterprise. Figure 10.1 depicts the most important areas where metadata collection will be vastly beneficial.

Metadata management is about capturing the definition, context, description, and lineage of all this information spread across the enterprise and storing it in an easily accessible repository for quick retrieval and wide distribution. Imagine being able to query a business term, know its definition and what business processes use it, understand its business rules and data-quality requirements, recognize its connection to technical elements, and track its usage and transformations across all systems, processes, reports, and documents across the enterprise. That is what metadata management can achieve if done properly. This information is invaluable to business teams, information technology (IT), data stewardship, and data governance.

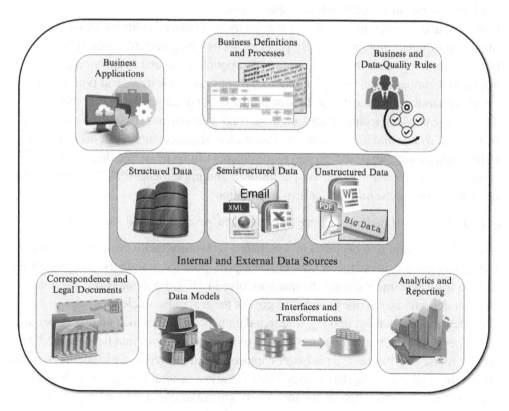

Figure 10.1: Islands of metadata

Here are the advantages of metadata management to business teams:

- Clear definitions of business terms, without ambiguity or dispute
- Origin of data, and its life cycle details and transformations
- The capability to identify data elements behind business processes and assess the impact if any of them changes
- The ability to locate which IT systems maintain data elements relative to those business terms and where to go to retrieve or change them
- Knowledge about all data elements referenced or contained within legal documents and reports, as well as their context
- Understanding of business and data-quality rules associated with each business definition

Here are the advantages of metadata management to technical teams:

- Data lineage allows technical teams to identify where data come from and where they are going, which is crucial for ensuring effective maintenance and making future changes.
- Documentation on data transformations allows technical teams to quickly assess and react to new business requirements or questions about existing issues.
- Data lineage and transformations are essential to understanding existing interface implementations or future interface requirements.
- Complete and accurate metadata information tremendously facilitates future data migration or integration projects. By properly recognizing current states, it becomes much easier to estimate the effort required to upgrade them and to carry on actual upgrades. Companies go through many rounds of system changes, and typically, the effort is chaotic each time due to lack of proper understanding of existing metadata.
- The linkage between technical data elements and their business definitions and usage is essential when validating potentially incomplete requirements. Systems are getting more complex with time, and certain requirements can be misstated due to a lack of complete comprehension of existing definitions and implementations. Proper metadata documentation can be used to confirm assumptions.

Here are the benefits of metadata management to data governance and stewardship:

- Unambiguous definition captured in a metadata repository facilitates good governance. Data governance is in charge of creating enterprise policies, standards, and procedures. If there is no agreement among the many involved LOBs about enterprise-level data element definitions, the rules needed to govern them are also unclear.
- Data stewardship is about making sure that data is fit for use, which clearly depends on proper documentation of business usage of the data, context, and business and data-quality rules. This information is better captured and managed in a metadata repository to ensure the meaning of the data is available to confirm general business user beliefs.
- Data quality is a critical discipline underneath governance and stewardship. But data quality is not an absolute statistic; rather, it is relative to a purpose. Proper metadata

information enables the documentation of that purpose unambiguously, and consequently, successfully guides data-quality efforts essential to governance and stewardship.
- Companies face many rules and regulations, and any type of noncompliance can have damaging consequences. Legal departments typically do a good job at understanding a potential compliance issue, but the problem is usually related to communicating and enforcing compliance. A metadata repository enables the dissemination of information by publishing rules and regulations related to data elements. Furthermore, since a metadata repository also documents the usage of the data, it facilitates compliance monitoring by data governance.

Master data is captured and maintained as structured data in traditional database management systems. But companies will have master data in many other forms and sources as well. Correspondences, emails, publications, social media, reports, reference data, and other elements will carry master data and any data associated with the master data. Those sources need to be understood and documented properly to identify if any master data need to be acquired from them or if the associated data are relevant to business practices.

Let's explore the islands of metadata depicted in Figure 10.1 and what kind of metadata information in each of them would be beneficial to capture in a metadata repository to support a well-implemented multi-domain MDM program. Remember that metadata management is valuable to any company looking to improve its data management practices, but good MDM implementation will include metadata management as a fundamental discipline.

Internal and External Data Sources

Every company will have structured data sources. As said previously, master data are stored and maintained structurally in traditional database systems. Metadata management is a must to properly convey the definition, usage, and maintenance of master data. The type of metadata captured from structured data sources is exclusively technical, such as data types, technical definitions, data transformations, and so on. This information is critical to stewards and technical teams to continuously provide high-quality support on master data to business teams. But metadata about master data is not the only element that should be captured from structured sources. Other data types, such as transactional and reference data, are certainly important to the business, and their definitions must be captured too. Furthermore, these other data types are likely to either affect or be affected by master data.

Semistructured sources, such as Extensible Markup Language (XML) documents, spreadsheets, and emails are also important resources of information. Metadata around the definition, context, and usage of semistructured information can influence decisions about what attributes related to master data should be captured at an enterprise level. In addition, understanding those sources can be critical to analytics and business intelligence. Do not ignore metadata information related to those sources. Many interfaces rely on XML files to distribute data. That means that the metadata information about those XML files are important to capture. Interfaces can be extremely complex and difficult to maintain if not properly documented.

Unstructured data can be very challenging to document and govern. For one, technology is still maturing when it comes to interpreting unstructured data sources. Likewise, metadata on unstructured sources can be very difficult to capture since the data in them are fuzzy. Big data are not necessarily unstructured, but a vast majority of sources of big data, such as social media, are. Capturing customer sentiment, for example, is one way that companies try to leverage social media data in their analytics. But it can be difficult to define what data to capture if metadata about those sources are not understood. Other sources of unstructured data, such as Microsoft Word and Adobe Acrobat Portable Document Format (PDF) documents, can also contain important information related to master data elements. Without metadata, the understanding of those sources is limited.

Data Models

Conceptual, logical, and physical data models are instrumental to convey, validate, and implement a solution that correctly meets business needs. But that is not the only consideration. A well-designed model is invaluable to support the integrity and quality of data, ease of maintenance, and scalability. Most metadata tools can automatically connect to popular data modeling tools and extract metadata information valuable to technical and business teams, data stewards, and data governance.

Much of the time, companies do not pay enough attention to data models and consider them a secondary artifact. The truth is that data models are extremely important, and they should be built by experienced people and reviewed by data modeling peers and data architects. Furthermore, conceptual and logical data models should be used to validate business definitions, understanding, and requirements. This can ensure that the ensuing physical model and eventual implementation are easy to maintain and extend if necessary. Unfortunately, project priorities and delivery timelines often force the implementation of a physical model while precluding the completion of conceptual and logical models. This will lead to later problems related to data lineage and traceability from enterprise data models to physical applications.

Conceptual and logical data models can serve as a connection between business terms, their definitions, and where they physically reside in the multiple sources of data in the company. If this information is properly captured in a metadata repository, the maintenance and governance of data are facilitated. When implemented sources follow proper data modeling best practices, the resulting product is much more robust, and data quality enforced through database constraints can be confirmed via the metadata tool for the benefit of all interested parties.

Master data are typically at the core of all data models across the enterprise. The understanding and dissemination of those models foster the comprehension of the relationships of master data within the multiple domains and their transactional counterparts.

Interfaces and Transformations

Since the advent of distributed computing, one of the purposes was for multiple systems to collaborate and coordinate their use of shared resources. This architecture should naturally lead to more specialized systems and consequently higher modularization, which obviously are very desirable outcomes. Higher modularization means that applications are written to serve a specific purpose, are used by distinct teams, and are maintained by specialized groups. All this leads to greater understanding and easier maintenance of the data behind those applications.

However, business processes are getting more complex, and applications are getting more flexible. More complex business processes typically require new functionality. Instead of adding more specialized applications, companies customize the more flexible applications to support the new requirements. Of course, this is not always bad, as there is an obvious advantage to using what is already available. However, it is possible to end up with applications running functions that were not originally designed for them. For example, a customer relationship management (CRM) system might be customized to run functionality that should have been deployed in an enterprise resource planning (ERP) system, or vice versa.

The reasons for this vary. They could be lack of available resources to develop the new functionality in the right technology, or the fact that the target users do not have access to a certain application. The bottom line is that this development could lead to additional data needed in a system that was not necessary before. Proper interfaces and transformation documentation are essential to handle this type of scenario.

In addition, every company will have a multitude of distributed applications, both internal and external. Vendor offerings are becoming more numerous and complex, with real-time applications available for integration. That means that more data are moving around, and as they do, they may undergo transformations. Metadata management can help documenting how data are mapped from one system to another and how they are transformed. This information is critical to understanding what data is required where, how data is changed as it moves around, and what impact an eventual change will have on all involved systems.

To be sure, capturing interface and transformation logic is important for any data element, but it is even more so for master data because they are more pervasive and subject to change as time passes. Also, data security is typically more important to maintain when dealing with master data. Customer information, for example, is extremely sensitive, and having the knowledge at your fingertips about what interfaces receive and send customer information is quite powerful. Product data can also be confidential, and its exposure could risk losing a very important competitive advantage. Again, knowledge of where that information is at all times is a must.

Analytics and Reporting

Bad decision making can happen due to either low-quality information or incorrect understanding of data elements in a particular context. DQM helps with the first issue, while metadata management helps with the second. Therefore, complete and accurate metadata information in support of analytics and reports is valuable to ensure that critical business decisions are based on correctly interpreted information.

The issue that metadata management can help address is to ensure that decision making is taking place and involving unambiguously defined data elements, that the context for those decisions is correct, and that the impact of any change to the underlying data elements is proactively determined. This overall assessment requires a combination of properly characterized data elements and their lineage to analytical components and reports.

Master data elements from multiple domains lie at the core of most analytics and reporting. Thus, metadata information on master data elements for multiple domains will have this additional benefit.

Correspondence and Legal Documents

Similar to analytics and reporting, correspondence and other legal documents contain important data. As such, it is necessary to understand where the data are coming from and their definitions in given contexts. In addition, there is the even-higher risk of noncompliance issues being exposed and subject to legal action.

Metadata information, such as definitions and lineage, can ensure that the right source is being used to determine what correspondence to send, to whom, and what content it should contain. As discussed throughout this book, the amount of duplicate and conflicting information across the company is overwhelming. The integration component of a multi-domain MDM will address the issue of uncovering the single version of the truth, and the data-quality component will make certain that the data are fit for usage. Still, there is the need to make sure that the data used across the many legal documents are sourced correctly, and if any changes do occur, the affected correspondence can be easily determined and changed accordingly.

Privacy issues are an increasing concern. Many companies still struggle with making sure that sensitive information is protected. But it is hard to do this if you cannot track where all the sensitive information is. Data lineage information is essential to having this knowledge at your fingertips. Data governance can highly benefit from this in order to ensure that proper policies, procedures, and compliance rules are followed.

Business Definitions and Processes

As described previously, metadata management can be divided into business, technical, and operational areas. The elusive enterprise business glossary is the foundation of the business metadata. This is where the entire data set of business definitions resides. Imagine having a single repository with all business terms clearly explained. That is what a business glossary can do for you. It allows the creation of a business-level glossary for the enterprise, and if necessary, specialization of certain terms at the organizational level.

Related to business processes, the intent is to capture in the metadata repository the definition of the processes, as well as the business terms associated with them—it is not to capture the actual process flow. This allows lineage between business definitions, business processes, and the data elements associated with them. Impact analysis can be quickly performed to assess the effect of any changes, which could be due to regulatory mandates, functionality improvements, mergers and acquisitions, new requirements, and so on.

As the discipline of multi-domain MDM grows, metadata around business definitions and processes becomes more critical. The integration of data across multiple sources requires larger collaboration and governance, which consequently leads to a higher need for coordination. In data management, effective coordination requires less ambiguity and more knowledge and understanding of the data elements, as well as their definition and usage across the multiple organizations within the company.

Business and Data-Quality Rules

In addition to definitions, there are many other characteristics of business terms that should be captured. One such category is business and data-quality rules. It is not sufficient to just describe a business term—it is important to clearly establish the rules around it. This is no easy task. Business is getting more complex, and rules can be quite difficult to document and keep updated. However, having a single location with clearly defined characterization of all rules surrounding business practices is pivotal.

Along with business rules, it is very important to document the expectations about the fitness of the data that is supporting those business definitions and processes. This is central information to DQM. It is often said that data quality is not maintained for its own sake—it is about data's fitness for use. A metadata tool is the perfect instrument to capture what is expected by the business regarding data health.

Entity resolution was previously described as one of the critical tasks within a multi-domain MDM program. There is a large number of data-quality rules behind entity resolution, and if these rules are not clearly stated, incorrect design and implementation, which can be very costly and present high compliance risk, can result. Data clustering is one of the key components of entity resolution, and proper business expectations regarding false positives and false negatives must be stated. Survivorship is another key component, and the expected quality of this is important to substantiate the decisions made about what source to use to create a golden record.

Business Applications' User Interfaces

A vast majority of business functions are carried on via a user interface (UI) to a business application. Of course, those business applications have other components behind them, such as data sources, middleware, and interfaces to other systems. But those have already been covered in other discussions in this book. Let's cover the UI component here.

Application UI is a user-friendly mechanism to expose data to users. It allows users to create, read, update, and delete information. However, it is not always obvious how data fields on the screen are related to business terms and processes. Since the UI is a window to data sources, it works as the connection between the business metadata and the technical metadata.

The association of UI elements and the database elements behind them, such as tables, columns, functions, and stored procedures, is normally provided by high-quality software. On the other hand, the association between UI elements and business terms is less straightforward. It is possible that a certain business term may be resolved by one application as multiple fields in the UI, or that a business term is referenced in more than one application UI. An example of the former is a customer name shown as separate fields such as First, Middle, and Last Name in one application, but as Full Name in another. An example of the latter is product taxonomy available in multiple applications.

The bottom line is that if there is good metadata information about UI elements and traceability to their data terms, it becomes much easier to understand the data life cycle. A business term tied to a business process can easily be traced to all applications, as well as to individual data elements and their usage in interfaces, analytics, correspondence, and so on.

Metadata Management Goals

It was stated earlier in this chapter that not all metadata is the same and that companies mistakenly attempt to go from no metadata information to exhaustive documentation instantly, with no transition. The previous section covered the many sources of information in the company from which collecting metadata can be extremely valuable. However, just like data quality, metadata documentation should not be kept just for the sake of it. Metadata must bring value to the enterprise by lowering costs, increasing revenues, lowering risks, or any combination.

Prioritization of metadata should not only happen based on the category of metadata, but also on the source of data and data elements within each source. For example, when prioritizing categories of metadata, creating an enterprise business glossary might have a higher priority than describing data transformations. Second, within a business glossary, stating business rules might be initially more important than creating a lineage between business terms and business applications. Finally, within the business glossary, prioritizing data elements associated with a given domain might be more important, depending on the MDM order.

Figure 10.2 depicts typical internal drivers and external factors that are most likely to influence the prioritization of what metadata information to capture. It also shows some of the categories of metadata collected from the many sources throughout the company.

Figure 10.3 depicts how tactical artifacts from metadata management form the foundation of an overall strategic improvement of the enterprise. By supporting many key activities and minimizing negative effects, metadata artifacts lay the groundwork for success.

Figure 10.3 indicates the following areas improved by metadata management:

- *Data governance:* The key to governance is knowledge. Metadata management supports data governance and business teams with a deep understanding of their data assets. It provides data governance with the capability required to monitor existing policies, assist existing business teams, and plan future changes. Data integration is fundamental to a multi-domain MDM program, and the more that data are integrated, the more governance is needed.

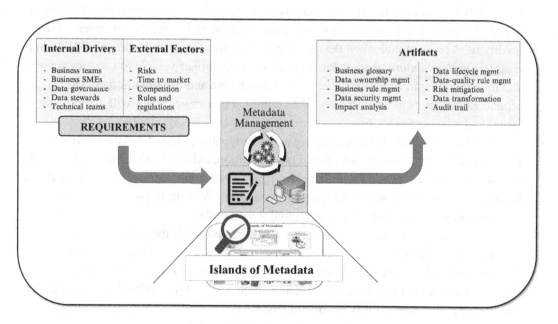

Figure 10.2: Capturing metadata

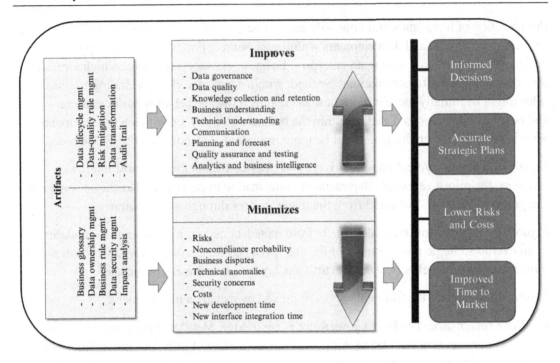

Figure 10.3: Metadata management benefits

- *Data quality:* The first step to achieving good data quality is to understand what high-quality data really means to the business. A good metadata repository will have the required data-quality expectations to serve the business well. Clearly, documented data-quality rules are essential when designing and implementing a multi-domain MDM hub.
- *Business understanding:* A metadata repository is the proper vehicle to use for capturing and disseminating information. There are so much data and different nomenclatures around all the assets in the company. Maintaining a proper inventory will avoid many issues and misinterpretations.
- *Technical understanding:* Data mapping and accompanying transformations are very important in many technical activities. Data migration, extract, transform, and load (ETL) operations, interface development, and real-time calls are just some of the tasks that can benefit from comprehensive metadata documentation. Without it, companies have to rely on fragmented documentation and the actual source code.
- *Knowledge collection and retention:* A metadata repository is the perfect tool to use to document data. Companies normally underestimate how many rules exist behind every data element. A lot of these rules are known only to a handful of subject matter experts (SMEs). They are not formally captured anywhere, and if those SMEs leave, so does the knowledge they possess if it is not documented.

- *Communication:* A metadata tool facilitates the dissemination of information, which is the basis of communication. Communicating definitions, context, business and data-quality rules, data life cycles, and all other elements surrounding data is key to encouraging knowledge and dialogue. Increased dialogue will bring up more clarifications and lead to fewer mistakes.
- *Planning and forecast:* The more information, the better the planning. If there is enough information about where data elements are used, the easier it is to estimate and plan future changes. If a phased MDM approach is in place, metadata information can help plan better for each of them.
- *QA and testing:* Several metadata artifacts are useful to QA teams. In a data migration project, for example, data mapping is a critical element of testing whether data conversion was done correctly. Many times, QA is performed based only on requirements, which can fail to identify where all data elements are used. Data lineage can help fill the gaps in the requirements.
- *Analytics:* Business intelligence is not only about using good data, but also about understanding the data being used. The documentation provided around data will certainly increase the probability that analysis is done correctly.

Figure 10.3 also indicates how metadata management can help minimize undesired conditions, such as the following:

- *Risks:* Stated plainly and simply, more knowledge leads to less risk. Decisions are made based on correct assumptions, and guesswork is reduced.
- *Noncompliance probability:* Legal organizations generally have a good understanding about noncompliance rules issued by specific authorities in their respective fields and industries, but those same organizations typically lack knowledge of the many data elements across the company related to those rules and consequently are vulnerable to noncompliance. Documentation on full data life cycles and transformations lead to better tracking of sensitive information.
- *Business disputes:* A business glossary and a business process glossary bring clarity to potential divergences and differences of nomenclatures throughout the many organizations within a company.
- *Technical bugs:* Many times, bugs are caused by missed dependencies. A full data lineage can indicate where dependencies exist, and if any changes do occur, what other components might be affected.
- *Security concerns:* Sensitive data elements need to be tracked properly to account for any undesirable exposure. Master data especially can be very susceptible to security issues, and as such, understanding their context and flow can proactively prevent negative effects.
- *Costs:* Reduced costs is an automatic consequence of increased positive effects while decreasing negative ones.

Overall, it is clear that these factors can lead to better-informed decisions, more accurate strategic plans, lower risks and costs, and improved time to market. A data-driven organization is more apt to plan, act, react, and adjust to market forces.

Organizing Metadata Management

Not all metadata is the same, and not all metadata should be managed in the same way. For example, building a business glossary is very different from documenting transformations on an ETL interface. Therefore, it is recommended to separate the management of metadata into separate tracks. Business metadata should be managed as part of a business track, while technical and operational metadata should be managed as part of a technical track. Figure 10.4 depicts that idea.

Each of these tracks will have different drivers, requirements, processes, and complementary artifacts. Let's cover those tracks next.

Business Track Organization

As you might expect, a business track will handle business metadata. Figure 10.5 depicts a process of collecting business metadata in a global organization with distributed business units. SMEs submit metadata information to a centralized governing body, which will review them, manage a voting process, and approve or reject them. Approved information is collected into a metadata repository for easy distribution across the enterprise. Of course, the more business definitions, processes, systems, rules, and data can be shared and defined at the enterprise level, the better. But there is always going to be a need to specialize certain terms at the LOB level. That is all right, so long as there is an attempt to establish an enterprise definition first.

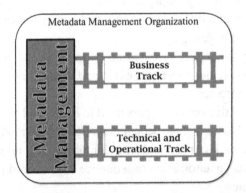

Figure 10.4: Metadata management tracks

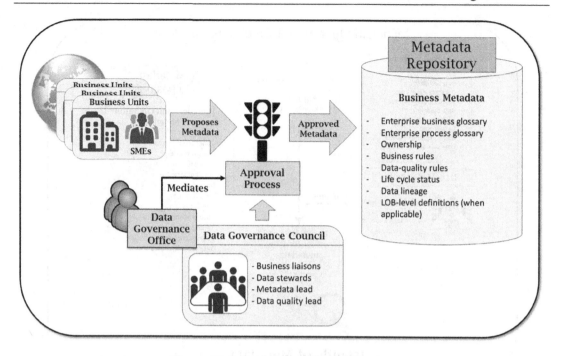

Figure 10.5: Business track organization

Technical Track Organization

Technical and operational metadata can be better managed by a technical track. Figure 10.6 depicts a process of collecting technical and operational metadata from multiple sources across the company. Technical metadata can come from many different places. Metadata tools will often offer plug-ins that can automatically collect metadata using many different technologies. For example, metadata from databases, ETL tools, XML files, and data modeling tools are likely to be either automatically or semiautomatically loaded. Other sources might have to be manually entered.

One major difference between the technical and business tracks is the approval process. When technical data elements are loaded, they likely have already been through some type of review. For example, data models should have been revised by data modeling peers and a data architect; or data sources are generally at the production level, and hence they have been designed and tested, so there is no question about what to load. The same is applicable for other sources of data already deployed across the organization. Still, a data management board is recommended to oversee what goes into the repository.

Be sure to maximize what can be automated. Be creative. A real-life example from our past experience is parsing source code, such as Procedural Language/Structured Query Language

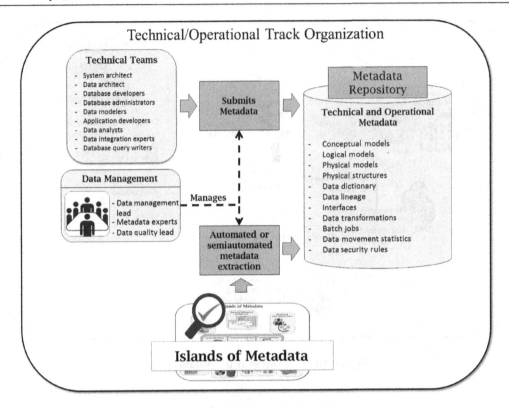

Figure 10.6: Technical track organization

(PL/SQL) stored procedure, Java, and JavaServer Pages (JSP), to extract data mapping. If source code is developed following a recognizable set of patterns, it is possible to write regular expressions to identify those patterns and extract important metadata information. Still, much metadata information will come in the form of spreadsheets and other media that cannot be automatically parsed. Those will have to be manually loaded into the metadata repository.

Connecting the Business and Technical Tracks

The management of business and technical/operational metadata is quite different. But obviously, there is a connection. Behind business rules and definitions lie data elements, which exist in multiple systems throughout the enterprise. A mapping can be created between business terms and their equivalent technical counterparts. Through data lineage, it is possible to establish this relationship. The result is astounding, as one can locate a given business term and trace it to multiple applications, data sources, interfaces, reports, models, analytics, reports, and other elements. It is the ultimate goal of metadata management: search for a business term, learn and understand its definition, and track it throughout the entire enterprise. Imagine how powerful this information is to data governance, data quality, data stewards, and business and technical teams.

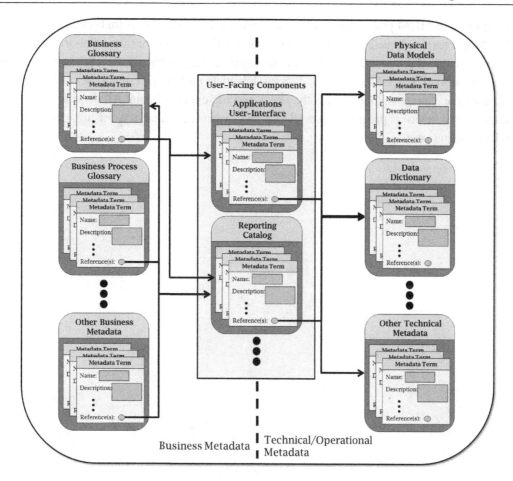

Figure 10.7: Simplified data lineage

Figure 10.7 depicts a simplified data lineage to convey this idea. Notice the application UI is being used as a connecting point. Business terms are mapped to labels on the screens of multiple applications, which are mapped to databases, which in turn can potentially be mapped to many other elements. This daisy-chain effect allows any metadata object to be a starting point that can be navigated from wherever data are flowing.

Conclusion

This chapter covered the discipline of metadata management. It is obvious that metadata management is not only beneficial to companies implementing multi-domain MDM. It is a core discipline for companies looking to improve their data management practices. Still, in a multi-domain MDM implementation, whether it is a one-time deployment or a phased approach, properly documenting metadata will avoid many issues.

A multi-domain MDM program amplifies the need for collaboration from both business and technical teams. A metadata tool becomes the conduit to foment this collaboration. It provides a standard approach to define, identify, and manage enterprise-level metadata assets such as business terms, reference data, data models, data dictionaries, and other artifacts used throughout the enterprise that express the flows and life cycles of data. All these artifacts are fundamental to business practices, as well as data governance, data stewardship, data quality, and data integration.

PART III

Sustainability and Improvement

CHAPTER 11

Performance Measurement

This chapter discusses how to establish a robust performance measurement model across a multi-domain Master Data Management (MDM) program. Many vantage points and factors need to be considered when measuring the program's performance, including measurement from a strategic, tactical, and operational perspective, from a cross-domain perspective, from a financial and compliance perspective, and in relation to the MDM disciplines of data governance, data quality, metadata management, reference data management, and process improvement. This chapter provides performance measurement examples from each of these perspectives. Figure 11.1 illustrates the various performance measurement areas that will be addressed here.

As was mentioned in Chapter 1, there is no one-size fits-all plan for multi-domain MDM. There are too many factors that will differ from one company to another, or within a company from one domain to another. However, expanding to a multi-domain model and being able to manage the program consistently require an effective top-down management approach

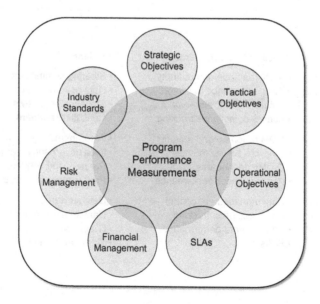

Figure 11.1: MDM performance measurement areas

involving strategic, tactical, and operationally focused measurement levels. Specific metrics and status updates are required at each level to enable management actions and decisions.

Because of the impact that master data and an MDM program can have on many functional areas, having a variety of well-focused performance measurements defined throughout the program is critical to the effective execution, management, and success of the program. Prior chapters of this book have touched on the importance of program and process area measurements such as those related to maturity, data quality, data integration, data governance, and data stewardship. Specific measurements in each of these areas are needed for the operational and tactical management of the program and contribute to summarized views and executive dashboards needed at the strategic levels. Figure 11.2 provides an example of these types of measurement at the different levels.

Without these types of performance measurements, program management will operate with limited vision. Even if other evidence exists that can reflect areas of program performance, such as meeting minutes, intake log activities, stakeholder testimony, or ad hoc reports that can be pulled together from various MDM and data governance processes, the inability to produce comprehensive, consistent, and well-grounded performance metrics impairs the ability to demonstrate the end-to-end value of the program. The performance of a multi-domain MDM program has many opportunities for measurement at the strategic, tactical, and operational levels. Let's examine each of these measurement levels more closely.

Level	Types of Measurements	Audiences
Strategic	• MDM roadmap and maturity • Key performance indicators • Program financials • Audit & compliance tracking	• Steering committees • Data governance council • Stakeholder reviews • Consulting partners
Tactical	• MDM roadmap and maturity • Program activity metrics • Quality dashboards • Partner/vendor performance	• Program management office • Data governance teams • Partners and vendors • Project managers/leads
Operational	• Data management control • Issue resolution tracking • Data steward performance • SLAs	• Data stewards • Data administrators • IT support • Third-party support

Figure 11.2: MDM performance measurement levels

Strategic-Level Measurements

At the strategic level, steering committees and other executive audiences need to know how the MDM program is tracking to its goals and how this benefits the company, particularly in respect to improving business and information technology (IT) operations and reducing business risk that can result from poor data management. The program goals and objectives should tie back to the MDM value propositions described in the program's initial business case or return on investment (ROI) analysis (if any) conducted during the program's planning stages. In order to provide the strategic level of support and ongoing investment needed to sustain a program, a steering committee needs to clearly see progress being made with the program goals and objectives and be informed of any critical path issues that may be affecting this progress. A MDM program will not reach its full potential if the executive sponsors are not well informed and engaged at the strategic level. Let's take a closer look at important strategic-level performance measurements.

MDM Roadmap and Maturity Tracking

As noted in Chapter 5, MDM domains will likely be at different maturity levels at any particular time depending on the program strategies, priorities, implementation roadmaps, and domain-specific data management capabilities. Data governance and data quality commitment will have the greatest influence on domain maturity. A domain with a high level of data governance focus and Data Quality Management (DQM) capability will enable MDM practices to mature much more rapidly. As data governance practices mature, less effort will be needed for DQM because better-governed data need less correction. Figure 11.3 provides a high-level example of this concept.

Defining and communicating the relationship that data governance and data quality have with MDM maturity will help a program's steering committee and data governance council recognize the governance and quality investments needed by each domain. Some domains will have more enabling factors to mature than other domains. For example, a *Customer* domain may have many more opportunities to leverage consultants, best practices, third-party solutions, industry reference data, and other industry standards for managing, maintaining, and measuring customer master data, whereas with *Product* and *Manufacturing* domains, MDM has more unique and proprietary aspects and less opportunities to leverage external solutions and services. Fewer enabling factors and opportunities can result in slower progress and maturity of the MDM practices in these domains because more internal planning, resources, and effort are required to move these practices forward.

When planning the MDM program roadmap, the Program Management Office (PMO) should quickly identify the information needed to serve as the foundation and baseline

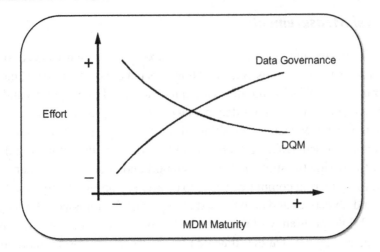

Figure 11.3: Data governance, quality measurement, and MDM maturity

data for maturity measurement for each of the major MDM discipline areas—namely, Data Governance, Data Stewardship, Data Integration, Data Quality Management, and Metadata Management. In Chapter 5, Figure 5.2 showed examples of various maturity milestones in each discipline area that can serve as the basis to identify and define more discreet metrics and evidence needed to support the measurement of these maturity milestones. Figure 11.4 provides examples of measurements or evidence supporting the maturity milestones introduced in Figure 5.2.

MDM maturity should not be subjective or hard to articulate. Activity measurements and decisions associated with defining and tracking the program or domain level maturity should be captured as meeting minutes and/or in a program decision log. These will serve as reference points and evidence to support data governance or MDM program audits.

Key Performance Indicators

Key performance indicators (KPIs) should focus on the primary factors that drive the MDM program, improve master data quality, and reduce business risk. Here are some examples of where KPIs should be defined:

Program Performance

- Progress toward the achievement of delivery goals and objectives
- Progress toward the achievement of domain-specific goals and objectives
- Improvement of key capabilities targeted in the program roadmap and maturity model
- Reduction or increase of business risk factors associated to MDM

Maturity Milestones	Maturity State	Measurement or Evidence
Data Governance		
Governance team and charter have been identified	Structured	Charter ratification and audit verification
Master data have been identified	Structured	Governance approved master data list per domain
Data management policies and standards are enforced	Managed	Monitoring and auditing of policy requirements
Metrics and dashboards are driving master data control	Optimized	MDM program metrics and quality dashboards
Data Stewardship		
Processes, tools, and training needs are defined	Structured	Handbook and operating procedures exist
Master data control points and practices are defined	Structured	Control points in data flow and life cycle models
Data stewards identified and assigned to MDM practices	Managed	Names, roles, and responsibilities are communicated
Data stewards are meeting quality control requirements	Optimized	Performance reviews with job requirements and goals
Data Integration		
Data integration projects reviewed by data governance	Structured	Project reviews with data governance signoff
Data stewards engaged in data integration project teams	Structured	Data stewards identified and active in project teams
Agreement on ETL rules and data acceptance criteria	Managed	Business acceptance signoff by data governance
Integration and quality rules are standardized and reusable	Optimized	Rules repository and usage tracking exists
Data Quality		
The data quality team is aligned with data governance	Structured	Engagement rules are defined and adhered to
Analysis of key data quality issues has occurred	Structured	Tracking and prioritization of data quality issues
DQM policies and standards are enforced	Managed	Policies and standards exist with regular auditing
Data quality is maintained within control targets	Optimized	Monitoring and remediation is maintaining quality
Metadata Management		
Metadata management scope and approach identified	Structured	Governance approved metadata management plan
Metadata management priorities have been established	Structured	Metadata management roadmap exists
Metadata management policies and standards are enforced	Managed	Policies and standards exist with regular auditing
Key data definitions are distinct with data steward control	Optimized	Data steward gated change control processes exist

Figure 11.4: MDM maturity measurement

Data Quality Performance

- The overall state of data quality across each domain area
- Data quality improvement associated with data governance, data stewardship, data integration, or metadata management
- Operational improvement associated with data quality improvements

Program Financials

- Program budget versus program spending/costs
- Running costs of third-party software and data
- Costs related to external consulting services and contingent workforce
- Return on investment (ROI)

Audit and Compliance Tracking

- Performance against MDM program audit requirements
- Performance against regulatory compliance requirements
- Incidences of breaches related to data security and data privacy

Tactical-Level Measurements

At the tactical level, performance measurements will focus more on the program's key initiatives and processes to produce a more granular set of end-to-end program measurements. These measurements will allow the PMO to have a clear picture of what is driving the program, what is affecting the program goals and objectives, and where adjustments are needed. The results and observations from many of the tactical-level measurements will contribute to the KPIs reported at the strategic level.

MDM Roadmap and Maturity Tracking

The maturity of each domain in relation to the program roadmap and maturity model should be tracked very closely at the tactical level. The maturity milestones noted in Figure 11.4 need to be tracked for each domain in the program scope. Because there will be maturity-enabling or -constraining conditions that will vary with each domain, these conditions must be recognized, monitored, and evaluated at the tactical level to ensure that the MDM program's plans and priorities can be adjusted when needed to address the variables and maintain program momentum.

For example, each domain can have different types of challenges with executive sponsorship, data steward resources, quality management, data integration, or metadata management. If the PMO does not have sufficient understanding and articulation of the variables, strengths, and weaknesses influencing these domain conditions, the program can struggle with where to focus attention and the tactical plans that are needed to manage the sustainability of the program. Monitoring these conditions across each domain will enable the PMO to best gauge how these conditions are affecting or influencing the program maturity goals and roadmap.

Program Activity Metrics

Program activity metrics are measurements that track important, ongoing program activities that support the fundamental foundation, processes, and disciplines that make up the MDM program. This should include the tracking of key program activities and decisions across data governance, data stewardship, data integration, data quality, and metadata management.

As noted in earlier chapters, the MDM PMO needs to monitor the application and process areas that interact or influence the flow and life cycle of master data. Examining these application and process areas will reveal a significant number of activities associated with the creation, quality, usage, and management of master data. This information can be leveraged to build a program activity measurement model that will support the tactical measurement needs and, in many cases, can be looked at more closely to measure performance specifically at the activity or operational level. For example, at the tactical level, the key quality management initiatives, decisions, and issues across each domain that influence the overall program goals and objectives should be regularly tracked. But to better understand the dynamics that are driving progress or causing issues, there needs to be the ability to closely examine more specific operational and data management activities to understand the process and quality control factors that are influencing positive or negative conditions.

Quality Dashboards

Because of the impact that master data quality has on business operations, customer interactions, and the ability to meet compliance requirements, measuring and managing master data quality will attract the most attention. At the tactical level, the MDM program's data quality management focus should include not only the quality measurement and management of the master data elements themselves, but also the quality of the business metadata and reference data associated with the master data. Effective tracking and quality control of the master data elements and the associated metadata and reference data will demonstrate a solid DQM and measurement strategy that should be reflected through various metrics and dashboards.

Chapter 9 described quality measurement of the master data elements. A similar approach can be taken with the measurement of the associated metadata and reference data. That is, the quality of the metadata and reference data can also be measured using quality dimensions such as completeness, accuracy, validity, and uniqueness. These types of quality measurements, along with measuring how much of the master data elements and the associated metadata and reference data are under data governance control, should be regularly tracked and reported at the program level. For example, if the most critical master data elements have been identified within each domain, measurements should be established to track the domain performance against the program's overall quality and improvement goals established by the PMO and data governance teams for these critical data elements and their associated metadata and reference data. A dashboard can be established to compare this DQM performance across each domain.

In general, being able to track the focus and effectiveness of an MDM program's quality management performance will require a broad understanding of what aspects of master data are being measured and how the quality is being controlled. Data governance and stewardship will play a large role in the quality management approach, which is an important reason why the PMO and data governance teams will need to work closely together on data-quality priorities and initiatives.

Partner/Vendor Performance

Many aspects of a company's master data can involve external partnerships and third-party vendors. This is particularly true in a multi-domain model, where various partners and vendors can be engaged at many levels; and in many process areas with products and consulting services or vendors of third-party data. All partner and vendor engagements should have a contractual arrangement with delivery or performance requirements described through statements of work, service-level agreements (SLAs), or other binding agreements. This performance, along with the budgets and costs associated with the contracts, should be regularly tracked and evaluated, particularly when approaching contract renewal periods and program budget reviews.

Poor partner and vendor management can contribute to MDM program cost overruns, quality management issues, or other conditions that can negatively affect the program roadmap and maturity. For all partner and vendor contracts, the MDM PMO should ensure that there is an account representative closely engaged with the MDM program so that all necessary interactions and performance reviews with the partners and vendors can be effectively and directly managed.

Operational-Level Measurements

Performance measurement at the operational level will focus more on the processes, applications, and data steward activities associated with master data touch points, quality control, and issue management in each domain. The operational level of performance measurement reflects the degree to which the domain teams and operational areas have a good sense of the day-to-day management and control of the master data. The next sections describe some examples of these activity areas.

Data Management Processes

At the heart of MDM are the processes and controls established to manage the quality and integrity of the master data. These processes and controls are embedded in the key discipline areas that have been discussed throughout this book. The performance of these processes and controls at the operational level must be tracked sufficiently within each domain in order for the MDM program and data governance teams to influence them. Let's break this down further by looking at some of the key areas of MDM performance at the operational level.

Data Quality Monitoring

Master data quality monitoring (such as that described in Chapter 9) and the performance of the surrounding data steward processes associated with these monitoring tasks should be tracked and regularly reviewed at the domain-team level and contribute to overall data quality assessment at the tactical and strategic levels. Because each domain will have different DQM and improvement requirements, it will define and implement quality monitoring and data steward support practices in tune with its specific requirements and operational processes. For example, the business rules required for monitoring and controlling the quality and integrity of master data associated with user customer accounts will be different from the rules for partner or vendor accounts. Similarly, the business rules required for monitoring the quality and integrity of master data associated with medical products will be different than the rules for financial products.

The priorities for data-quality monitoring and the expected quality performance depend on the company's business model, strategies, and objectives. From an MDM perspective, this will typically resolve to what the PMO and domain data governance processes have identified as the company's critical data elements (CDEs). As described in Chapter 2, each MDM domain should identify a CDE list that will determine where MDM and quality control should be primarily focused at the operational level.

Metadata Management

Metadata management involves a connected set of processes, roles, and rules involving data modeling, data governance, and metadata administration. There should be data governance-driven policies and standards for how metadata should be handled and maintained across a data life cycle. Governance policies and the governance teams should set the scope and priorities for the control of metadata. As previously noted, the priorities for metadata management should be closely aligned to quality control priorities for MDM, particularly as related to the most critical data element defined within each domain.

When examining processes, policies, and rules and associated with the creation, use, and documentation of metadata, there should be a number of process points and expectations for how metadata should be managed and controlled. For example, there should be metadata requirements and standards established in solution design processes and with administration teams supporting metadata repositories and data stewards engaged in change control support of business-oriented metadata. From these process points, activity can be measured against the requirements, rules, standards, and policies. These are all opportunities at the operational level for measuring and tracking metadata management performance.

Reference Data Management

Similar to metadata management, there should be various policies, standards, and processes that influence and control how reference data is managed. Many master data elements will have associated reference data, such as industry or internally defined code sets. Because many applications and processes can share in the use of standard reference data, data governance and stewardship are critical for the consistent, enterprisewide use and control of this reference data.

Reference data requirements will typically be defined during the business requirement and data modeling phases of a solution design process. The deployment and management of reference data usually occur through a reference data application where the registration, change control, and deployment of the reference data are controlled. Where there are common reference data widely used across the enterprise and where this reference data are associated with master data, there should be data governance-driven policies and standards for how this is managed and controlled. It is important that reference data associated with master data is unambiguous and has data steward oversight. Priorities for reference data management should be closely aligned to quality control priorities for master data.

With specific reference data management processes and controls in place, activity can be measured against the requirements, rules, standards, and data governance policies, similar to the approach for metadata management measurement. Again, these are all opportunities at the operational level for measuring and tracking data management performance as it relates to master data.

Data Integration and Entity Resolution

Earlier chapters of this book have addressed the fact that data integration and entity resolution are critical functions of MDM. Correct data integration and entity resolution are vital to the accuracy of many types of master data, such as customer, partner, sales, service, and financial data. The performance and quality results from data integration and entity resolution functions need to be monitored and managed at the operational level, evaluated at the tactical level, and reported appropriately where the quality is driving business improvement or affecting business operations.

The performance of entity resolution is particularly critical where it involves or affects the identity, requirements, or interactions with customers, partners, financial transactions, and regulatory agencies. The accuracy of customers, products, and accounts requires precise processes and rules to correctly resolve data from many sources of transactional data and reference data. These entity resolution processes need to be governed by very specific standards and quality requirements. Any exceptional or unexpected results need to be quickly recognized and addressed to avoid or minimize business impacts and costly remediation efforts.

Issue Resolution Tracking

Chapter 5 discussed the need for the MDM PMO to work with the incident tracking and resolution processes within the company to establish rules and methods that can flag master data issues as they are being reported and progressing through these processes. Being able to characterize these incidents and the actions taken provides valuable insight about how well the company is handling master data issues. How master data issues are being reported, what is being reported, what is not being resolved, and the reasons why issues are not being resolved all provide valuable insight to allow the PMO to better capture, evaluate, and report what is happening.

Being able to assess and categorize master data issues and resolution information in relation to the data governance, data stewardship, data integration, DQM, and metadata management helps provide a more granular view of MDM and any support improvement opportunities for the PMO to pursue. There are many points in the flow of master data where issues are being caught and resolved, but also many points where issues are not. Missed opportunities at the source and during other touch points result in master data quality and integrity issues downstream in the data hubs or enterprise warehouses, where there is more exposure to data issues and where more cost and effort are often required to correct them.

Earlier in this chapter, it was mentioned that as data governance practices mature, less effort will be needed for DQM because better-governed data needs less correction (refer to Figure 11.3). Issue resolution tracking and the ability to determine where more monitoring and control can be implemented earlier in the master data flow is a key factor in producing better-governed data.

Data Steward Performance

Chapter 7 indicated that data stewards need to be closely aligned to the touch-point and consumer areas where master data entry, usage, management, and quality control can be most influenced. Being able to achieve and maintain a well-functioning and well-positioned network of data stewards within a master data domain is a maturity factor that needs regular evaluation and attention. At the operational level, data stewards should have clear, measureable data management or quality management responsibilities, such as in support or gatekeeper roles related to master data integration, entity resolution, metadata management, code set change control, incident resolution, quality monitoring, and so on. All of these roles should have clear job descriptions and performance expectations that can regularly be evaluated and adjusted as needed.

Across a multi-domain model, data steward positioning and performance can vary greatly. Some domains can be well advanced with their data steward objectives and practices, whereas other domains may be further behind or even struggling to put data steward resources into place at all. Similar to the ability to track and characterize master data issues and resolution actions, the ability to measure data steward performance across each domain at the operational level and across each MDM discipline will provide valuable insight for the PMO to evaluate and articulate further at the tactical and strategic levels.

Well-positioned data stewards provide a front line of defense for detecting master data issues within operational processes or that flow from one system to another. Operational-level data stewards can help characterize how the source applications and local processes work, their limitations with regard to master data quality control, and the opportunities to better manage this, and they can even take the lead locally to improve awareness and training at the data creation and touch points where quality issues emerge. Even without formal data monitoring and quality controls in place at the source level, data stewards that have a good sense of these process areas can help define and enforce MDM policies and quality standards that can greatly reduce the potential for issues to occur at the operational level. Therefore, the PMO should work closely with these data stewards to define operational level performance measurements.

Service-Level Agreements

Having SLAs is common at the operational level, where there are time-critical requirements associated with data management and corrective action activities. It is important that SLAs reflect reasonable and achievable performance expectations; otherwise, they quickly become an ineffective instrument that may only result in creating contention between parties if expectations cannot be reasonably met. Also, consider that it is far better to allow some latitude and demonstrate patience while getting the support needed than to regularly disparage a support team for not always meeting the SLA terms and conditions.

Support teams generally want to meet their obligations and have happy customers, but backlogs, resource issues, and shifting priorities are all realities when dealing with service delivery and issue resolution. Quality improvement needs typically compete with, and often have a lower priority than, operational support needs. So keep this in mind and be prepared to accept or make adjustments to SLAs from time to time.

By working with the issue resolution teams, with data stewards at the operational level, and with the application support teams in IT, the MDM PMO should be able to determine which SLAs are most important to the quality, support, and timely availability of master data. From that, the PMO can determine where SLA performance should be tracked and adjusted where needed. Here are just a few examples where SLA performance may need to be tracked:

- Refreshing of third-party master data or industry reference data
- Corrective action time for entity resolution process issues or exceptions
- Availability of master data from service partners
- Master data support or data maintenance activity from offshore workers
- Vendor response time related to MDM product issues

In general, SLAs should be tracked in all areas where there are critical data management functions that affect the quality and integrity of master data. These SLAs provide yet another opportunity within each domain for the PMO to examine and understand the many factors that can influence MDM in a multi-domain model.

Other Factors That Can Influence Performance Measurements

Other external or internal conditions can emerge that can influence MDM program performance focus and require additional attention. MDM program priorities and performance goals can be influenced by changes in corporate strategies, mergers and acquisitions, new industry standards, or government regulations. For example, significant changes in a company's sales numbers, marketing strategies, or financial performance will likely create shifts in data management and analytical strategies. Master data need to be monitored and managed in line with a company's business priorities. Therefore, the MDM PMO and steering committee need to constantly evaluate these priorities to keep the program focused on providing business value.

Each business unit within a company will have some form of strategic roadmap aligned to the corporate goals and strategies. Often, these are three- to five-year strategic roadmaps. The MDM PMO, steering committees, and data governance council should work together to review and align their data and quality management goals with the strategies and goals at the business unit and corporate levels at least annually.

Customer satisfaction issues that result from master data problems can also have a significant influence on the master data management priorities and performance focus. Customer dissatisfaction can often result from data-quality issues that affect customer identity, customer analytics, and service delivery, or they can stem from data management and information security bugs that create data privacy and regulatory compliance problems. When these types of issues occur, the MDM PMO and data governance need to respond quickly to help the mitigation and status reporting efforts.

Also, MDM programs will always have many processes and performance improvement needs that will be reflected in the program's roadmap and maturity model assessment. As new MDM products, new benchmarks, and industry best practices emerge, a MDM PMO should take opportunities to evaluate performance of their current products and practices against latest products and practices, particularly where improvement can lead to competitive advantage. Attending industry conferences, engaging a consulting firm to do a program or process assessment, or simply staying in touch with the many MDM-oriented blogs, forums, user groups, and social media channels will keep you up to date on the latest MDM trends and perspectives that can help you identify if capability enhancements should be explored to improve program performance.

Conclusion

This chapter discussed how to establish a robust performance measurement model, including examples of various types of metrics needed to measure MDM activity and performance factors consistently across domains and in relation to the disciplines of data governance, data quality, metadata management, reference data management, and process improvement. It also covered performance measurement from the strategic, tactical, and operational perspectives, indicating how measurement at the operation level influences what is reported up to the strategic level and how many KPIs reported at the strategic level need to be studied to identify the performance factors at the domain and operational levels.

Defining performance measurements and KPIs is a necessary step in the MDM planning and readiness process in order to avoid blind alleys at implementation. Through regular MDM program reviews, the PMO needs to keep a watchful eye on these measurements from both a data-management and quality-performance perspective. As with any performance or quality measurement, the requirements, rules, and criteria likely need to be adjusted over time as quality improvement occurs or corporate strategies change, or if unexpected business impacts emerge that must be addressed.

The MDM PMO and data governance council should conduct an annual review of the existing metrics and performance measurement goals to determine the need for any new metrics or to refocus performance measurement to ensure that MDM program maturity and performance continue to be measured effectively across the MDM model and are aligned with corporate strategies. It will be incumbent on the MDM PMO and data governance council to define a robust set of measures to track program performance and quality of the master data across each domain so that it can fully understand how people, process, and system events affect this data. As is often said, it is very hard to control what cannot be seen and measured. Therefore, the PMO should be diligent about the many scenarios that affect MDM and the opportunities to set expectations or goals and measure performance.

Be sure that performance measurements have a purpose, track important aspects of the program aligned to the key goals and objectives, and will influence decisions that improve the program's ability to manage and control master data. Over the long haul, a multi-domain MDM program risks failure if there are insufficient performance measurements to navigate and manage the program at the strategic, tactical, and operational levels. The next and final chapter will address the topic of continuous improvement, which will be directly influenced by what the program is able to measure and where improvement can best be focused.

CHAPTER 12

Continuous Improvement

This chapter discusses the need and opportunities for continuous improvement in a multi-domain Master Data Management (MDM) program. While not always addressed as a specific program initiative within a company, continuous improvement is an implied ongoing focus expressed in the MDM program's roadmap and maturity goals. Continuous improvement requires many enabling factors involving people, process, and technology that need to be examined across each MDM discipline to determine what improvement opportunities can most benefit the program and where lack of improvement will be an inhibiting factor. Without comprehension of and foresight about continuous improvement needs, an MDM program's momentum can slow down or even disappear altogether if certain enabling factors, needed capabilities, and improvement opportunities are not achieved because they were not forecast and positioned as critical dependencies and program success factors.

Continuous improvement cannot just be one-time recommendations waiting for positioning and recognition. It needs to represent an ongoing focus that can be translated into reasonable and applicable improvement targets needed to support the program's sustainability and maturity. These targets need to be clearly related to the program roadmap and part of annual budget-planning decisions. Chapter 5 discussed how to define and establish a cross-domain maturity model; this chapter addresses how continuous improvement focus throughout the MDM program is a key enabling factor for achieving these roadmap and maturity goals.

In order for the MDM domains and the overall program to move forward in the maturity model, continuous improvement is assumed, but not a given. Achieving many of the maturity milestones will require specific capabilities and process improvements to occur. These capabilities and improvement needs should be examined in relation to each of the five MDM disciplines, along with how and where such improvement opportunities exist within each domain. Figure 12.1 is an illustration of the relationship that continuous improvement has with these MDM disciplines and the maturity of the MDM program.

Improvement opportunities will vary with each domain, but the end goal of the Program Management Office (PMO) is to continue to move each domain forward in the maturity model to eventually achieve a highly manage and optimized state. But let's first step back to better understand continuous improvement as a general methodology, and then examine continuous improvement opportunities in relation to each of the five MDM discipline areas.

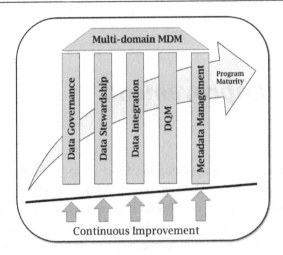

Figure 12.1: Continuous improvement in a multi-domain MDM

Continuous Improvement in a Nutshell

Many companies already employ some type of method to constantly evaluate and improve their processes, services, and products. They just need to look at expanding those methods to support and mature the functions behind MDM. It is not the intent of this chapter to specifically describe or recommend any particular continuous improvement approach. Rather, continuous improvement should be understood as a general concept to apply to the MDM program scope, regardless of the specific method used.

There are semantic differences between the terms *continuous improvement* and *continual improvement*. Using the more particular definition, continuous improvement presupposes a more linear and incremental improvement within an existing area. Conversely, continual improvement is broader, encompassing multiple continuous improvement programs. For the purpose of this book, those two terms are used interchangeably to mean the broader scope, where companies are constantly seeking incremental improvement over time or breakthrough improvements to many processes, services, and products in many areas.

Among the most widely used tools for continuous improvement is a four-step quality model—the plan-do-check-act (PDCA) cycle, also known as the *Deming Cycle* or *Shewhart Cycle,* which steps can be summarized as follows:

1. *Plan:* Identify an opportunity and plan for change.
2. *Do:* Implement the change on a small scale.
3. *Check:* Use data to analyze the results of the change and determine whether it made a difference.
4. *Act:* If the change was successful, implement it on a wider scale and continuously assess your results. If the change did not work, begin the cycle again.

Other widely used methods of continuous improvement—such as Six Sigma, Lean Six Sigma, and Total Quality Management—emphasize employee involvement and teamwork; measuring and systematizing processes; and reducing variation, defects, and cycle times.

The use of a defined approach along with some consulting services can significantly aid in the preparation and analysis work needed with continuous improvement initiatives. In other words, often the MDM program team itself will not have sufficient bandwidth to conduct an effective or objective continuous improvement assessment. With a good approach, and after an initial assessment is conducted, the format and approach can be reused and updated each year to provide year-to-year continuity with improvement evaluation. Also, if a company has an internal audit department, there may be some opportunities to apply that process each year to evaluating program progress and improvement.

Let's take a closer look at continuous improvement for multi-domain MDM.

Continuous Improvement in Multi-Domain MDM

Continuous improvement for multi-domain MDM is multifaceted. There is the natural expansion related to incrementally adding additional domains to an MDM hub, which, due to the many variables within each domain, cause both leading and lagging conditions. At a minimum, an annual assessment should be conducted to align requirements, roadmap, priority, and maturity-tracking processes.

But in addition to continually expanding the management of master data for more and more domains, or even expanding the number of master attributes for a given domain, it is also important to apply continuous improvement to the five primary focus areas surrounding MDM: data governance, data stewardship, data integration, Data Quality Management (DQM), and metadata management. This is covered in the next sections.

Continuous Improvement in Data Governance

In many respects, the definition and charter of data governance reflect a continuous improvement focus in itself. In Chapter 6, this definition of data governance was presented (from DMBOK 2010):

> *Data governance is the exercise of authority and control (planning, monitoring, and enforcement) over the management of data assets.*

We know that applying and achieving a successful degree of data governance requires a long-term commitment to execute a governance framework that can drive policies, standards, and decisions aimed at the effective management and quality control of data assets. A data governance charter typically has a broader focus than just master data. Data governance authority will usually span many types of data and various data environments. A data governance program will often have its own maturity model that covers the broader scope.

Throughout this book, we have focused on the relationship and alignment needed between data governance and an MDM program. This also assumes alignment of continuous improvement efforts.

Because of the broad use and importance of master data with a company, master data improvement needs are likely to command more priority and attention during the data governance process than other improvement needs for other types of data. The MDM PMO owns much of the responsibility for defining and reviewing these improvement needs with the data governance process. From a MDM program perspective, continuous improvement should in many respects align with broader data management improvement goals that an enterprise data governance program also has in scope. In fact, effective governance of master data may be the single most important objective of an enterprise data governance scope. For example, in Chapter 5, these data governance–oriented milestones were presented as part of an MDM program's maturity model:

- Domain-based data governance charters, owners, teams, and the decision authority have been identified.
- The master data associated with the domains have been identified and approved by data governance from an owning and using perspective.
- Data management policies and standards have been defined and implemented.
- Measurements and dashboards are in place to measure and drive master data quality and control.

Achieving each of these milestones will not only improve the management and control of master data, but also greatly contribute to improving the roles and effectiveness of data governance as a whole across the company. The ability to align and organize data governance focus with master data domains to improve MDM and quality-control focus will provide the foundation and capabilities that can be extended to other types of data and data governance needs.

What this is suggesting is that continuous improvement of the data governance discipline in the MDM program will be a highly influencing factor for the recognition and success of a broader enterprise data governance program. If master data governance is inadequate, the perception of data governance in general will be negatively affected. Therefore, the MDM PMO and a data governance council need to share common direction and continuous improvement goals. Here are a few specific recommendations of where the MDM PMO and a data governance council can collaborate to drive continuous improvement that supports both the MDM program and enterprise data governance objectives:

- **Help sponsor and support an Enterprise Data Governance model.** The MDM PMO should have an active and influential role in a data governance council to help build a comprehensive enterprise data governance model where MDM data governance needs can feed into. Often, a data governance initiative starts from requirements associated with a specific program or functional area then tries to expand outward or upward from there. A good practice in one area can certainly get attention in another area where similar data governance interest exists, but without a more formal enterprisewide program charter and a broad level of executive sponsorship, not all business areas will respond because data governance is not part of their business plan and priorities. In this situation, developing an MDM and data governance footprint across multiple domains will be very difficult and will certainly inhibit the ability of a multi-domain MDM program to gain sufficient penetration into domain areas where data governance does not have sponsorship. Therefore, the ability to influence and help support enterprise data governance growth should be a key aspect of a MDM program's continuous improvement plans.

- **Ensure an ongoing alignment of the data domain definition.** Be sure that the data domain definition is aligned or has a clear mapping across MDM, data governance, and enterprise data architecture models. Chapter 2 indicated that data domain definition can vary depending on the company's industry orientation and business model. Within a company, the definition of data domains and data subject areas can be different or conflicting across a company's information, system, and functional architectures if there are no standards that apply to this. The MDM PMO and data governance program should work with data architect teams to agree on how data domain definitions and structure should align. Creating an aligned and commonly recognized data domain structure will greatly simplify the ability to focus data management, data governance, and data-quality-improvement initiatives.

- **Ensure that data governance maturity milestones are actionable and achievable.** Where MDM program maturity milestones represent data governance capability improvement expectations, be sure that these milestones align to data governance council or other steering committee priorities and budget-planning activities that will influence or affect the achievement of the milestone. For example, if a key data governance milestone is to ensure that data quality measurements and dashboards are in place to measure and drive master data quality and control, the MDM PMO needs to be engaged with the information technology (IT) and data governance planning activities, where decisions will occur about the technology and support capabilities needed for data-quality measurement and reporting. Having an influence on data governance investments and delivery of needed capabilities will help enable the MDM program meet improvement targets that advance the program's maturity.

- **Forge a strong, collaborative relationship with corporate functions.** The MDM PMO needs to maintain a strong relationship with corporate functions such as Legal, Compliance, Information Security, and Human Resources (HR) to regularly evaluate corporate issues and risk factors that the MDM program can assist with. Aside from being engaged in or responsible for specific issue mitigation activities where master data quality and management issues are involved, the MDM program can proactively work with these corporate functions on other general data governance or risk avoidance opportunities, such as alignment of data management policies, employee training, data steward support, and monitoring of conditions that can create risk and compliance issues. From a MDM maturity perspective, these are collaborative opportunities that will directly contribute to achieving a highly managed and optimized state.

As stated previously, continuous improvement cannot just be one-time recommendations waiting for positioning and recognition. It needs to reflect an ongoing focus that can be translated into reasonable and applicable improvement targets that a data-governance program will need to support the MDM program's sustainability and maturity.

Continuous Improvement in Data Stewardship

The build-out and positioning of data steward roles and practices may be the most challenging components of an MDM program. Continuous improvement in data stewardship is a constant factor in the MDM maturity model. In a multi-domain MDM model, data stewardship largely relies on the enlistment of personnel acting as data and process area experts who can truly embrace the data steward concept and focus on specific data governance and data management initiatives. The difficulty with this approach is that a data steward role is often not a formally defined role within a company. In such cases, data steward enlistment, positioning, and recognition can be affected when that role overlaps or conflicts with other roles and titles and there is no visible job ladder or career path for a data steward within the company. As was pointed out in Chapter 7, the purpose and function of data stewards are vital to maintaining good, trusted master data. Therefore, the data steward model and any improvement opportunities need continual evaluation to ensure that the MDM program goals are achieved. Here are some recommendations for how to keep improving data stewardship across the MDM program:

- **Create recognition and rewards**. People who are doing a good job and meeting goals in a data steward function need to receive recognition and rewards. Whether these employees are participating in a data steward team that provides perspective or makes decisions about important MDM concepts, issues, and solutions, or performing very specific data management or quality control tasks, the PMO and data governance leaders should coordinate on offering recognition and reward opportunities for them. This helps retain the focus and talent needed to fill these roles effectively, and from an MDM program maturity perspective, reflect a clear intent to build and maintain a high-quality culture.

- **Identify the enabling and constraining factors in a data steward role.** Like almost every job role, data stewards can be happy about where they are positioned but frustrated by the process and tools that keep them from being as successful and effective as they would like to be. In most cases, the person in the data steward role has some insight or recommendations for how their processes and tools could be improved. The domain data governance teams and lead data stewards should periodically assess their data steward processes to identify improvement needs and opportunities to make improvements. Obviously, not all process or tool improvements are feasible, but simply having a continuous improvement focus that results in at least some beneficial improvement will help increase data steward effectiveness and job satisfaction.

- **Keep pursuing opportunity to make "data steward" a formal job title.** If "data steward" is not a formal job title, but there are roles that resemble the data steward support role, and there are growing recognition and evidence of the value of these roles, the MDM PMO should keep demonstrating its appreciation. This should be demonstrated to the program steering committee, governance council, and HR leadership. If the appreciation is there and consistently demonstrated, executive leaders will recognize the need to support the creation of an actual data steward position as a necessary component of the enterprise data management strategy and goals. As there is a growing focus in data management on the data steward role and career path, being able to formally post open data steward positions will greatly improve a company's ability to target and recruit qualified candidates. Having formal data steward job titles, levels, and salary ranges will enable the MDM PMO, data governance program, or both to more specifically address resource and budget forecasting for program improvement needs.

As was also pointed out in Chapter 7, data stewardship should be a major component throughout all of MDM. Therefore, a multi-domain plan needs to develop a firm concept of how a data steward will look and function, where the data steward role will need to be best positioned, and how the right resources can be identified and engaged for optimum performance. As the program evolves, so should the data steward model and focus. Data stewards are critical to the improvement of master data quality and control, so the program's continuous improvement plans need to ensure that data steward needs and capabilities are factored in.

Continuous Improvement in Data Integration

Data integration involving master data can happen on many different phases and levels. And if a company is expanding, data integration plans and activities may also have to expand over time, such as in the following ways:

- **Manage more master data from additional domains.** It is very common for companies to start with one or two domains and add more as their MDM practice matures. This can potentially require the integration of additional sources, and consequently the possibility of different technologies and processing type (batch versus real time). It might also require the integration of additional external sources for reference data management.

- **Integrate more sources feeding data into an MDM hub.** Companies might choose to minimize risk by integrating only a couple of sources at a time. Instead of integrating master data for a particular domain from all existing sources, it might be more advantageous to start with one or two data sources, and in incremental phases, add more as needed. Of course, the actual MDM hub style and architecture chosen will have a direct impact on this. The registry-style hub, for example, does not affect existing data sources, but it obviously requires a data integration effort in the hub itself. Nevertheless, in addition to the typical technical challenges of data integration, it is necessary to review the roadmap, priority, and viability of integrating more sources.

- **Integrate more data sources due to mergers and acquisitions.** Many companies grow by acquiring other companies. This represents a great data integration challenge because the acquired company might have completely different systems, differing master data attributes and definitions, uneven levels of data quality, and varying levels of existing integration. Furthermore, the integration of the newly acquired company might have to be completed very quickly, which will certainly add to the challenge. If mergers and acquisitions are common, a company must focus on maturing its data integration practice, and methods of continuous improvement are certainly helpful to accomplish this challenging task.

- **Integrate more sources consuming data from the MDM hub.** Just as it can be less risky to start with fewer sources feeding master data into the MDM hub, it might make sense to have fewer sources use data from the hub at first. Downstream systems might have to be redesigned and rebuilt to accommodate a newly developed master data model. Depending on the overall architecture and how the MDM hub fits into the existing technological and business roadmap, downstream systems such as operational data stores (ODSs) and enterprise data warehouses (EDWs) will not necessarily be integrated with the MDM hub in its initial deployment.

- **Add more attributes to existing master data sets.** As more sources are integrated, the higher the probability that additional master attributes will be identified. Even certain master data attributes from previously integrated sources may not be in the initial scope, but now they are important to capture in the MDM hub as well. In either event, when a new master attribute is considered for inclusion into the MDM hub, an upgrade will be necessary to integrate the newly identified attributes. If the new attribute does not affect the identity of the master entity, the change is much easier. If it does affect the identity of the master entity, it will require a revision of the entity resolution process (see the next point).

- **Make additions and changes to attributes related to entity resolution.** This topic is a special case of the abovementioned point. New attributes are added to the scope of an existing master entity, either because of newly integrated sources or due to increased scope of previously integrated sources. If new attributes affect the identity of an entity or the survivorship rules, it is necessary to review the entity resolution logic. This is certainly more time-consuming than adding other kind of attributes that can be simply appended to the existing ones without affecting clustering and survivorship.

- **Upgrade from batch to real-time data updates.** Real-time MDM is typically more difficult to implement and maintain than batch-mode MDM due to the complex nature of keeping data in sync at all times. Granted, certain domains might not require real-time integration because business requirements can be met even with delayed processing. But there are cases where companies decide to start with batch mode to get the MDM hub operating quickly and opt to convert to real-time processing as their MDM system matures.

- **Change business rules.** Businesses evolve and change over time, and so do their data definitions, contexts, regulations, processes, and procedures. Data integration can be affected depending on the extent of those changes.

All these subjects can greatly benefit from a continuous improvement program applied to data integration. An MDM PMO would provide a roadmap for how some of those areas are expected to evolve, but a continuous improvement program might be better equipped to review, reprioritize, plan, and execute eventual changes over time. As always, data governance participation is critical. A data governance program in place can certainly facilitate and expedite steps when business engagement is required to review and approve modifications.

A continuous improvement program can document processes, guidelines, checklists, and other artifacts to increase the maturity of the company with regard to implementing each of the previously mentioned MDM-related data integration requirements. Using the addition of more data sources with time as an example, a well-documented set of guidelines will certainly help the completion of all necessary steps quickly and successfully. If a company goes through frequent mergers and acquisitions, creating a step-by-step recipe for the process would save a lot of time and money. To be sure, a process to revise and update those guidelines should be in place as well.

Continuous Improvement in DQM

MDM is obviously about the management, governance, and quality control of master data. But the charter and scope of data governance and DQM can be greater than the master data scope. Therefore, continuous improvement in data quality will occur beyond the boundaries of the master data program.

Maturity of DQM is a constant focus. Companies should strive to move from being reactive to data-quality issues to being proactive. Error prevention is preferred over data correction, and such practices are likely to be less costly if they can be feasibly implemented. The following sections list areas that require constant innovation and should be the focus of a continuous data quality improvement program.

Data analysis and profiling. Data analysis and profiling can and should be approached methodically. Therefore, it is important to create a repeatable and efficient process to explore, analyze, and profile data sources and potential issues. But a high degree of tailoring is also required when performing certain types of data analysis and profiling due to the uniqueness of some data scenarios. Both methodical and specific aspects of data analysis and profiling are discussed next.

From a methodical point of view, a data-quality program should establish certain standard types of data-quality checks to follow when analyzing a data source. These types of activities are usually more repeatable and require less resource specialization. Examples of elements to check include the following:

- Completeness of key attributes
- Uniqueness of potential primary key candidates
- Highest and lowest values of numeric attributes
- Frequency distribution of certain types of attributes
- Pattern analysis of attributes candidates to standardization
- Data match analysis across sources

More specific data scenarios and types of analysis are likely to require a high level of expertise and tailoring of data profiling techniques to find the root cause of data issues. Certain issues can be very convoluted and entail a very specific analysis that will go above and beyond any preestablished, step-by-step methods. Quite often, this requires great expertise, not only about data analysis techniques, but also about the existing data and their relationships. Improvement in this area must occur by properly training individuals in data analysis techniques, how the business uses data, and the structure of data at their respective sources.

A great enabler of data analysis and profiling is technology. Technology is constantly evolving and should be regularly sought out for improving existing practices, as well as expanding to new topics. For example, technology designed to explore and profile unstructured data is a lot less mature than technology designed to do similar tasks to structured or semistructured data. Therefore, it is important to regularly evaluate what is new in a given area of interest, and whether it is related to a master data domain. A great deal of data quality is required for the governance of multiple types of data, not only master data.

As companies expand their multi-domain MDM disciplines to other subject areas, it is advantageous to research what data-quality tools are available to enhance and expedite data analysis and profiling of any newly added entities. For example, data profiling of customer master data can be quite different from data profiling of product master data. Certain tools might offer better capabilities in one area than another.

Another important aspect of this idea is the usage of reference data to assess and validate the quality of the existing data. Reference data can be very specific to domains and industries. Here are some examples:

*   Credit bureau data can be used to validate a person's identity.
*   U.S. Postal Service data can be used to validate U.S. addresses.
*   Industry-specific catalogs can be used for validation. For instance, in the automotive industry, vehicle catalogs are vital to efforts to validate and standardize a vehicle's make, model, year, and trim.
*   Catalogs of companies can be used to validate information about a company, including its legal name, industry classification, and company hierarchy and subsidiaries.

Therefore, regularly researching and evaluating reference data offerings are highly recommended for enhancing and accelerating data-quality-maintenance capabilities.

Finally, the ongoing profiling of production MDM data is also important. The intent is to use data profiling to continue to measure and analyze master data attributes to ensure that previously established rules and resultant values are being established according to expectations. Details such as which sources are most frequently contributing new values, which sources are being refused, and what fields are becoming more or less distributed in value can help us evaluate if any adjustments are necessary.

Error prevention and data validation. A lot of times, data-quality issues have a ripple effect, making it difficult to truly measure the total cost of a problem that could have been altogether avoidable if proper measures had been taken to prevent it from happening in the first place. Error prevention is generally the most desirable approach, but clearly that cannot be achieved in all situations. Understanding those situations is important to properly plan a continuous improvement program in this area. Here are some situations to consider:

*   Technological limitations may prevent certain real-time data validations to occur due to the inability to collect and present valid options to the user in a timely manner. For example, as users make consecutive selections from multiple interrelated drop-down lists, it might not be viable to access one or more remote systems to dynamically filter invalid values. Data might have to be duplicated locally to allow the timely population of valid options, but this increases maintenance costs and the risk of inconsistencies. Certain system designs and architectures can be more conducive to performing data validation than others. Therefore, as system design and architecture evolve, opportunities to improve error prevention should be sought.
*   Reference data for different domains and industries are constantly evolving. Vendors keep advancing their expertise and data offerings in many areas, which can and should be considered when validating data and preventing data issues.

- Mergers and acquisitions require data from one company to be integrated with another. It could entail many systems within a single merger or acquisition. If a company is constantly acquiring other companies, it should work on creating a reliable process to efficiently integrate data, while at the same time validating what is coming in.
- Evolving business rules sometimes require system changes to fulfill new needs. Implementing new error prevention mechanisms may take time. If a company is highly susceptible to these types of changes, it should explore options to improve the speed and efficiency of any change processes associated with them.

Most of the time, there is little dispute that preventing a data-quality issue is the best remedy. But sometimes is not possible to do that due to high associated costs, technological constraints, highly demanding schedules, or any combination. In these situations, it is important to capture the rationale used in the decision process and revisit decisions on a regular basis to evaluate if conditions have changed and implementation has become viable.

Data cleansing or data scrubbing. Recall from Chapter 9 that the terms *data cleansing* and *data scrubbing* are often used as a catch-all for all sorts of transformations to data to improve their quality. Of course, a company looking to mature its DQM process will continuously look for opportunities to improve its data. It is true that the requirement to correct a certain piece of information will often be directly stated. However, in some cases, cleansing opportunities will arise as a byproduct of other activities. For example, when a bug affecting data quality is found, it is necessary to fix it, both to correct the existing issue and to prevent it from happening in the future. In another example, if a business rule changes, it is necessary to implement one or more changes to support the new rule, and sometimes to modify any existing data to comply with the new rule.

Therefore, from a continuous improvement point of view, it is important to identify situations when data cleansing can potentially arise as a subsequent or indirect requirement. This is part of being a proactive organization. Furthermore, regular data profiling can also help raise awareness of required data cleansing activities that the business may have not have noticed before. Mature IT organizations are capable of identifying certain types of data issues before the business does. Keep in mind that data quality is not maintained just for its own sake—it needs to fulfill a purpose. And businesses should always have the final word regarding the level of quality required. But an IT organization that can point out potential problems will go a long way to meeting quality standards.

Data standardization. Data are distributed across heterogeneous systems, leading to an ongoing battle to consistently represent the same information in the same format. New sources of information are constantly being integrated into existing ones. To require data elements from every system to conform to a particular standard is too much of a stretch. Therefore, data transformations are unavoidable when data is moving across systems.

This integration typically happens in one of two ways:

- Data are moved permanently from one system to another.
- An interface is created to move data regularly from one system to another.

When data is permanently moved from one system to another, data from the source system should be transformed to conform to the standards required by the target system. When an interface is added to move data from one system to another, the logic to conform the data across them needs to be added as data are moved. Refer to Chapter 9 for more details on this.

From a continuous improvement perspective, companies should tackle data standardization from multiple fronts:

- Constantly evolve data standardization as part of data migration projects. In general, data need to be permanently moved from one system to another due to data consolidation, system upgrades, and mergers and acquisitions. Data migration efforts require a repeatable process that can deliver successful and predictable results. Data standardization should be a permanent item in the list of activities required as part of this exercise, with enough details to correctly guide teams on how to identify and conduct data standardization activities during the migration process. Furthermore, this documentation should be regularly updated as the process matures.
- Companies should start and progress their data standardization efforts at their core systems, prioritized by the data elements that bring the most value to the business. Data governance should assist with the identification and prioritization processes. As standards evolve, they become the foundation of a full-fledged enterprise standard catalog, captured via a metadata management tool and published for general usage.
- Any new interface integrated should be evaluated from a data standardization perspective. Data elements not following a standard should either be corrected or properly defended in terms of why they are exempt from conformity. That could be so for a multitude of reasons, such as cost, technology, and risk. Regularly revisiting those decisions is wise because the landscape is constantly changing.
- Technology and reference data improvements. Many standardization efforts are dropped due to a lack of proper technology or reference sources to reliably standardize certain data elements. As technology matures and reference data are expanded, more can be improved in this area. Regular evaluation should be conducted to identify new opportunities.

Data enrichment. In general, data enrichment is accomplished by integrating trusted reference data sources. For example, integrating D&B allows augmentation of customer information; integrating Vertex allows augmentation of tax ID; integrating the Postal Service allows the adding of 4 digits to the standard 5-digit ZIP code; integrating Chrome allows augmentation of vehicle catalog information; and so on. As stated previously, the number of vendors providing reference data is growing. To continuously improve in this area means to regularly assess what is offered and what areas of the business can be improved by augmented information.

New business opportunities may arise by creatively tapping into these new sources of information. Marketing and sales campaigns can tremendously benefit from additional information about customers and products to improve their predictive analytics and their up-sell and cross-sell techniques.

Data monitoring, scorecards, and dashboards. It is probably easy to see how this category needs continuous improvement. The catalog of data items in need of metrics—monitoring, scorecards, or both—is bound to grow. As companies mature in DQM and become more proactive, the more items they will identify as needing regular assessment. As companies mature their data error prevention practices, one may wonder if they will need less monitoring. Typically, though, it is more likely that more data items will require monitoring as time goes by than that data items will become completely error-free. Even as anomalies are lowered due to better error prevention, chances are they won't be completely eliminated. Therefore, the number of anomalies will still need to be measured in many cases. However, while the number of items in need of metrics won't necessarily go down, the number of violations should.

Continuous Improvement in Metadata Management

The collection of new metadata and maintenance of existing metadata is a never-ending activity. The key is to properly prioritize sources where metadata would be most valuable, enhance the collection and maintenance process through automation and process improvement, constantly search for new ways to effectively integrate metadata management within other existing processes, and efficiently distribute metadata for better understanding and usage of information throughout the company.

Metadata management is perhaps the least-explored data management capability within a multi-domain MDM. Because companies often start their MDM plans with just a single domain, the number of master elements can be relatively small, and this may not justify having dedicated metadata management. But as the number of domains increase, there are more master data elements that need control and more data integration activities occurring, and so the need also increases for a more formalized and centralized metadata management approach.

The bottom line is that the core functions of multi-domain MDM—data governance, data stewardship, data integration, data quality, and metadata management—are all critical for the better usage of information. Furthermore, those five key components feed off each other, improving each other's efficiency and efficacy.

In the next several sections, let's look at some specific areas of metadata management that can benefit from a constant focus on improvement.

Sources of metadata. Recall from Chapter 10 the many islands of metadata throughout the company, such as internal and external data sources (structured, semistructured, and unstructured), data models, interfaces and transformations, business applications, business definitions and processes, analytics and reporting, correspondence and legal documents, and business and data-quality rules. Collecting business, technical, and operational metadata information related to these sources can tremendously improve the capability to better use these sources of information correctly and effectively. Companies are constantly making incorrect decisions because they lack a full understanding of their data assets.

Completing a full picture of all these sources of metadata is a tenuous process. Depending on the size of a company, each of those islands of metadata can have thousands of data attributes, and documenting all the metadata will take a long time. Therefore, it is important to have an efficient process to recognize what sources would mostly benefit a company if its metadata information is exposed. To prioritize future sources requires understanding of what has worked in the past.

Metadata management can suffer quite a bit of resistance from existing organizations because they cannot quite see an immediate benefit of metadata management to what they are doing, or they see metadata management as an additional overhead to their already understaffed teams. Therefore, forward-thinking companies may start with their metadata management program tied to a data governance office, but first without full engagement from the business, or even from IT application owners. That will require the metadata team to build a case by exploring islands of metadata on their own to show their value. This will result on hit-or-miss scenarios where certain metadata groupings will offer more benefits than others. Of course, that is not an ideal scenario.

The ultimate goal is to have a fully integrated metadata management discipline, with priorities driven by the added value that they bring to the many organizations within the enterprise. A continuous improvement process should make sure that this happens and metadata management does not become a fad. It is important to learn from what has worked in the past and adjust to what has not. Regular evaluations should be conducted to ensure that proper adjustments are made.

Collection and maintenance of metadata. Metadata is data, and as such, it can suffer from typical data-quality issues, such as duplication, inconsistency, incompleteness, and accuracy. It is necessary to realize how important creating a sustainable and reliable process to collect and maintain metadata is. It is not unusual to see thousands of metadata items become practically unusable because they are now obsolete.

Companies capture quite a bit of metadata on a regular basis, with or without a formal metadata management function. But there is a problem: This information is distributed in many forms. Manually captured metadata is typically stored in unstructured or semistructured form, such as Microsoft Word documents or Microsoft Excel spreadsheets. These documents will usually contain business term definitions, data dictionaries, data mappings, business rules, data-quality requirements, and other elements. In addition, metadata also exists in technological components, such as databases, data-modeling tools, extract, transform, and load (ETL) tools, reporting tools, business rule engines, and so on. Examples of metadata in those sources include data models, data types, data structures, attribute names, data mapping, transformations, business rules, and calculations.

A mature company will have a repository that can capture metadata from all these channels and store them in a single and integrated location for easy retrieval. However, the collection of metadata is truly twofold. The first part is the initial collection of metadata; the second is the continual update of what has been collected. If the collection of metadata can be automated, the ongoing activity is simply a repetition of the initial load process for the purpose of regularly refreshing the metadata repository. But if the process is manual, it is necessary to decide if the maintenance after initial load will be done directly into the metadata repository, or if it will continue at the original source and require constant synchronization.

Let's use an example to illustrate this point. Assume that before a metadata repository tool is acquired, a team of users maintain data definitions and mapping between systems in spreadsheets. Once a tool is acquired, it is only logical to load the metadata from those spreadsheets into the tool. When the metadata is in the repository, the maintenance team needs to decide if it will make changes directly into the metadata repository or continue to use spreadsheets. There are pros and cons to both options. Using spreadsheets is a known process, but it requires regular refreshes of the repository. Using the metadata tool will require training and availability, but the most up-to-date and unique metadata will be available immediately for distribution.

Continuous improvement in collection and maintenance of metadata is about addressing the following main issues:

- *Continue to explore tools that can automate the process of collecting metadata.* Metadata tools typically offer capabilities to import metadata from certain technologies, but vendors will continuously improve and expand their features. Stay abreast of newly added options.
- *Evolve the relationship with producers of metadata.* Have them seek to use an enterprise metadata tool in their metadata-collecting process. For metadata management to be mostly effective, companies need to approach it similar to the way that Wikipedia content is created: multiple people contribute content. Sometimes it is necessary to confirm that the content is right. In those cases, an arbitration process can be led by a data governance program.

Metadata within other processes. There needs to be a metadata team to establish the foundation, manage the metadata repository, define standards, provide expert guidance, and ultimately be accountable for the health and proper delivery of metadata throughout the enterprise. But metadata is documentation, and as such, it needs to be close to the experts generating it, and collected within the existing processes that these experts already perform to avoid duplication and rework. For metadata management to be most effective, metadata documentation should be a byproduct of already-existing processes, but captured in a more formal way, following predefined standards and techniques. The resulting metadata can be utilized as a self-feeding artifact within existing processes to improve itself. In addition, the exposure of metadata related to data elements within a process can highly benefit other interested parties in the company.

Some teams may not agree that the activity of collecting metadata is part of their responsibilities, so they may resist or refuse to become engaged in these efforts. A key element of continuous improvement is finding ways to overcome this resistance. The following actions should be considered to increase adherence to metadata collaboration:

- Work with the data governance council to define and implement an enterprisewide metadata management policy that will help drive specific metadata management expectations and requirements across the enterprise.
- Improve the metadata repository constantly. The more the repository is populated, the more teams will want to be part of it. It is a chicken-and-egg situation. The repository needs contribution from subject matter experts, but these people will resist doing so if they do not see potential return. Metadata teams will have to look for the low-hanging fruit, which means to find areas where metadata can be easily extracted to sell the metadata management idea to other teams.
- Improve training. Much of the time, teams resist certain changes because they are not properly educated about them. Training sessions with resisting teams can help overcoming their reluctance and make them more welcoming. Experiences from other metadata user teams can be presented as case histories to show value.
- Propose that a metadata management team member work more closely with subject matter experts in that group to aid the process of collecting metadata information and provide training at the same time.
- Collect metrics from contributing teams to use them as proof of value added, and publish them accordingly.

Metadata management has to become part of the culture. To achieve that goal, it is important to embed metadata practices into existing processes. Organizations are constantly capturing metadata, but they need to formalize it and gather it collectively in a shared repository to be most effective.

Metadata distribution. If metadata is not used, there should be little or no reason to collect it. Companies might sell the idea of the importance of metadata management and allocate the proper resources for collecting metadata, but if consumers do not buy into it, that completely defeats the purpose. Companies will have to go to great lengths to effectively collect and maintain metadata. But the effort cannot end there. They need to make sure the published metadata reaches the right audience.

A metadata repository with an easy-to-use and easily accessible interface is a great start. Training in its use is also very necessary, and it needs to be tailored to specific audiences due to the wide range of user skills. Remember that a metadata repository can have a large number of metadata types and categories. It can include many business, technical, and operational types of metadata, and it will be used by business and technical teams. Therefore, to get the most out of it, its users must know how to find the information they are looking for. If the repository's usability is poor, they will tend to stop using it, hence compromising the value of the metadata management program. From a continuous improvement point of view, it is important to understand the issues that users are having with the repository and find ways to make it more user-friendly.

Another path to pursue is to integrate the metadata repository with applications or other technological components within the company. For example, some metadata tools can associate a Uniform Resource Locator (URL) address to a particular piece of metadata. This URL can be used within the user interface (UI) screen of another application. When users are navigating through the application, they have the option to click a link associated with a UI element, which will take them to a metadata page with descriptions of that element and other metadata associated with it. This approach will increase the usage of existing metadata and will create demand for more. A continuous improvement process must explore and test alternatives to make metadata information be more permeated and seamless across the enterprise.

Conclusion

This chapter discussed the need and opportunities for continuous improvement in a multi-domain MDM program, indicating that continuous improvement is an implied (if not explicit) activity in the MDM program's roadmap and maturity goals. Continues improvement is implied because the overall MDM program is expected to mature. However, this is not a given, as continuous improvement requires many enabling factors involving people, process, and technology that need to be examined across each MDM discipline to determine what improvement opportunities can most benefit the program and where lack of improvement will be an inhibiting factor. This chapter pointed out that an MDM program's momentum is likely to slow or stop if certain enabling factors, capabilities, and improvement opportunities are not achieved because they were not forecast or coordinated well with appropriate planning processes and decision-making groups.

Continuous improvement needs to represent an ongoing focus that can be translated into reasonable and applicable improvement targets that will support the program's sustainability and maturity. Improvement targets should relate to the program roadmap and be part of annual budget-planning reviews.

Because this chapter concludes this book, it is important to reiterate a few key points about planning and implementing a multi-domain MDM program:

- A multi-domain MDM strategy requires patience, persistence, adaptation, maturity, and the ability to act on opportunities as they emerge across the enterprise.
- Multi-domain MDM can be very much like a jigsaw puzzle—a big picture that you have to piece together. These pieces can come together from various locations in the puzzle, but it should not be a random process.
- The strategy has to consider how to address and improve certain parts of the MDM plan first and others later.

A multi-domain MDM program requires a constant focus on planning, prioritization, and improvement. When these activities are well positioned and well orchestrated, the puzzle pieces will continue to come together to form a big picture that will represent achievement of the program goals and objectives.

Index

Note: Page numbers followed by *f* indicate figures and *t* indicate tables.